SUNBURST

SUNBURST

The Ascent of Sun Microsystems

Mark Hall and John Barry

Foreword by Tom Peters

CB
CONTEMPORARY
BOOKS

CHICAGO

Library of Congress Cataloging-in-Publication Data

Hall, Mark.
    Sunburst : the ascent of Sun Microsystems / Mark Hall and
John Barry ; foreword by Tom Peters.
       p.   cm.
    Includes bibliographical references.
    ISBN 0-8092-4368-7 : $19.95
    1. Sun Microsystems.   2. Computer industry—United
States.   I. Title.
HD9696.C64S794   1990
338.7'61004'0973—dc20   90-1601
                                          CIP

Copyright © 1990 by Mark Hall and John Barry
All rights reserved
Published by Contemporary Books, Inc.
180 North Michigan Avenue, Chicago, Illinois 60601
Manufactured in the United States of America
International Standard Book Number: 0-8092-4368-7

In memory of my father, Everett I. Hall
                                        —MH

For Sean, Eva, Fred, Jane, and Jim
                                        —JB

Contents

Foreword

Sun Microsystems has emerged as one of the most intriguing success stories of the 1980s. As we enter the 1990s, the company's winning streak shows little sign of abating in the long term. In *Sunburst: The Ascent of Sun Microsystems*, authors Mark Hall and John Barry examine Sun's first eight years, concentrating on how Sun achieved its remarkable growth. Sun started as a workstation company, but it continues to expand its horizons in the direction of becoming a general-purpose computer company. Although Sun operates in the high-performance computer arena, its strategies and actions are applicable to any company rocketing to the top of its market. *Sunburst* is important reading for anyone piloting such a company or wanting to experience the rocket ride.

Sun has successfully sold its products, in large part, because it understands the needs of its customers. It has an overarching strategic plan that guides its entire organization. That plan is effectively communicated throughout the company so that nearly everyone understands the logic behind decisions. Sun builds excellent products and brings them to market in a timely manner. It takes chances but is not reckless; it makes mistakes but does not repeat them. By these and other criteria Sun Microsystems qualifies as a company in constant pursuit of excellence—so much so, that the company went from zero to nearly $2 billion in revenues in less than eight years.

Sunburst examines the core strategy that propelled Sun to the top of its market. It documents the pressures and the possibilities of working in a company in the throes of hypergrowth. The book reveals the motives and aspirations of the men and women who make things work at Sun.

Sun's president, Scott McNealy, has made no secret of his and his company's ambition to become one of a predicted handful of major computer companies in the 1990s—and beyond. I, with other observers of aggressive, successful companies such as Sun, will be watching to see if McNealy's ambition is realized.

Tom Peters
Author of *Thriving on Chaos*

Acknowledgments

The authors are deeply indebted to several people who contributed in many fashions to this book. Besides the obligatory mention of spouses, children, pets, and dutiful mothers, we want to note the support and help we received from Eva Langfeldt, Lisa Levine, Rich Wyckoff, and Stan Baron, all of whom read the manuscript in its raw form. Their comments improved the accuracy and style of the book. Tom Peters was gracious enough to review our book and provide the foreword. Former Sun executive Carol Broadbent also found time to comment on and critique our effort. Longtime Sun manager Carl Swirsding opened up to us his collection of materials published by Sun over the years. Everyone's assistance added immensely to the value of the book, while all faults belong in the laps of the authors.

Introduction

Sun Microsystems exploded into the computer industry with amazing speed and force. In less than five years, the Mountain View, California, company qualified for the Fortune 500 listing. In just over six years of existence, it cleared the $1 billion revenue hurdle. In its seventh year, Sun grew another 70 percent, to more than $1.7 billion, becoming the hottest company in Silicon Valley, one of the most dynamic economic regions in the world. Sun's growth rate exceeded Apple Computer's expansion history. Longtime Silicon Valley luminaries, such as Hewlett-Packard, Intel, and Atari, could not match Sun's march to the top.

In the history of high-tech business, only the equally amazing Compaq Computer has exceeded Sun's growth in terms of speed and size. The significant achievements of Compaq are undeniable, but that Texas outfit reached its peak by simply following a technology path established by IBM and distributing its wares through established retail outlets such as ComputerLand and MicroAge. Sun, on the other hand, created its own technology and product lines while building a worldwide direct-sales force. Where Compaq imitated, Sun invented. While Compaq jockeyed for shelf space, Sun sought for share of mind.

This distinction is vital. Sun's success is based on its creation of technologies that served a pent-up demand. Although not a unique raison d'être for a business, the way in which Sun built its market dominance, maintained its independence, changed competitive strategies, and altered the way people compute is worth a detailed review.

An appropriate corporate comparison with Sun might be Digital Equipment Corporation. Both companies appealed to technologists, selling their products primarily to skeptical and savvy engineers, scientists, or technically inclined managers. DEC and Sun achieved their initial victories by leapfrogging customers' traditional data-processing approval processes and buying cycles. Both companies went to the departments and individuals with a chronic need for more efficient, more flexible, more advanced computer power. DEC and Sun have been equally heralded as high-technology marvels. Each one attracted top-quality engineers and computer scientists.

Few firms engaged in growth plans as ambitious as have DEC and Sun. Yet it took DEC more than twenty years to pass the billion-dollar mark and nearly as long to reach the Fortune 500; even accounting for inflation, Sun's phenomenal growth outstrips DEC by a dozen years. The generation that separates the founding of these two similar organizations accounts for some of Sun's distinctive track record, but timing alone does not explain the company's achievements.

The rapid ascent of Sun is not a fluke. It is not a company whose products depend on the passing whims of a fickle consumer society, where what's hot one year can propel a company to dizzying revenue heights, only to cast it into cascading losses as the fad fizzles. The Silicon Valley area has seen more than its share of such companies; Atari and Osborne come to mind. Sun is not one of them.

Sun has staying power. It sells its wares to organizations that have decided to build their computing future around Sun technology. These organizations like the hardware and software Sun produces, to be sure. But more important, they agree with Sun's philosophy of computing, its vision about what's in store for the future of the computer industry. They have faith that Sun will nurse that vision into a reality, one they can use and profit from. As much as anything else, they like the company's attitude.

These are ingredients you can't cook up in the engineering lab. You can't program them into your software. They are simply part of the package, the intangible benefit a customer gets whenever a purchase is made. They are also the stuff that makes Sun different from Compaq, DEC, or any other company in the industry. Not better. Just different.

That difference gives Sun an advantage. The company's image is easy to discern. Its messages are clearly understood. It is distinctive amidst a gaggle of clone makers and me-too also-rans. That difference is also a disadvantage. If a company takes an unambiguous position, it's easy to take a stand against it.

Sun, for all its friends, has no lack of enemies. It has become a target not only for DEC, but also IBM, Hewlett-Packard, and Apple. These and other companies are investing billions of dollars in marketing, sales, and product development to unseat Sun as the leader in the workstation segment of the computer market. "Sun-killer" machines are already available from nearly all these companies. The competition's obsession with Sun has arisen not because the company has found a high-tech niche and is exploiting it; rather, it is because they feel that Sun has the potential to change the way people work with computers and, therefore, the way in which they buy the machines.

The purpose of this book is to identify and explain the distinct characteristics of Sun and how they propelled the company to become the fastest-growing direct-sales company in the history of capitalism. The brief history of Sun Microsystems is an object lesson in how to build a major corporation able to compete internationally with companies ten, twenty, even fifty times your size. It is a lesson in avoiding failure as much as it is in achieving success. The swiftness of

Sun's expansion undercuts the value of a straight chronological history of the company. So the book focuses on the major themes—the corporate cultural traits, you might call them—that have contributed to Sun's success. These are the essence of Sun, the filament that makes it successful. They might even represent a formula for what it takes to establish and sustain new companies looking to the 1990s and beyond.

The first chapter quickly summarizes the company, the people, and Sun's structure over time. The events and ideas touched on here are expanded later in the book. Chapter 2 covers Sun's amazing knack for making deals. Nothing exemplifies a successful corporation better than its ability to work with another organization; whether it's a simple sale or a complex trading agreement, the deal is the bedrock of business. No deal, no business. Sun makes deals as well as, maybe even better than, anyone else in the computer industry. Chapter 3 looks at the competition, the companies trying to take the deals away from Sun. This chapter pays special attention to Apollo Computer (before and after its acquisition by a competitor), DEC, and Hewlett-Packard.

In the fourth chapter, the shift is to the technology that inspires Sun. Chapter 4 focuses on the UNIX operating system, the foundation for all of Sun's technical achievements. Sun's CEO repeats over and over to anyone who will sit still long enough to listen that Sun is the *only* billion-dollar, exclusively UNIX company in the world. It is no mean feat in his eyes. Chapter 5 extends the notion of UNIX from the laboratory into the boardroom, examining how Sun works as an engineering-driven organization. Chapter 6 discusses the unique methodology Sun has adopted for making its technology tops in the workstation market: it gives it away. Sort of. Sun's licensing strategy, which even includes putting its inventions in the public domain, is arguably one of the most brilliant plans in the computer industry. Or one of the dumbest. It certainly has been controversial and stands as one of Sun's boldest moves, continuing to raise debate inside and outside of the company.

Chapter 7 moves from technology to people. In a company

that blasts upward like a rocket, there are immense and complicated management issues. How do you manage employees? How do you finance growth? How do you efficiently expand manufacturing? Chapter 8 investigates the kind of people who work at Sun. How do you recruit them? How do you organize them? How do you inspire them? How, amid the frenetic pace, do you simply keep them alive? Chapter 9 looks closely at the idea of openness. Is it exclusive to Sun? How is it reflected in Sun's corporate culture?

The final chapter recaptures the crucial two-quarter period when Sun suffered setbacks on nearly all fronts. It reviews what management did to avoid disaster and keep growth on track. The book concludes with an authors' coda, which describes the writing of the book and the authors' relationship to Sun. There is a glossary of terms, which can be helpful when you are slogging through the company's lexicon. Some of the words are technology specific; some are Sun specific.

As of this writing, Sun continues to set records for revenue growth. Its influence persists and expands, and it has a chance to become one of the major computer companies in the industry. In this era of megatakeovers and nail-biting economics, however, it may become a footnote in some other company's ledger, or a paragraph in a future history of Silicon Valley.

It's clear that Sun has an opportunity to become the ultimate Silicon Valley success story, eclipsing Apple Computer, even Hewlett-Packard. If Sun's rocket acceleration retains its fire, there may be nothing ahead of the company but the stars. Control is the critical question. It is the one that everyone rightfully addresses. It is the one that only the future can answer, but knowing something of the past can give us some clues.

SUNBURST

1
Insurmountable Opportunity:
The Founding of Sun Microsystems

In May 1982, Silicon Valley's major newspaper, the *San Jose Mercury News*, published a cover story in its Sunday supplement, *West* magazine. The feature depicted the dangers of living in Silicon Valley in the event of nuclear war. The region was high on the Soviets' list of targets, the author suggested. In addition to being the nation's leading technology center, Silicon Valley boasted the notorious "Blue Cube," the satellite tracking and control center for the military and intelligence communities. The area was also populated by NASA's Ames Research Center, Lockheed, a nuclear-weapons division of Westinghouse, Moffet Naval Air Station, and a host of other national security operations. Wiping it all out would be a priority task for Russian military planners. The article proposed to tell its readers where, exactly, ground zero was in Silicon Valley—where, if the denizens of the "Evil Empire" had only one place to drop the Big One in the area, the best place would be.

The article was widely read and discussed by the engineers and employees of a four-month-old startup company called Sun Microsystems. In 1982, long before the relief of *glasnost* and armament agreements, the specter of nuclear annihilation seemed far too near. Unnerving reports of superpower conflicts, such as the one in *West*, constantly peppered the news, adding tension to a country already on edge from years of political and economic uncertainty. For Sun's youthful staff, the article spurred many a discussion as to how military and foreign policy ought to be handled. More often, the piece generated a wisecrack or some black humor.

According to *West*, ground zero for Silicon Valley was Walsh Road and San Thomas Expressway in Santa Clara, California. Those street corners were the likely coordinates in the Soviet computers targeting the area for destruction. They also happened to be the location of Sun Microsystems' first headquarters—one the company left later that month for its current home in Mountain View.

In May 1982, Sun's fame rested solely on its proximity to ground zero. But soon after it abandoned its dubious address, the company began a sustained and explosive growth in the business world, expanding at rates never before seen for a manufacturer and direct seller of computer products. That month, Sun shipped its first computers, beginning a virtually unblemished seven-year record of quarter-to-quarter growth and profits. And though it escaped from the nuclear bull's-eye, Sun landed at the center of the fastest-growing segment of the already torrid computer industry.

Sun's entry into the computer industry in 1982 caused tremendous controversy. Its business philosophy and strategy significantly changed the huge and fast-growing high-technology marketplace, influencing the technology, marketing, research and development, and investment strategies of all major computer makers and users alike.

The Sun success story is an object lesson for business in the 1990s. The company's genius for developing and exploiting markets is an excellent model for others in the midst of their own success story or on the verge of building one. The exact traits and themes that have made Sun so extraordinary are examined in detail in subsequent chapters. Here, however, it is important to establish the foundation of the company, to identify some of the key people, and set the stage for one of this country's most intriguing business ventures.

COUNTDOWN

The workstation, an extremely fast and highly functional computer that fits on an engineer's desktop, was not a novel idea in 1981. Priced from $80,000 to $100,000, workstations as powerful as minicomputers, but nearly as compact as personal computers were already reaching the market. Because of their expense, however, they were used mainly by highly paid employees for whom superior computing capacity was essential. Competition and technology improvements were bound to lower the cost and expand the market. One of the first to see the unmined potential for inexpensive workstations was Vinod Khosla.

Khosla was born in New Delhi in 1956, the same year the other three founders of Sun Microsystems were born. He came to Silicon Valley via the Indian Institute of Technology, where he picked up a bachelor's degree in electrical engineering, and Carnegie-Mellon University in Pittsburgh, where he was awarded a master's degree in biomedical engineering. He signed up for Stanford's M.B.A. program and was infected with the region's entrepreneurial ambitions.

His own ambitions led him to help found Daisy Systems, a computer maker that specialized in machines for engineers who built other computers. This demanding craft was known as computer-aided engineering (CAE). The systems that helped accomplish it were expensive computers with dedicated software to assist engineers in designing the circuitry on the boards that fit inside another computer. CAE systems were also used to design printed-circuit boards for a variety of products that worked in everything from automobiles to microwave ovens.

Khosla concluded that Daisy's specialization limited the company's growth potential. He also believed that a general-purpose, less expensive computer was necessary, both for the CAE market and other technical environments where such powerful systems were in demand. At this time, from 1980 to 1982, engineers and scientists had few choices about what kinds of computers they could use. For all but the most advanced and well-financed companies, powerful mainframe systems from IBM or Control Data Corporation were not affordable. Newly popular personal computers, such as the IBM PC and the Apple III, were woefully inadequate for the technical problems facing engineers and scientists.

These demanding users gravitated to minicomputers from firms such as Digital Equipment Corporation, Prime, and Data General. Minicomputers had a lot of power and cost much less than mainframes, so they were quite successful in the technical marketplace. But because they were often shared by many users, their performance tended to be slow. A single, complex program run by one engineer generally bogged down a minicomputer for everyone else who was using it.

In 1980, Apollo Computer of Chelmsford, Massachusetts, unveiled its first workstation. Less powerful but much cheaper than a minicomputer, the Apollo workstation provided enough performance to satisfy many technical users. Khosla and others at Daisy reviewed the Apollo system as a possible alternative to designing and building their own CAE computer, but they decided that a dedicated, specialized CAE machine was the right choice. The idea of a general-purpose workstation, however, took hold in Khosla's mind as the way of the future. Although he felt certain Daisy would be successful, he concluded the success would be limited. Khosla's personal ambition was to retire by the time he was thirty years old, so he decided to leave Daisy and start a new firm, one that had a greater vision of the market for powerful, general-purpose desktop computers.

Well versed in the recent history of computer technology, Khosla thought that a workstation company could be built on a product that used many standard components and technologies. Although an engineer by training, Khosla's personality and ambitions were entrepreneurial. He realized that standard technologies were readily available and relatively cheap.

They did not have to be designed from scratch—an expensive and time-consuming process. So he started to ask knowledgeable people a lot of questions about what technologies and what components would be best for his envisioned workstation. He also nosed around to see who was doing what with those technologies.

In his research Khosla discovered that a Stanford University graduate student, Andy Bechtolsheim, had developed a computer along the same lines as Khosla's own workstation idea; it was a machine considerably different from the others making their way into the market. Because he could not afford the time and expense of designing a completely new machine, Bechtolsheim had created a workstation by combining already available components. Khosla shared this notion. He believed that by combining standard, off-the-shelf technologies, he could build a workstation that exploited and built on the research and development skills of many different companies. This method would also lower the unit cost for each computer and give his standards-based workstation a price, if not a performance, advantage over the competition. At that time, only Apollo offered a real workstation product. Hewlett-Packard had announced an intention to build one but had not yet delivered anything. Minicomputer makers were still enjoying record growth and showed no interest in jumping into such a small, untested market.

In January 1982, Khosla, a handsome man with quick intelligence and a persuasive intensity, easily convinced Bechtolsheim that there was more opportunity outside of Stanford for him and his computer. Bechtolsheim had been searching for outside backers for his idea before meeting Khosla, so he was primed for a chance to build a product and company around the computer he had created.

Bechtolsheim, who is much more comfortable in an electronics laboratory than in a boardroom, joined Khosla in the hunt for venture capital. Armed with a four-page business plan, the two men, both still in their mid-twenties, met with Robert Sackman on Lincoln's Birthday. A general partner in the Silicon Valley–based U.S. Venture Partners, the older man listened carefully to the young men's idea. Sackman, a degreed engineer, had held various jobs in the electronics industry for more than thirty years, including a vice presidency at Ampex Corporation, a highflier in the region before the term *Silicon Valley* was coined. He had also held the top executive position for a research and development agency for the Department of Defense. Having Sackman as friend and backer was clearly a boon to Sun's success.

Khosla knew Sackman as an investor from the founding days at Daisy Systems and had earned the money man's trust. After considering for less than a week one idea for a general-purpose workstation for engineers, Sackman, who is currently on Sun's board of directors, agreed to underwrite Khosla's and Bechtolsheim's initial development. He gave them a check for $100,000 immediately and another $200,000 when Sun Microsystems was officially incorporated ten days after their first meeting.

Khosla knew that it would take more than himself and Bechtolsheim to make the company fly. He invited a friend he knew from the Stanford M.B.A. program to join him for lunch. Typical of Khosla's reputed tightfisted approach to money, he did his recruiting at the local McDonald's. There he met Scott McNealy and persuaded him to leave his job at Onyx Computer and join the fledgling Sun as director of operations. At Onyx the twenty-six-year-old McNealy directed the minicomputer company's manufacturing floor. He did not take long to ponder his future. At Onyx he was a middle manager. At Sun he would be a founder. The idea immediately appealed to McNealy's aggressive sense of adventure. He jumped ship and became Sun's third employee. By then the young cofounders had decided to call their venture Sun Microsystems.

For the next two-and-a-half months, the team prepared for the development and production of the Sun-1 workstation. In May a prototype was ready. That same month, Bechtolsheim recognized that operating system software was critical to the success of the new workstation. He had used the UNIX operating system while devising his computer, a common approach among engineering students in the 1980s. Generally, though, when prototypes turned into production models, UNIX was renounced in favor of specialized, proprietary operating systems, which in the early 1980s was considered the prudent approach to take.

Sun's engineers could have developed a proprietary operating system for the hardware, but that would have meant a long development period, something Khosla wanted to avoid. Personal computer operating systems, such as MS-DOS, did not have the functions, power, and flexibility necessary for the technical market that Sun planned to serve. And, of course, existing operating systems from DEC and IBM, which had the capabilities that Sun wanted, were proprietary. Keeping with Khosla's and Bechtolsheim's collective vision of a computer based on standards, they opted for the UNIX operating system, which was popular in universities and, increasingly, in the commercial world. More important, it was in the public domain and readily available.

The young founders knew they needed a master of the internals of UNIX, the tricky and complex raw programming code that organizes and manages the silicon transistors so people can use a computer. They went to the University of California at Berkeley, which was leading the world in UNIX development. At Berkeley, the undisputed thinker on the subject of UNIX was Bill Joy. Bechtolsheim insisted that Sun recruit him.

Bill Joy enjoyed puzzles. He was also very good at them. One of the thorniest puzzles in the computer industry was getting computer software to match the much more rapid progress of hardware. Computers kept getting faster, less expensive, and smaller, while operating systems seemed slower, more costly, and cumbersome. At Berkeley, Joy was renowned for manipulating UNIX so that it could run efficiently on lots of different computers. He took advantage of computer hardware as well as anyone in industry.

As the principal architect and designer of Berkeley's version of UNIX, Joy's reputation and influence had spread. Like the other three founders, he believed in the propagation of computer standards. To him, standards meant better, cheaper, quicker computers. More important, standards meant more computers because their popularity would soar as costs plunged and capabilities rose. Although Joy is often considered purely a technical genius, his analytical mind quickly assesses marketing, manufacturing, and distribution issues. Khosla once noted that Joy "is also a brilliant marketing strategist because of his ability to match the best combinations of existing technologies to what a customer needs." Joy understood more than the technological possibilities open to him by jumping from academia to corporate life. He knew that the time was right to build a major company based on standards. The world was ready.

The importance of Joy's arrival cannot be overstated. Although he was Sun's sixteenth employee, arriving months after the company opened its Santa Clara offices, Joy was given founder status, both in stock and prestige. With Joy, the Sun team was complete and ready to launch itself into the computer industry.

At the time of his recruitment, Joy, like Bechtolsheim, was working on his doctorate and agreed to join the company with the understanding that he would someday return to the halls of academia to complete his studies. More than seven years later, neither man has returned to school. The challenge of building a company and designing new technologies is apparently more satisfying to their inquisitive intelligences.

On Target

Before he and Khosla met, Bechtolsheim had spent well over a year defining the hardware of Sun's first workstation. It took them only a few months, then, to get the first products ready. Initial shipments began in May 1982, a bare three months after the company's founding. The entire company, fewer than twenty employees, saw the first boxed machines packed away in a truck for delivery.

In 1982 the heady atmosphere in Silicon Valley made embryonic companies such as Sun good bets for venture capitalists. Almost anyone with a dream and a business plan was funded in those days. After the first trickle of Sun workstations emerged from production, the company needed more funds to finance full-scale manufacturing. Sun made its case to several venture capitalist companies, and two of them—Kleiner Perkins Caufield and Byers of San Francisco and Technology Venture Investors (TVI) of Menlo Park, California—joined Sackman and his group with a total investment of $4.5 million. The venture capitalists at both Kleiner Perkins and TVI accepted the standards-based–computers philosophy of Sun's young founders. They were careful, though, to add members of their companies to Sun's board of directors. From Kleiner Perkins came L. John Doerr, while TVI added David Marquardt. Both men held engineering degrees and M.B.A.s, giving them insight in both the technical and business opportunities Sun faced. The money from the two companies was committed by July 1982, allowing Sun to increase hiring and begin volume production of its products.

Sun's first customers for the ten-thousand-dollar workstations were the easiest buyers in the computer business: universities. Schools with advanced computer-science programs, such as Berkeley, Stanford, and Carnegie-Mellon, were the first buyers. Academics love new, fast hardware. They also get deep discounts. Selling to the university market will not make a company rich, but it does get the products into a market in which they will be tested by the most demanding and curious users. The feedback to Sun's engineers, both good and bad, about the Sun-1 was critical to the development of the much more successful Sun-2, which went into development in the summer of 1982, immediately after shipments of the Sun-1 began in volume. Fewer than two hundred of the Sun-1 computers were sold, and few are in use today. But they established a pattern that Sun has been known for since 1982: building relatively fast and modestly priced machines. In comparison to DEC and IBM minicomputers, the Sun machines were a steal. Sun-1 users had nearly the power of a minicomputer for one-tenth the price.

In addition to the price and performance advantage they gained, users did not need to share their computer with other users, which was generally the case with minicomputers.

Because nearly all computer makers sell to the major university computer-science departments, these manufacturers soon heard about the "hot new box" from Sun. Original-equipment manufacturers (OEMs), which repackage other companies' systems under their own name, began to call on Sun, curious about the fast (for that time), inexpensive workstation that was built from standard components.

The switch to workstations from minicomputers had begun, but ever so slowly. In 1982 and 1983, most OEMs that had begun integrating workstations into their products were going to the workstation industry leader, Apollo. Sun was still too small, too unknown—its managers perceived as too young. Each of the four founders turned twenty-six the year Sun staked its claim as a computer manufacturer. Most of the rest of the employees were around the same age.

Sun's youth was a real impediment to striking deals with companies. OEMs in particular wanted the assurance that management was experienced and savvy enough to endure the inevitable tough times a business will face. Seeing no wrinkles on the faces and no gray hair at Sun made them think twice before buying into the Sun product line. Apollo, whose seasoned managers came from Prime Computer, an already established and successful minicomputer maker, exuded the experience that comforted the OEM marketplace.

Within Sun, however, the youthful atmosphere was part of its charm and appeal. Sun's founders knew that it took more than charm to motivate employees, especially talented ones who were sought after in the aggressively competitive Silicon Valley region. As a result, all Sun employees, regardless of position, became stockholders in the company. Many of the new workers took the thousands of offered shares lightly. Most, however, were inspired by the incentives; stock that cost them pennies a share might be worth considerably more in just a few years. It gave employees the added bond of working together in hopes of making their individual and collective fortunes. They were eventually proven right beyond their most optimistic expectations.

Sun, like other Silicon Valley startup operations, was known for its weekly beer busts. In the early years, when the company numbered fewer than two hundred people, the employees chipped in to buy bottled beer, with special consideration given to individuals' favorite brands. New employees were introduced to the entire company at the beer busts, where they received T-shirts and other Sun trinkets. Once a month, people at the beer bust would pitch in and help the shipping crew, putting workstations into boxes and loading them onto trucks for delivery. The sessions often ran late, but generally a few people would amble back to their offices and continue working until the early morning hours.

It was at these early beer busts that McNealy began to exhibit his leadership qualities and gift for public speaking. As director of operations, he was the man with the most important numbers—the number of workstations shipped, the amount of money in the door. Because every employee was a stockholder, that information was particularly vital, although the employees also took a palpable pride in knowing that their collective work was succeeding in the market. McNealy stood on a chair and traded jokes and insults with those at the gathering while swigging his favorite brew, Stroh's. His personality was perfect for a public forum, whereas Khosla appeared too humorless, Bechtolsheim too shy, and Joy too intellectual. Unconsciously, McNealy refined his talents as a leader and public figure at the weekly festivities.

As a youthful company, Sun was famous for its desire "to party." But youth has its other advantages, not the least of which is energy and optimism—traits that came to Sun's aid at a critical time in its history.

BULL'S-EYE

In late 1982, Computervision, the world's leading supplier of systems to the computer-aided-design (CAD) market, let it

be known that it was considering new technologies to replace
its previous reliance on minicomputers. The CAD market
was becoming price-sensitive, and minicomputers were too
expensive. Additionally, competition was heating up in the
CAD area.

Sun joined a stream of competitors, including the leading
suitor, Apollo, to woo Computervision. Khosla and others on
Sun's board of directors believed that a more mature senior
management might give the young company a better chance
at winning favorable consideration at Computervision and
other major OEMs. So Khosla recruited Owen Brown from
Digital Equipment Corporation to be vice president of sales
and marketing.

At DEC, Brown had held various marketing and sales
titles, including worldwide operations manager for the technical volume group, an organization with more revenues and
employees than all of Sun. He held engineering degrees from
Auburn University and the navy's Nuclear Power and Sub-
marine Training Program. While at DEC, he had earned a
reputation as a bright, enthusiastic salesman and an intelligent marketer. He understood the needs of the technical
community and eloquently articulated DEC's product positioning. Khosla and the board of directors wanted that same
intelligence and advocacy for Sun.

During the recruitment process, the salary and stock options were agreed on, but Khosla was unwilling to offer
Brown any higher position than the top spot in marketing
and sales. Brown insisted on the job of president of the
company. Sun's board considered the demand reasonable.
Sun needed a seasoned top executive, and Brown had the
necessary qualities.

Khosla wrangled with the board, not wanting to relinquish
that much authority to an outsider. Longtime Sun employees
remember Khosla as having been dictatorial and, at times,
arbitrary in his decisions. His hard-driving personality did
not tolerate dissension, and it was obvious that he did not
want to share power with Brown or anyone else. But the need
was compelling. The board of directors insisted that their

wishes be carried out, and Brown was hired as president of Sun Microsystems.

Once inside Sun, Brown's style conflicted with Khosla's. More easygoing than Sun's founding CEO, Brown established a rapport with lower-level managers in a way that was impossible for the impatient Khosla. While Khosla wanted to have his hands in virtually every decision, Brown was willing to delegate responsibility to the budding managers in the company. As a result, conflict grew between the two men.

Prior to Brown's arrival, Khosla had insisted that all purchases of more than one hundred dollars be approved by the office of the president. He regularly questioned every buying decision, rejecting many of them. This process not only slowed the company's ability to act, it soured individuals on Khosla's style of management. Once the president's title came to Brown, he regularly and virtually without comment approved purchases. Soon everyone took their buying requests to Brown. Khosla quickly managed to rescind Brown's signature authority, causing more conflict between the two men and disgruntlement below. But it was the battle for the Computervision contract that finally severed their relationship.

Nearly everyone inside Sun knew how vital winning Computervision was to the long-term success of the company. If Apollo took the account, Sun would have little hope of overtaking its number-one competitor; if Sun won, it would mean that Sun had made it as a viable computer firm.

Bidding with their new Sun-2 workstations, which were twice as fast as the Sun-1 series and cost less, Sun's young team felt confident they would get the nod from Computervision. Inside the big CAD outfit, engineers and midlevel managers led the Sun team to believe that its products were superior and that the price was right. Enthusiasm began to course through Sun.

Then in July, on a day still remembered as Black Monday, Khosla got a call from a midlevel purchasing agent at Computervision. Sun had lost the deal. Apollo had won the contract. Khosla couldn't understand it. He was furious, with Computervision, with Apollo—and with Owen Brown, who

was gone for two weeks completing his duty in the Navy
Reserve.

Rejection is not something young people take gracefully.
So Khosla grabbed McNealy, and they took a red-eye flight
from San Francisco to Boston. Uninvited, they planted
themselves in the plush lobby of Computervision's headquarters. From there they called everyone they knew inside Computervision, asking for another chance, demanding an opportunity to revise their bid.

To some Computervision staff members, the two young
Californians were an embarrassment. The review process was
over. The decision was made. Sun had lost. Why weren't they
mature enough to accept no for an answer? Others admired
the unrelenting energy and the unconventional approach of
the Sun executives.

After hours of frustrated waiting, during which no one
would even venture into the lobby for fear of being considered a traitor to Computervison's decision process, the vice
president of sales came to see McNealy and Khosla. He
acknowledged that Sun had many friends inside Computervision and that the technology Sun offered was far more intriguing than Apollo's products. But more than technical
wizardry went into business decisions. Khosla requested an
opportunity to discuss the matter one last time with Computervision's president, James Barret. The VP of sales said he'd
arrange it, but added, "Please, just leave the lobby. He'll call
you at your local sales office."

When the call came, Khosla knew it was his last opportunity to sell Sun. So he sold hard. Winning Computervision as
an OEM would prove to industry watchers that Sun was real,
that the California upstart had made it. Going one-on-one
with Barret, he pushed hard on the advantages that teaming
up with Sun would provide. He cut his prices so that there
was virtually no margin. He highlighted the flexibility Sun's
use of standards gave Computervision. Khosla was compelling; Barret was interested again. He told Khosla to go home,
and he'd call back. Within a week Khosla and Barret met in
Chicago to negotiate a new contract, a three-year, $40 million
agreement, one that McNealy said "put us on the map."

Apollo had lost its first in a long series of deals to Sun. It was, perhaps, the most important. Apollo executives were furious with Computervision. They tried to win the contract back, crying foul all the way. But having switched positions once, Barret and his team were not about to do so again. When the news was released, industry observers sat up and took notice of this small, forty-person Silicon Valley operation. Inside Sun jubilation broke out. McNealy announced the news at a beer bust, which turned into a raucous party that lasted into the wee morning hours. In a later celebration that summer, the notoriously miserly Khosla sprang for a party on a rented boat for a meal, dance, and cruise on the San Francisco Bay for the entire company.

DEALING WITH THE BIG GUNS

The bad feelings Khosla and others inside Sun harbored for its president, Brown, over the Computervision deal eventually pushed him out the door. Khosla wasted no time blaming the near failure of the Computervision deal on what, to Khosla, was Brown's unnecessary absence during such a critical period. He felt that Brown could have rescheduled his navy duty or resigned his commission altogether. Being the president of a company in the young Indian's eyes was more than a full-time job. He pressured the board to relieve Brown of his duties. In February 1984, Brown left Sun. Although the board acceded to Khosla's demand, they recognized that Khosla could not get all the executive reins in his hands again. They insisted that he share his power with someone else. Khosla was adamant about not bringing in another outsider, so they looked inside Sun for another top executive.

McNealy's successes in manufacturing and his involvement at all levels in the company propelled him to take over the office of president. As a cofounder, classmate, and friend, McNealy was an acceptable candidate to Khosla, who remained as chairman and chief executive officer. The two men were faced with, in McNealy's words, "insurmountable opportunity."

The Computervision deal attracted a lot more business—

both OEM and end-user sales. This success was wonderful, but it also began years of Sun's struggling with the spiraling effects of hypergrowth. From $8 million in its first full fiscal year, Sun closed the books at the end of year two with nearly $40 million in sales. Managing and financing such expansion was, and continues to be, Sun's major problem.

By early spring 1984 it was clear Sun needed more cash to finance its growth. McNealy was dubbed the chief Sun fund-raiser. The chosen investor was Eastman Kodak. After a close look at Sun's books and an optimistic assessment of the workstation market, Kodak's money managers poured $20 million into the two-and-a-half-year-old company that summer. Besides a seat on the board, Kodak picked up 7 percent of Sun, one of its best investments in the decade.

As is often the case, the company's success created new problems. Sun's rapid expansion brought change and conflict. Tension mounted in the executive suite, and conflicts inevitably arose between the tightfisted Khosla and the board of directors. Khosla ultimately resigned in the fall of 1984, worth several million. The board picked McNealy as his successor, adding the responsibilities of chief executive officer and chairman to his role as president. They chose him over industry veteran Paul Ely, Jr., who was being considered for the position. Ely, then the president of Convergent Technologies, a maker of small office computers, wanted more than the small company was willing to offer. Besides, board members felt, McNealy was an ideal transitional leader. The idea at the time was to let McNealy run the show for a while and then eventually recruit a seasoned manager who could guide Sun to even greater success. That was more than six years and billions of dollars ago. Today McNealy is still at the top, holding maximum control of a multibillion-dollar organization that threatens the market stronghold once secured by DEC, Apple, and IBM.

The departure of Vinod Khosla brought a major change to the company. Together with Bechtolsheim and Joy, he imbued Sun with a philosophy of using existing standards in its product lines. Standards would bring the cost of goods down, making Sun's workstations more competitive on the market. Although the basis for Sun's eventual leadership in so-called open systems technology, the use of standards alone did not propel Sun to where it is today. That took new leadership with a grander vision. Though the new vision was not held by McNealy alone, but by Bechtolsheim, Joy, and the rest of Sun's UNIX engineers, it was McNealy who espoused it best. What McNealy provided was an articulate and unflagging voice for that vision.

McNealy's power rests in part on his infectious attitude. He does not accept the idea of failure. His confidence—some say his cockiness—is unbounded. His public presence is palpable. His main audience, Sun employees, pack rooms to hear him. His accessibility makes him seem involved with everyone's problems. He personally answers electronic mail sent to him by his workers. When department managers feel their group needs its spirits lifted, McNealy will give the group a pep talk, charging its intellectual and emotional batteries.

But Sun's board of directors did not place power in McNealy's hands because he was the company's top cheerleader. He understood the market. He had an overall vision of Sun's future, defining the aggressive market-share strategy that has propelled Sun's amazing growth for more than half a decade.

In addition to being a powerful spokesman and strategist, McNealy impressed the board with something else: he was a deal maker. His negotiating skills gave Sun an advantage in almost every situation. McNealy reveled in the bargaining process. He hammered out agreements that were bold and innovative and that have made Sun one of the most controversial and successful companies of our time. Under his guidance Sun's deal making has obliterated one competitor and scared the pants off most of the rest.

2
High-Five Deal Making:
Teamwork to the Top

Scott McNealy, the president of Sun Microsystems, and Vittorio Cassoni, the president of AT&T Information Systems, were on the precipice of a major deal. Each felt in his gut that when they put ink to paper their companies and the entire computer industry would change dramatically. As events played out, the changes were more significant than either man had anticipated.

For more than a year, the two companies had been in thorny discussions, hammering out an agreement that would bind them together in a complex business and technology venture. Both men had personally taken responsibility for the collaboration, investing a significant amount of their individual credibility in the deal. McNealy, the then thirty-two-year-old boyish-looking chief executive of Sun, had led the Sun negotiating team from the start. After it was over, he apologized to some of his close associates, saying that the process had "obsessed" him for nearly all the twelve-month negotiations. Cassoni, the urbane Italian chief of AT&T's computer-products division, was looking for the final element to finish the restructuring of his group—to complete the turnaround he had instigated upon his arrival from Olivetti eighteen months earlier.

The New York City hotel suite where they negotiated the final details in October 1987 was comfortable but not ornate, an unintentional compromise between McNealy's innate austerity and Cassoni's natural flamboyance. Down the hall in other hotel rooms, Sun and AT&T negotiating teams went over the ramifications of every phrase, every percentage point, every dollar mentioned in the complex proposals. Virtually everything had been finalized beforehand. Now it was only a matter of each team's leader making the final and ultimate assessment of his counterpart. Too much was at stake to overestimate the value of the other. Once the commitment was made, there was no turning back. The hotel rooms were charged with anticipation and excitement.

After many tension-filled hours, the last of the documents arrived before McNealy and Cassoni. Executives and lawyers from both sides had combed through them for the final time. All that remained was the signatures. The two men glanced at each other; with steely calm and contained self-assurance, they signed the papers. When it was over, they shook hands and exchanged a few words; then McNealy left for his own suite.

Back in his own room, McNealy let out a war whoop. He and his team danced around the room, slapping each other's hands with "high fives," like basketball players who had just won a tournament. They leapt over couches and hooted and hollered with glee. It was party time for Sun Microsystems once again.

FUN IN THE TRENCHES

The agreement with AT&T illustrates Sun's combination of clearheaded professionalism and youthful enthusiasm. The deal that Cassoni and McNealy had signed committed the giant company to buy up to 15 percent of its relatively young ally over a three-year period, at Sun's discretion. The shares of outstanding common stock acquired by AT&T would be purchased at a 25 percent premium above the average price for a given twenty-day trading period of Sun's stock on the NASDAQ exchange. AT&T was allowed to pick up another 5 percent of Sun on the open market, but AT&T was limited in the contract to owning no more than 20 percent of the company for ten years, or until 1998. In the first eighteen months of the arrangement, Sun agreed to sell at least a 7½ percent ownership, or AT&T would be allowed to accumulate that amount on the open market, with the proviso that it limit itself to owning no more than 12½ percent of Sun through strictly open-market stock purchases. Analysts estimated the deal to be worth $300 million.

The criteria and timing of AT&T's investment in Sun were as shrewd as the investment was lucrative. The agreement buttressed Sun's reputation as the most vital player in the computer industry's hottest markets, workstations and the UNIX operating system. It gave Sun the capital necessary to sustain its dizzying growth rate and its rapid seizure of market share, and it freed Sun from dependence on short-term expectations in the stock market. The deal solidified a business relationship between Sun and one of the major corporations of the world, while giving Sun distinct advantages. It also provided Sun with one of the industry's most critical, though intangible, assets: a reputation as a leader in technology.

The AT&T deal was one of Sun's more spectacular announcements in its brief history, but it was consistent with the company leadership's capabilities and style. Since its founding in February 1982, Sun has regularly won key accounts, signed critical OEMs, and opened new distribution channels for its products. It did so at the expense of established and larger competitors, until it eventually became the leader in its market. Sun's deal making has often caught competing companies off guard, angering and frustrating them. But they have apparently been unable to stop Sun's momentum, as each year the company has grabbed increasing market dominance (see figure 2.1). Between 1987 and 1988, for example, market researcher DataQuest estimated that

Sun's market share jumped from over 24 percent to more than 28 percent. In the strictly UNIX workstation market, according to analysts at IDC, Sun's dominance reached 43.4 percent of the installed base of high-performance computers (see figure 2.2).

Figure 2.1

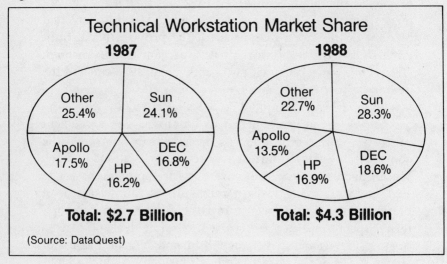

Technical Workstation Market Share

1987

Other 25.4%
Sun 24.1%
Apollo 17.5%
HP 16.2%
DEC 16.8%

Total: $2.7 Billion

1988

Other 22.7%
Sun 28.3%
Apollo 13.5%
HP 16.9%
DEC 18.6%

Total: $4.3 Billion

(Source: DataQuest)

Sun established an early track record of persistent and impressive growth (see figure 2.3). Its revenue expansion paralleled an intellectual shift on the part of computer users. Organizations, in particular, were radically reconsidering their attitudes about the nature of computing operations. *Distributed computing*—a concept espoused by Sun, among others in the market—emerged as a popular methodology for information-processing requirements. Large mainframe and minicomputer operations lost relative share of a company's total processing capacity as local area networks of desktop computers proliferated.

Producing high-performance, networked workstations, however, was not the only reason for Sun's skyrocketing expansion. Offering such a system was a basic competitive ingredient. A company could not claim to be in the workstation market without paying homage to the values of computer

Figure 2.2

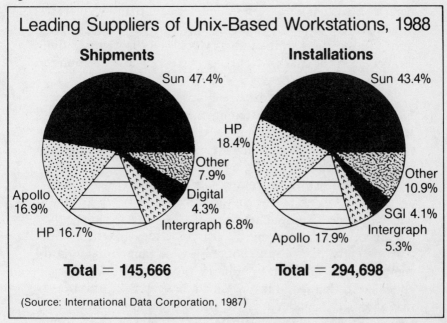

Leading Suppliers of Unix-Based Workstations, 1988

Shipments

Sun 47.4%
HP 18.4%
Other 7.9%
Apollo 16.9%
Digital 4.3%
HP 16.7%
Intergraph 6.8%

Total = 145,666

Installations

Sun 43.4%
Other 10.9%
SGI 4.1%
Apollo 17.9%
Intergraph 5.3%

Total = 294,698

(Source: International Data Corporation, 1987)

Figure 2.3

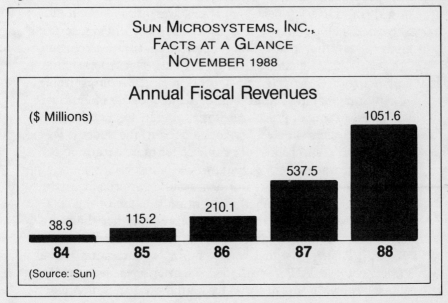

SUN MICROSYSTEMS, INC., FACTS AT A GLANCE NOVEMBER 1988

Annual Fiscal Revenues

($ Millions)

84	85	86	87	88
38.9	115.2	210.1	537.5	1051.6

(Source: Sun)

performance and networks, delivering at a minimum a fast box attached to a wire. Sun was better able than its rivals to build on these basics and exploit its advantages with a single-mindedness others in the industry could not match, turning its success in the market from mere technological triumph to business victory in the process.

Sun did not reinvent the wheel of distributed computing, but it made it roll in a different direction. It was a concept with a healthy lineage, going back to the 1960s and the first minicomputers. Sun did, however, expand the notion to the desktop with the promulgation of the idea of *open systems*. It was the first workstation company to fully grasp that customers were serious about moving to standardized technologies, which enabled these customers to escape, in part, the "planned obsolescence" built into proprietary systems.

In its early years, Sun adopted a wide range of standard components with which to build its products. This approach appealed to users, and it quickened development, improved manufacturing, and added to the bottom line. Standards such as Ethernet (local area networks), Motorola chips (central processing units), Multibus and VMEbus (system buses), and UNIX (operating system) were incorporated into Sun's technology and touted by both Sun and some press analysts as what made Sun "open" and the competition "closed." The strategy worked. Users flocked to Sun, eschewing the proprietary attitudes of the competition. When Sun expanded its standards strategy—the Open Systems Networking approach, as it was called—to include complementary technologies developed at Sun, the success was even more pronounced. (See chapter 6 for more details on the company's strategy for "giving away" its inventions.)

The steamroller of Sun's open systems approach in the workstation industry gained momentum because of the company's unwavering commitment to gaining market share. To do so, Sun established itself as "the price/performance leader." That is, its goal was to build products that had a lower cost per MIPS (million instructions per second: the industry's measurement for determining the speed or performance of a given workstation) than any other firm. Bernard

Lacroute, Sun's executive vice president, maintained that the price/performance edge was what gave his company the opportunity to bid on contracts that were previously locked in by the competition. Offering less-expensive workstations in the early years got Sun's foot in the door, allowing the company to bid against industry giants such as IBM and DEC. It also set Sun apart from the market leader of that time, Apollo, whose own initial product, the DN100, carried a hefty sixty-thousand-dollar entry price, three times the price of Sun's first workstation.

Lower prices at Sun were possible, in part, because of the incorporation of standard components. Sun did not have to recoup the development costs for designing a lot of proprietary equipment. More important, however, was the sacrifice Sun was willing to make at the bottom line. As such, Sun kept its margins much lower than the competition's (see figure 2.4). These low prices gave Sun instant appeal in the United States. But equally vital was the advantage it gave to Sun's workstations abroad. In Europe, for example, where high-technology goods sell for 50 to 300 percent more than in the United States, Sun's sales and market share blossomed immediately.

The importance of attaining the long-term advantage of

Figure 2.4

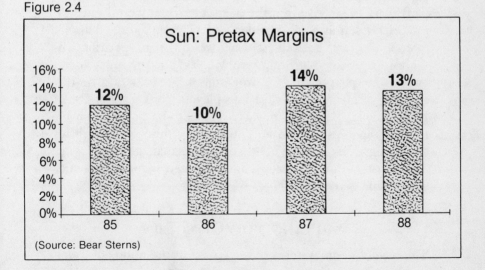

(Source: Bear Sterns)

market share, rather than short-term profits, cannot be overstated in Sun's case. It was the basis for many key decisions, including the AT&T investment. McNealy, Sun's CEO, grew up in the house of a U.S. automotive executive: his father was a vice chairman of American Motors. He learned from visceral, firsthand experience how a company can lose its raison d'être when the competition steals away its market position. McNealy also learned, from the Japanese entry into the U.S. car market, that achieving an advantageous market share takes vision, resolve, and perseverance. These were traits he wanted to embed in Sun's business strategy.

Of Sun's four cofounders, McNealy was part of the "business half," with Vinod Khosla; Andy Bechtolsheim and Bill Joy were the "technical half." Khosla was the business genius who helped put the company together, but it was McNealy who had to carry on when Khosla left.

Sun tenaciously pursued the vision of open systems because it gave the company an immediate distinction over the competition. The company also saw that riding the open systems wave was the most effective way to become a long-term major player in the computer industry. Sun's managers had set their sights on being dominant not simply in the workstation arena, but in the realm of general-purpose computers as well. In the view of Sun management, if the company were to survive into the next century, it would have to establish itself as a multibillion-dollar organization that offered a clear and desirable alternative to the competition. In the minds of some at Sun, with McNealy as the most vocal and visible proponent, the workstation arena would be reduced to four, maybe five, serious players, consisting of IBM, DEC, Apple, Sun, and perhaps Hewlett-Packard. Each of these companies offered a popular and unique approach to technology. Each had a solid and stable management team. And most important, each had cultivated a consistent and sustainable market share.

SELLING THE CONCEPT

The idea of open systems did not arise in the minds of users out of the blue. People had become accustomed to the concept through years of selling practices by personal computer (PC) makers and their attendant local-area-network (LAN) manufacturers. PCs and LANs preceded workstations by a few years. IBM and Compaq were followed by the likes of 3Com and Novell. The idea of sharing resources predates PCs; LANs originally legitimized themselves through resource sharing for minicomputers. "Sling a string of minis onto a network and share printers and disk drives" was the pitch to users. And it worked. From 1979 to 1985, LAN companies were the darlings of the industry.

Workstations took the appealing notion of PCs and LANs and added muscle to it. PCs were fine for word processing, spreadsheets, and games, but in the world of engineers, scientists, and what became known as "power users," PCs did not make the grade. Power computer users needed machines with more memory, better displays, faster networks, and most critically, more speed. They had bigger tasks that had to run faster. For years these users were handcuffed to timeshared minicomputers. One large program could bring a system to its knees, forcing other users to either learn the exquisite value of patience or burn an ulcer into their stomachs waiting for their programs to run. In some organizations, the cost of adding minicomputers became prohibitive, despite the processing needs of the technical staff.

Engineers and other technical users in organizations were among the last to experience the desktop computer revolution because PCs were too underpowered for their tasks. They needed much faster machines, but they also needed to be unshackled from timesharing inadequacies. The introduction of workstations offered a viable alternative. At first these desktop units were not nearly in the same league as minicomputers, but soon they passed the more expensive minicomputers in performance, gaining ground on the even pricier superminicomputers. "Minis thrived in the 1970s because they cut costs by sharing expensive resources such as processing power and memory among dozens of office workers, each with a terminal. Now the role has been taken by desktop computers . . .," concluded *Business Week*.

This change occurred because of performance. Speed was the crucible in which PCs were tested and failed; workstations passed with ease. Performance, then, rose above most other distinguishing criteria for what defined a good workstation. Like the rest of the industry, Sun pointed to the speed of its computers, and it contributed its share to the industrywide notion that a computer manufacturer can never make a machine too fast or too inexpensive.

If making the latest, swiftest machine was all there was to the game, Sun might not have fought its way beyond its combatants in the workstation industry. Every year Sun introduced new computers. Some of them set the temporary standard for high performance, but it was inevitable that a competitor would beat the MIPS numbers a Sun workstation had established. The technology moved too quickly for one company always to have the quickest machine. But Sun steadfastly held its advantage in the price/performance category, one it essentially created and promulgated in the industry and one the customers clearly understood and appreciated. If a competitor came out with an equally fast system at a comparable price, it was a sure sign that Sun would lower its prices, as it did in 1987 with the price cut for the popular Sun-3/50 computer; industry foes were forced to drop prices for similar machines. When Sun introduced its Sun-3/60 color-display workstation at a price drastically below those of products in its performance class, the competition had to reconsider its pricing. Even after Sun later increased the cost of the Sun-3/60, the machine was still less expensive than any similar computer. Such moves were applauded by users, even those who suffered long delays in getting delivery of their Sun systems because of the phenomenal demand. Lead times on some workstations stretched to 120 days, but the orders continued to pour in.

In addition to price distinctions, Sun offered a wide range of products. Between 1985 and 1988, the company was busy.

• Sun introduced the Sun-3, Sun-4, and Sun386i series of workstations, broadening the product line to appeal to diverse customers.

- SunLink (data communications), SunIngres and Sun-Unify (data bases), and SunTrac (project management)—products to help gain further access to the business community—were unveiled.

- For more technical customers, Sun introduced NeWS, the Network/extensible Window System.

- Sun's PC-NFS networking product, which could link Sun workstations to the thousands of PCs in place in business and industry, entered the market.

- The company released the TAAC-1 graphics accelerator, which made graphics applications run faster.

- For programmers, Sun introduced the SunPro and NSE software development products, as well as ongoing releases of the Sun Operating System (SunOS). The product diversity appealed to the company's broad base of users and was considered "one of Sun Microsystems' strengths."

Sun kept research-and-development investment high, producing fast desktop systems based on Motorola 680x0, Intel 80x86, and its own Scalable Processor Architecture (SPARC) microprocessors. The scope and mix of Sun's products matched many of its larger competitors', so that the company appeared to have the depth and strength of companies many times its size. If one machine was not perfect for the job, Sun was ready to demonstrate another to a hesitant buyer. Each workstation, Sun reiterated, uses the same *software architecture*. Don't worry about the hardware. That will always change, always improve. The real issue is the software architecture, the operating system. That's where the investment is tangible and critical. As John C. Levinson of Goldman Sachs defined it for his readers: "The Open Systems environment contains the basic elements of an operating system, user interface, communication protocols, languages, database management system and so on." Levinson referred to open systems as a "common software chassis."

This was exactly the preaching customers wanted to hear.

It was the gospel of open systems, and there were no greater
proselytizers than those at Sun. They had many converts.

The open systems mentality Sun fostered succeeded primarily because the vast majority of computer users, from PC
players to supercomputer jocks, viewed the machine, the
hardware, as a mere "platform," something on which their
programs ran. Geophysicists working for Exxon in Louisiana
or Petrobras in Brazil are not concerned about the MIPS
rating of the computer's CPU (central processing unit), the
speed of the system bus, the number of pixels on the screen,
or at how many megabits per second the network chugs
along. Their goal is to run a program as quickly as possible
and have it usefully displayed on the monitor. They want to
be able to share it with their colleagues, whether over a
network or through a timeshared device. Their objective is to
locate oil and natural gas beneath the earth's crust, not to
wow their coworkers with the bits, bytes, and bauds of a
computer.

The same holds true for mechanical engineers; artificial-
intelligence researchers; oceanographers; electronic publish-

Figure 2.5

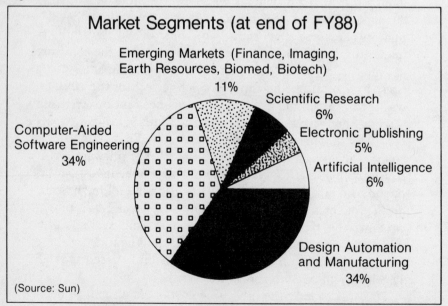

Market Segments (at end of FY88)

Emerging Markets (Finance, Imaging,
Earth Resources, Biomed, Biotech)
11%

Scientific Research
6%

Computer-Aided
Software Engineering
34%

Electronic Publishing
5%

Artificial Intelligence
6%

Design Automation
and Manufacturing
34%

(Source: Sun)

ers; financial analysts; scientists; electrical and electronic engineers; and to some extent, even software developers. All these people use Sun workstations, and most of them do not care whether their system comes from Sun or IBM (see figure 2.5). They simply need a platform to run their job-related programs.

Sun took maximum advantage of this trend. Users were tired of being locked into a company's computer hardware because that was the only platform the software ran on. While Sun's competitors talked at great length about the superior nature of their computer "architectures"—the configuration of the CPU, memory, bus, and other hardware elements—Sun talked about its architecture in a radically different fashion. It described an architecture of software, an operating system architecture that ran on a variety of platforms, three of which it offered (MC680x0, 80386, and SPARC)—and others were widely available. Sun may have earned the lion's share of its revenues from shipping workstations, but it *sold* people on its software architecture.

Expansion and improved market position came to Sun primarily through the steady sales of its workstations. There were, however, some notable, if small, acquisitions. Sun acquired companies not simply because they would add more immediate revenue or profits, but because they filled a hole in the company's product offerings or contributed to the vision of open systems.

First, Sun acquired Trancept in 1986 for its TAAC-1 graphics coprocessor, a hardware product that improved the graphics-processing capabilities of Sun's computers. TOPS, a networking-software company (originally called Centram Systems West) acquired in 1987, and Folio, a font-scaling developer picked up in 1988, both extended the open systems philosophy in new ways. For example, the TOPS product linked Apple Macintosh computers to IBM personal computers, fostering at a lower performance the open approach that Sun adhered to. TOPS eventually offered a Sun-Macintosh-PC link. Sun's management understood that it would not be able to provide Sun machines for every desktop, but there was no reason Sun workstations couldn't communicate effectively with all these lower-level systems.

TOPS software was one of the hottest-selling products in the personal computer field. Folio offered a software technology that gave virtually everyone the ability to build scalable fonts for their own use. This was a potentially explosive technology that, when fully matured, would rival the success of Adobe's PostScript, the wildly successful program for computer-generated fonts that popularized the use of laser printers. In both cases the acquired companies were small, growing in fledgling markets. They dovetailed nicely with Sun's strategy of introducing its machines into new areas of workstation computing while sustaining earnings from older, established markets. These deals with small, growing companies complemented Sun's ability to bargain effectively with giants such as AT&T. In each instance Sun increased its advantages.

The blend of diverse products and an aggressive market-share strategy was the foundation of Sun's success. Although such a combination might be claimed by any aspirant in the computer industry, Sun's appealing open-systems philosophy and creative methods of doing business made it dominant in its field and has positioned it to become one of the major forces in the industry.

The Lay of the Land

The geography of the workstation market in its early years was simple; it could be likened to an undulating plain, fairly consistent, with only an occasional dip or bend in the landscape. When Sun entered the market, three years after Apollo had pioneered the concept of computer workstations, that market was dominated by electrical computer-aided design (ECAD) and computer-aided software engineering (CASE). Although customers in these areas still comprise a significant and expanding part of the workstation market, Sun's arrival changed the territory of workstations. The lay of the land became much more diverse and interesting.

The world of computing into which Apollo thrust the

workstation consisted of mainframes, minicomputers, and personal computers. Mainframes were behemoths directly accessible only to system administrators and their ilk; users were at the mercy of the administrators. Mainframes required a large, climate-controlled room in which to operate. The mainframe market was controlled by IBM and clone makers.

Minicomputers were smaller, nimbler, and cheaper—and more accessible by their users than mainframes were. Users' terminals were connected to the computer, which was also located off in a separate room somewhere. Minicomputers could be networked together. The minicomputer market was created and largely controlled by DEC.

Personal computers put the user one-on-one with the machine. The entire system could fit right on top of the user's desk. For immediate, personal access to their data, however, PC users paid with anemic performance.

Workstations combined the power and networking of minicomputers with the immediacy and compactness of PCs. For demanding applications such as computer-aided design, workstation users could have a lot of power and data storage right at their desks and have immediate access to their data. Furthermore, they could share necessary data with colleagues, since a hallmark of these new machines was their networking capabilities.

When Apollo first established the differences between workstations, personal computers, and minicomputers, the initial interest was among OEMs serving the ECAD world. Apollo landed some lucrative contracts and set about building ancillary markets in other areas. The price tag for Apollo's Domain product line, however, intimidated quite a few users and software developers. Limited software for Apollo workstations curtailed the number and breadth of viable markets. In 1985, six years after the company was founded, Apollo managed to claim that only five hundred software packages from third-party developers worked on Apollo's Domain computers.

Six years after Sun began, it had three times as many

third-party products for its systems. The main reason was Sun's greater number of units in the field. Sun workstations appeared everywhere and in sufficient numbers to encourage software developers in many areas to port their programs to Sun computers; that is, to rewrite their existing software—a program such as WordPerfect, say, meant for a personal computer—so that it ran on Sun systems.

Another reason was the aggressive marketing program, called Catalyst, that Sun initiated to promote availability of third-party software. Market-segment managers determined the most attractive software in the various fields—CAD/CAM (computer-aided design/computer-aided manufacturing), for example—and these managers actively wooed their third-party firms, convincing them of the sales they would get from Sun workstation users. Occasionally, key developers received porting fees, cash to offset the programming time it took for a developer to revise a program to work on Sun workstations. The third-party developers reimbursed Sun for these fees over time as they sold goods to Sun users. Sometimes workstations were swapped for porting fees. For less critical software, another approach was to offer significant developer discounts. The Catalyst program generated significant interest and, as it grew in popularity, became much more selective, actually eliminating third-party products that did not meet increasingly refined standards. By 1988 it was considered a prize achievement to be listed in the mammoth, slick biannual *Catalyst* catalog.

Third-party support, primarily with software, made a product viable. Without it the workstation was only a machine running an operating system, of value to software mavens and hackers but precious few others. It was vital to deliver a machine with an extensive catalog of compatible programs.

When the Sun386i debuted in April 1988, Sun could boast sixty vendors with application programs destined for the workstation. The company's goal was to have at least a hundred vendors ready to announce their products for the Sun386i at its introduction, but that proved to be impossible.

As a result, the initial sales for the new workstation did not meet Sun's forecasts. A major push by the Catalyst group under its new boss, Bill Larson, focused on turning that situation around. By November of that year, Sun was able to claim that two hundred products for the Sun386i were available, an average of more than twenty additions a month. Concurrent with software availability came dramatically increased sales for the machine, reinforcing the idea that users bought computers for the value of the software, not the cleverness embodied in the hardware.

Sun did not discover most of the markets in which workstations would eventually prosper. Apollo and others followed minicomputer firms into those areas, including ECAD, CAD/CAM, image processing, animation, scientific research, and electronic publishing—anywhere technical users thrived.

While these companies were cautiously testing the waters, preferring the safe, familiar shallows, Sun dived in headfirst. In November 1985, for example, Sun went to its first trade show for automated manufacturers, AutoFact, in Detroit. AutoFact (short for automated factory) was spearheaded by General Motors, largely to get computer manufacturers in line about industry standards, especially networking standards. GM and other industrial giants, such as Boeing and Ford, were fed up with computer vendors jumping on the latest high-tech bandwagon in order to make their systems run faster. They were equally displeased about the incompatibility among the different manufacturers' computers. "Why can't you guys talk to each other?" they pleaded. Then they demanded communication and an end to "islands" of manufacturing automation. Having to buy new computer technology every few years was costly and disruptive on the factory floor.

AutoFact was the first show at which the computer users exercised their collective muscle to yank computer vendors over to their point of view. Given the strength of the customers involved, most computer companies positively tripped over themselves to claim their sudden adherence to industry

standards. The most reluctant was IBM, imperious enough to
withstand most user demands, but even Big Blue dragged
itself up to the industry-standard table set by customers.

The demands were actually quite modest. No one was
asking DEC, HP, and IBM to relinquish their tradition of
using proprietary technology in their computers. What the
users wanted, however, was compliance with network standards. To enforce this compliance, AutoFact participants
agreed to use a version of the International Standards Organization's Open System Interconnect networking model
(called ISO/OSI, or OSI) known as MAP, for *manufacturing
automated protocol*. Companies that did not offer MAP networks would simply lose business.

Sun prepared for AutoFact in a big way. It joined a booth
with a dozen other vendors to demonstrate how its workstations could work on the same network with competitors'
products. At that time Sun was a smallish company, having
just turned in its first $100-million-plus fiscal-year perfor-
mance, and was not considered much of a threat to the likes
of DEC or HP. The smallness of Sun and its commitment to
standards from its inception made the company's task of
complying with MAP much easier than that of the other
firms. A handful of Sun engineers, led by Mike Cox and Don
Hoffman, put together a network of Sun systems using MAP
protocols, which greatly pleased GM's network managers.
Hoffman attributed his team's alacrity to its smallness, lack
of bureaucracy, and committee mentality. The Sun engineers,
who referred to AutoFact as the "OSI Olympics" because of
the rigorous training and preparation required to get ready
for the show, witnessed these same network managers berat-
ing their counterparts at IBM, DEC, and HP for being unprepared.

In early 1987, fueled by the efforts of Bruce Golden, the
company's financial-services marketing manager, Sun waded
into a new market, as yet unexplored by other workstation
makers: Wall Street. In mid-1986 the company concluded
that the financial world needed Sun workstations. Traders on
stock exchanges from Tokyo to New York to London were

generally linked to powerful mainframes that processed huge volumes of data on virtually everything. All traders had their own favorite series of indicators, stocks, commodity futures, currency fluctuations, international market results, interest trends, and a dozen other computer-generated factors. To see them all at once, as was preferred, traders often had up to twelve terminals stacked on their desk. With millions, even billions of dollars at stake whizzing across these terminals, traders became technically inclined as a survival precaution. When Sun opened its Wall Street sales office in 1986, these technically savvy money people wanted to get the mountain of terminals off their desks and add some local computing power, which was impossible with the mainframes' dumb terminals.

According to Rich Edwards, an analyst for investment bankers Robertson Stephens & Company (formerly Robertson Colman & Stephens), "Sun workstations on Wall Street for automating the trading desk . . . [have] a lot of long-term potential due to the factors that distinguish the Sun workstation: high-performance color graphics with an effective window manager; high-performance computational capabilities; access to files on the network . . . ; and availability of third-party applications software. . . ." The multiple windows on the large workstation display particularly caught the attention of the stock traders. Technically, up to sixty-four windows could appear simultaneously on a workstation screen, although their small size might limit their usefulness. Still, many more windows than terminals could run in a much more confined space. The color capability meant significant changes could be highlighted in various shades. The networking, of course, meant that all the existing information on the mainframe hardware would still be accessible and useful to traders.

With so much money riding on any proposed change from dumb terminals to workstations, nobody was going to throw out the old technology on a salesman's promise or an analyst's estimate. The first workstations crept into the data-processing areas of the financial concerns. Morgan Stanley was one of the first, in March 1987, giving the computers to its software developers. These were the creative folks who built programs to process all those numbers, aiming to supply traders with an edge in the hectic handling of the world's economies. Since all the traders and financial analysts had their own predilections about what data and software machinations combined for the best planning information, these software developers were kept incredibly busy. What people at Morgan Stanley and other financial houses learned quickly was how fast programs could be developed on Sun systems, which had always excelled in software engineering. Furthermore, by working on the Sun computers, the developers did not bog down the company's IBM mainframes. Also, the programs were relatively easy to port to the mainframes once the traders were happy with them.

Later that spring, Sun announced a string of deals that cemented its role in the computing realm of Wall Street. First, on May 13 it announced a series of financial software packages for its workstations. Companies adapting their products to Sun systems were Fame, a subsidiary of Citicorp, with a financial modeling program; The Athena Group, with two artificial-intelligence-type programs; QV Consulting Services and its portfolio management product; and Speakeasy Computing Corporation, with a product for economic calculations.

Two days later, Sun signed an important OEM agreement with Quotron, a Los Angeles–based firm that was one of the world's largest real-time financial services. Its product, called the Quotron 1000, made market data immediately available to investors, no matter where they lived or worked. The Quotron software let users process the data in a way they believed gave them the best predictions on whether to buy or sell. Quotron Marketing Vice President George H. Levine contended that the deal was worth $300 million. The importance of the Quotron deal was so significant that the Securities and Exchange Commission scrutinized Sun executives' stock transactions around the time of the announcement. Although nothing came of the SEC investigation, it underscored the importance of the deal to Sun.

Less than a week after the Quotron announcement, Sun and Stratus Computer unveiled a strategic partnership in which Stratus agreed to comarket its fault-tolerant computers—machines with backup systems that would kick in in the event of such disasters as power outages, fires, and earthquakes—as servers in a network of Sun workstations. This agreement notified the financial community that Sun was serious about providing the range of products necessary to meet Wall Street's needs, with an emphasis on system reliability. If a trader's system went down—even for seconds—billions of dollars could fall through the cracks. Although Sun was happy to install backup systems for the financial community, fault-tolerant computing, pioneered by Tandem Computers and Stratus, was considered essential to legitimize the use of Sun machines in this venue.

Throughout 1987 Sun's workstations kept squeezing their way into different trading houses. Then came the crash of October and the partial blame cast on automated trading. The financial community briefly slowed its buying of workstations in view of revived public sentiment against computers, and one firm after another announced that it had discontinued the policy of automated trading. Almost as soon as these mea culpas were offered, however, Wall Street began flooding Sun with more orders. Although instant trades triggered by the most current data ceased, traders still relied heavily on the data for their decision making. Paine Webber, Bear Stearns, and others publicly declared that Sun computers were their preferred workstations. By 1989 Sun, among workstation makers, owned Wall Street.

Slipping into Wall Street offices or onto factory floors was just the beginning of Sun's user appeal. One of Sun's consistent strengths, one that got it through the rocky computer-industry recession years of 1985 and 1986, is its diverse customer base. The complexion of Sun workstation users not only cuts through multiple markets but also transcends multiple boundaries.

In the last calendar quarter of 1988, 43 percent of Sun's business occurred overseas. European sales were only slightly higher than those in the Pacific Rim, a lead expected to change hands before the end of 1989, not because the European sales were slowing in growth, but because the Pacific Rim expansion raced ahead so quickly, including multimillion-dollar sales to the People's Republic of China. In 1986 Sun started an aggressive Japanese subsidiary, Nihon Sun Microsystems, which quickly established Sun as the number-one workstation company in that country. Besides making all-important end-user sales, Nihon Sun closed a variety of OEM deals, including a huge $280 million pact with Fujitsu and several smaller ones, such as a $15 million agreement with Tokyo Electron.

Sun vice president of marketing Ed Zander, whom Sun had wooed away from archrival Apollo, projected that by the end of 1990, between 50 and 60 percent of Sun's revenues would derive from international sales. Again, this was not because of a forecast slump in North American sales but because of the expanded overall market and accelerated growth abroad. That growth would in part be fueled by an aggressive move into South America, where, in 1988, Sun concluded deals with twelve distributors.

Although no company is immune to economic hardships, the worldwide spread of Sun computers from Mountain View, California, protected the company from regional slowdowns in the economy. If German bankers tightened the fiscal belt by raising interest rates in Frankfurt and Bonn, buyers in Singapore took up the slack. If new business in Australia dipped for a quarter, nascent markets in Brazil made up the difference. Industry analysts have consistently been impressed with Sun's ability to carve out such wide geographic interest in its products.

Combined with its worldwide sources for revenue, Sun designed its growth without depending on any particular outside organization. No single institution, including the government, has accounted for more than 10 percent of Sun sales. More important, despite doing major business with the government, to the point where Sun established a separate division with its own president, there was no single government entity—federal, state, or local—that dominated the revenues. Sun's major sales to the government covered the gamut, including, among other groups, the U.S. Patent Office, intelligence agencies, the General Services Administration, and the New York Health Department and Department of Transportation.

THE OEM COUNTDOWN

In mid-1989, Sun claimed more than three hundred OEMs. Some of them, granted, were small, consuming only a few workstations a year, amounting to much less than $1 million in annual revenues. Others were volume buyers, however, spending close to $100 million a year at Sun. The most important aspect in terms of Sun's long-range strategy, however, was not necessarily the size of an OEM but rather where it fit in the mix. For Sun management it was vital that the company not depend on one or two large organizations for its revenues. Such was the fate of Sun's archrival Apollo: when the major customer suffered hard times in 1987 and 1988, Apollo's sales and profits were crippled.

The strategy of market, geographic, and customer diversity has been the bedrock of Sun's penchant for striking such a variety of deals. For example, although workstations are considered ideal for technically demanding or information-rich applications, Sun and Olivetti USA signed an OEM agreement by which the latter company would sell Sun computers as servers in its expanding market of automated law offices. One of the world's largest office-automation companies, Xerox, signed a five-year, $200 million agreement with Sun to incorporate its workstations into the Xerox product line.

In office automation, more than in any other computer market, software has determined the success of hardware. Aside from the specialized programs Sun offered through its key OEMs, Sun lagged in this area until 1988, delivering only a few relatively unsuccessful products—such as the lackluster office-automation software product SunAlis, jointly developed with Applix, Inc. In the fall of 1988, however, the SAS

Institute moved its mainframe- and minicomputer-based
project-management software over to Sun workstations.
SAS's product was more powerful and sophisticated than Alis
and was popular among management information systems
(MIS) professionals. In early 1989, the popular PC-level
word-processing program WordPerfect became available to
Sun users. Coupled with the Sun386i, these products improved end-user sales in office automation for Sun.

Identifying and targeting new markets is common to virtually all growing companies. Timing an entry into those
markets is the difference between spending money on market
research or earning revenue from product sales. A case in
point is the architecture, engineering, and construction
(AEC) market. Here, personal computers broke through to
the desktops of AEC professionals, a previously underauto-
mated area, especially among architects, whose labors would
have benefited from more powerful computational machines;
yet most architects did not use them because of the high cost
of minicomputers. PCs held some promise, but they did not
have the performance capabilities necessary for the large
projects in which automation was necessary. Still, PCs gave
the market a taste for a computer's potential.

Workstations, however, had the processing power necessary for tasks such as material management, surveying, large-
scale drafting, and architectural design. Packaged by Sun,
workstations also carried the right price. In spring 1988 Sun
pounced on the market by inking OEM deals (a $10 million
deal with ICG, a major supplier to the home-building industry, and a $3 million civil-engineering pact with Digital
Matrix Services) and unveiling fifteen new software applications targeted at the AEC market. By the time Sun attended
the AEC trade show in Chicago that May, the company had
built such momentum that fifty different vendors were demonstrating more than eighty products on Sun workstations.
Sun's quick achievement in this area was so profound that it
prompted one AEC supplier to refer to the California company's products as being "in the mainstream of computer
technology," despite Sun's relatively short history and shorter
time in the AEC market.

A market Sun dominates is electronic publishing, often called computer-aided publishing (CAP), desktop publishing, or Epubs. Electronic publishing is the rubric under which many types of documents fall, from company newsletters and political leaflets to four-color magazines and best-selling books. Electronic publishing automates page composition, typography, and graphics and assists in the design of printed pages.

Early in the history of electronic publishing, specialized systems, both hardware and software, were the only options. Proprietary software on top of proprietary hardware locked users into a vendor-controlled situation. It also kept the costs artificially high, which was a stumbling block to many small- and medium-size publishing houses because their work is generally a cash-flow, low-margin operation.

At the low end of the power spectrum, personal computers' proprietary technology and cost were not factors. Personal computers—particularly the Apple Macintosh—virtually gave birth to the notion of "desktop publishing" for small publications such as newsletters and fliers. At the high end, however, there were few liberating forces until the mid-1980s. Up to that time, Epubs vendors bought equipment, generally minicomputers from DEC or HP, and then modified the hardware with their own specialized coprocessors (chips that work in conjunction with the CPU) to run their own publishing software. Occasionally the underlying operating system from the computer maker would even be discarded, making the machine task-specific and tying the user to the vendor.

As the 1980s progressed, some electronic publishing suppliers sensed the user revolt. The noise about standards was no longer an irritating sound heard mostly at technical conferences, but a roaring crescendo that drowned out the vendors' claims about the advantages of their specialized systems.

One of the first to recognize the sounds of user discontent was Compugraphic Corporation, the world's largest supplier of typesetting and graphics equipment to commercial printing operations. In the fall of 1983, it signed a three-year deal with Sun. Its transition from proprietary technology to Sun's workstations signaled a change. Other major suppliers—including Atex, Docupro, 3M, Interleaf, Monotype, and Kodak—followed Compugraphic's lead. Brand-new software products designed specifically for Sun's systems emerged, such as Frame Technology's FrameMaker program and Unda's Color Design and Production System.

By the end of 1987, Sun had taken the market lead among high-end suppliers. By 1988 it dominated the workstation portion of the market by signing more OEM deals—with, among others, Bedford Computer, Miles PLC, Scribe, and Auto-Trol, all major suppliers to the Epubs market (the last formerly an OEM of Apollo). By 1989 Sun led all other vendors, including PC makers, with the most electronic publishing applications available on its computers.

Although not the dominant player in heavier industries, Sun also expanded its OEM relationships in those realms. In the factory area, Sun and Cimlinc signed a $25 million deal that gave Sun equipment entrée into a variety of manufacturing and factory settings. Nippon Steel inked a $15 million pact with Sun that moved Sun into factory-automation operations in Japan. In oil exploration Sun has followed DEC as a supplier of workstations, to the tune of $40 million in fiscal 1988. Modest OEM deals with companies such as Generation 5 Technology gave Sun certain advantages in the oil market. End-user sales, however, put Sun in the number-two spot in that market. Virtually every oil company installed at least one network of Sun workstations between 1985 and 1989. More important, key international oil industry consortiums, such as Teknica Resource Development in Alberta and the Stanford Exploration Project in California, adopted Sun workstations as their desktop machines of choice to link with more-powerful mainframe systems. As in the financial market, what cinched those sales was Sun's open systems approach of connecting to non-Sun technology.

The traditional workstation markets of CAD/CAM and ECAD require a lot of computing and networking power. Workstations have proved adept at providing the computing punch needed to run factory floors and handle the complexities of designing integrated circuits, for example. Sun is well known in these markets, sharing leadership with DEC, HP, and Apollo. Sun holds a slight edge in the ECAD market because of its key OEM arrangements with Valid Logic, Daisy Systems, and others. It broke into these areas primarily through establishing key OEM agreements for its Sun-2 workstation series—with companies such as Chromatics in 1984 and Gould Information Systems in 1985.

Until 1987 Sun lacked the depth of applications software to spur end-user sales, the other half of the company's selling strategy. From 1985 to 1987, however, Sun's New Business Development group, managed by Rob Kuhling and JoAnn Kahn, attracted virtually all the key software players in ECAD and CAD/CAM to port their products to the Sun platform. Besides providing porting fees in some cases, Sun offered a creative marketing program that included everything from team sales calls to coproduced data sheets. By the beginning of 1988, any software-application advantages held by DEC, Apollo, or HP were gone, and Sun continued to steal their market share.

In the programmer-dominated computer-aided software engineering (CASE) market, another traditional workstation stronghold, Sun clearly rules the roost. In CASE, computers are used to build and perfect the programs that will run on computers. The operating system is more important than the application programs because the software engineers are developing programs themselves. Critical in the CASE arena are fast, efficient compilers (computer programs that translate programs written in one computer language into another) for a variety of languages and an effective set of developers' toolkits (the extra software that helps developers write programs). From its outset, the UNIX-based SunOS was considered among the best environments for software development. SunOS came standard with compilers for C, FORTRAN 77, and Pascal—all major program-development languages. SunOS was so prized by software developers that competitors purchased Sun's equipment for programming.

PARTNERS IN PRIME GROWTH

These dramatic successes in so few years, with only a few major setbacks, would have been enough to swell the heads in any organization. By 1988, when Sun's pronouncements on the necessity and inevitability of open systems began to look all too real to its competitors, some said the company had become too full of itself and needed a dose of humility. Despite Sun's reputation for arrogance (one that McNealy and others feel is a misinterpretation of the company's youthful confidence), its approach to computing technology strikes users and industry watchers as modestly realistic.

It is axiomatic with Sun's leadership that the company cannot go it alone. Partnership, cooperation, and teamwork with other companies, even competitors, is the way to do business and sustain high growth in the next decade, perhaps the coming century—especially in the eyes of certain American business analysts who advocate moving away from stratified theories of business. These partnerships must run the gamut of business operations, in everything from marketing and manufacturing to development and distribution.

On the technological front, Sun Vice President of Research and Development Bill Joy best articulates this point of view. Joy told Stuart Gannes of *Fortune* magazine, "Cooperating with technology leaders . . . is the only way Sun can grab a permanent place out front." In Joy's opinion, invention and advancement occurred in companies, laboratories, universities, and even in people's garages throughout the world. To suppose that Sun could devise every possible hardware and software product for every application niche was absurd. It was not so absurd, however, to pal around with those who were doing what Sun was not. And that's what the company set out to do.

Sun desperately wanted to enter the high-end scientific-computing market, so it mandated Gordon Short, a Sun marketing manager, to penetrate that market. In this realm, users ran massive programs on supercomputers from Cray Research or minisupercomputers from companies such as

Convex and Alliant. Short understood that these users would not be satisfied with simply chugging along with a Sun workstation, so he and his counterparts at other firms hammered out agreements by which users could connect Sun's computers to the more-powerful machines. These agreements benefited all three parties—Sun, supercomputer makers, and end users. First, Sun made long strides in a new market. Second, supercomputer companies were able to offer more-flexible products. Third, users were able to take a load off their expensive machines during various stages of running the supercomputer-based programs. Organizations such as Texaco, Lawrence Livermore Laboratories, and Cray Research itself found this combination of powerful desktop machines and the world's most powerful CPUs appealing.

Sun entered other technology agreements by being flexible with its technology in order to gain leverage in new markets. An agreement with Xerox in 1987 paved the way for the next year's $200 million deal. In this technology alliance, Sun and Xerox agreed to modify SunOS in such a way that Sun workstations would be more adaptable to office-automation software. The work with Xerox helped Sun into the lucrative office-automation market—one in which Sun had not had a large presence before. In the more esoteric realms of artificial intelligence (AI) and parallel processing, Sun joined forces respectively with the multinational conglomerate Schlumberger (AI), Topologix, and AMT in late 1988 and with Transtech Devices in 1989.

Even in the area in which Sun was hailed as the best in the industry, UNIX operating system development, the company linked its fortunes with another company, AT&T. Chapter 4 explores this arrangement in more detail, but it's important to note here that inside Sun there was a lot of discussion about whether the company should "go it alone" with SunOS or tie itself to AT&T, which owned UNIX. In the end the idea of partnership prevailed. In view of the potential headaches and delays involved in working with a relatively slow-moving organization, Sun management's philosophy of open systems demanded that Sun swallow its corporate pride

to remain faithful to its stated mission—providing an industry-standard software architecture for high-performance
workstations. For Sun to spurn a relationship with AT&T
because Sun's engineers felt they could do a better job would
have meant turning its back on the very premise of open
systems. It would, in effect, have changed the direction of
the company. It would have given ammunition to the competition, giving competitors reason to claim that Sun, too,
developed proprietary technology.

Sun remained true to its mission, however. A few engineers, unaccustomed to the molasseslike bureacracy of
AT&T, stepped aside during the codevelopment work. A
couple even left the company. But the work with AT&T was
applauded by the industry—nearly all of it. Sun's competitors were anything but pleased. To them it meant the success
of open systems would overwhelm them, unless they attacked
it and did so creatively. Which, of course, they did.

3

The Performance Game:
Workstation Technology and Market

Sun's extraordinary talent at cutting profitable deals was not due simply to being in the right place at the right time with the right product. Luck, after all, can be good or bad, depending on how well you're prepared. Sun management never let up on preparing for the workstation market.

One morning in early 1986, not long after moving the corporate headquarters into Building 6 on its Mountain View campus, Sun's top executives gathered in boardroom 2. The new furniture and the floor-to-ceiling white-board wall still elicited a few admiring comments from the high-level attendees. Conditioned to working close to the bone in cramped quarters for so long, everyone saw the expansive room and its furnishings as a new standard of luxury.

The meeting had been arranged by Carol Bartz, who was then vice president of marketing. Attendees included President Scott McNealy, Executive Vice President Bernie Lacroute, Vice President of Sales Joe Roebuck, Customer Services Vice President Bob Lux, Software Vice President Eric Schmidt, Engineering Vice President Wayne Rosing, co-founder and Vice President of Technology Andy Bech-

tolsheim, Product Marketing Director John Hime, and others. Among Bartz's tasks was to uncover just *who* or *what* Sun
was in the customer's mind. What differentiated Sun from
the competition? What did customers think when they considered the raison d'être of Sun Microsystems?

Bartz, a degreed engineer and former manager at DEC,
had long been dissatisfied with Sun's stated position as "the
price/performance leader" and as the maker of "the workstation for the technical professional." These notions were becoming cant throughout the entire industry—so much so that
PC makers were beginning to use the same kind of language.
Industry analysts and trade journalists were writing about
the blurring of distinctions between personal computers and
technical workstations. Salesmen were complaining about
customer confusion over just what was what.

Sun's management was determined to sustain a singular
role in the marketplace. At all costs, Sun had to avoid being
considered part of a turf already well staked out by Apple,
Compaq, and IBM. But as PCs edged up the ladder in performance and workstations tumbled in price, differences
between computer technologies diminished. Even Sun's
championing of the hallowed concept of "open systems" was
increasingly being usurped by the competition. Bartz's fear,
shared by others in Sun's hierarchy, was that Sun's added
value to the customer would not be clearly understood; that
Sun's machines would devolve into commodity products,
getting lost in a morass of minute technical details, as workstation manufacturers and PC makers attempted to out–high-
tech each other.

Bartz's charter, as she understood it, was to define how
Sun was perceived by customers, especially general-purpose
computer buyers. This "positioning," as it was called, was
not taken lightly by anyone in the room. To Bartz the clarity
of her company's position revealed the luster of the organization and the strength of its products. Up to that point, many
people believed that the market was so hot that it was inevitable that Sun and every other workstation builder would be
a success. It was almost impossible not to succeed, given the
overall industry growth. No other segment of the systems

market had grown as quickly as the workstation market between 1983 and 1987. Workstation makers were delivering
desktop dream machines, designed by technologists and for
technologists hungry for the latest, fastest device available.
Making a fast buck was no great accomplishment; staying
power was something else again. Real success lay with a
wider audience of users, not merely the aficionados of high
tech. In the future, Sun's top brass knew, things would be
much different: only companies with an unmistakable identity in the customers' mind had a chance to survive, let alone
triumph. Yet Sun's nascent technology and youthfulness
obscured the clarity of its identity.

Although some Sun executives cracked the usual jokes
during this winter 1986 meeting, everyone was very serious
about its intent. It was not an excuse for idle chatter or web
spinning, nor was it some faddish marketing technique
picked up from the Stanford Business School or the current
wisdom of a well-tailored and -coiffed California guru. It was
a serious exercise in critical self-examination, a corporate
version of the Socratic dictum that the unexamined life was
not worth living, with the added urgency that the unexamined corporate life meant death in the marketplace.

Bartz kicked off the discussion with some critical questions. What makes customers choose Sun's products over
Apollo's, DEC's, IBM's, Apple's, Silicon Graphics's, and
those of the lesser lights in the market? What do they think
when they consider Sun, the corporation?

The group immediately erupted with a plethora of characteristics they believed distinguished Sun from all comers in
the customers' minds. McNealy attacked the white-board
with a red marker and scrawled: "Barriers to Entry." These
were the points, they believed, that separated Sun from the
pack of other workstation companies—something Sun alone
possessed that would thwart competitors' success in the
market. Words spewed from the roomful of executives. "Networking." "UNIX." "Performance." "Cost-effectiveness."
"Breadth of the product line." "Software-development environment." "Availability of applications."

Each item was debated. Executives interrupted each other

like rowdy and friendly patrons in a neighborhood pub. As
each point was considered, at least one person took a dissent-
ing view. No sooner did McNealy write something on the
board than someone raised a cogent argument against it.
Sometimes voice votes overruled the naysayers, and a point
survived as a barrier to entry. Consensus was reached on a
few items, but universal agreement on a single barrier to
entry seemed impossible. What did Sun have that no one else
could claim?

Roebuck, the vice president of sales, had been generally
quiet during the rollicking exchange, adding only an occasional joke, for which he was well known. Finally he piped
up: "You want to know why customers buy from Sun?"
Pause. "Because we have Bill Joy."

"You can't call a person a barrier to entry," someone
chimed in.

"Why not? No one else has him. And the customers know
that with Bill we'll be light-years ahead of the competition."

And with no more debate, Joy's name stood as a barrier to
entry for the competition. Everyone agreed.

THE VISION OF JOY

Every Tuesday, members of Sun's engineering team gather in
the large assembly room (formerly the cafeteria) of Building
6 to eat cookies, drink coffee and soft drinks, and hear a
presentation. This tradition has gone on for years. Despite
Sun's reputation as a workstation manufacturer, garnering its
revenues from shipping hardware, the majority of the Tuesday talks deal with software. As with every other company in
the industry, Sun's hardware capabilities surpass those of
software, so most of the ticklish engineering issues swirl
around software, not hardware. Sun's edge in the marketplace stems from its software engineers' skill and luck at
squeezing more from the machine—more speed, more functions, more tricks, more possibilities. It is not unusual, then,
to have programmers expound on the importance of faster
processors while hardware developers emphasize the need for
more-compact programs.

These gatherings tend to be freewheeling affairs and are generally well attended, although some regulars joke that a true hacker will sit through almost any lecture for free Coca-Cola and chocolate-chip cookies. Speakers, not always from Sun, cover a variety of subjects. The audience can be merciless to the unprepared presenter. The question-and-answer session tends to be tough.

In late 1985, it was still possible to shoehorn Sun's engineers into the small Building 5 lunchroom, and on a wet December day there was standing room only to hear Bill Joy expound on what he called "The Future of Computing." Joy, who is clean shaven and well coiffed these days, wore his hair long and had a scraggly beard as he stood before the audience of engineers. He looked much like the "mad" scientist he depicted for the cover of *UNIX World*, which dubbed him "the father of 4.2 BSD." His role at Sun has remained constant since he joined as a founder. In a quarterly video shown to Sun employees in December 1988 about "the state of Sun," Scott McNealy described Joy as Sun's "thinker and guru." He drew an organization chart on a pad, on which Joy was listed above and beyond everyone, including McNealy, with an arrow pointing heavenward, indicating Joy's direct report.

Joy gave voice to the ideas and aspirations of Sun's engineers and technologists. More than original insight, his words had the genius of collective wisdom. His 1985 presentation was a speech he had begun delivering to existing and potential clients. For some audiences it was perceived as a "blue sky" narrative about an undetermined point in the vague years ahead, just as its title indicated. If Joy's musings sounded farfetched, that was fine. After all, it was mere speculation. To those in the close and stuffy quarters of the Building 5 lunchroom, however, it was a mission statement, a call to arms. Joy gave them dates and specific performance values for machines, Sun machines. In effect, Joy was describing their marching orders.

In an easygoing and lighthearted manner, Joy delivered his presentation, using an overhead projector for his transparencies or to quickly doodle an image, scrawl a few words, or calculate an elaborate equation. Throughout his speech, the audience interjected comments and questions that Joy fielded with aplomb. These were his people. He was preaching to the converted.

Joy said he wanted a desktop computer by 1992 that ran at 100 MIPS. He claimed it was necessary for the computing tasks that lay ahead: There was speech processing, a workstation understanding a user's native language as it was spoken, eliminating the need for keyboards. There was 3-D processing—so, for example, aircraft designers could spin a turbine on the screen as it simulated the passing of air through its titanium blades. There was a need for live video, distributed databases, elaborate worldwide data communications. As the processing power of desktop machines dramatically increased to the level of mainframes, they would finally extend beyond their specialized and more mundane uses of that day.

Such comments from a company executive might have unnerved the more sober-minded investors in Sun. Joy's words sounded almost like science fiction, a literary genre akin to high art among many of Sun's computer experts. Even in IBM's mainframe world, 100 MIPS was an awesome and rare experience. Coming from a Sun executive whose company produced a mere 2-MIPS workstation, Joy's words conveyed as much hubris as they did fancy.

But Joy was not simply peddling fiction or some hacker's gee-whiz notion. In all areas of computer-aided design, testing, manufacturing, and engineering, faster processors were critical, particularly during the development phases, when the time to test a program dramatically affected the time it took to bring the product to market. Boiled down to its essence, processing time meant money. There was a market, a lucrative one, that craved the fastest machines available. The company that got those machines onto the desktop first would be knee-deep in profits.

Fantasizing about a 100-MIPS workstation was one thing. Defining and designing one was something else. So Joy was telling his listeners how they were going to achieve the task. One way was with RISC, the reduced-instruction-set com-

puter. A RISC microprocessor required fewer instructions
and so ran faster than traditional CISC (complex-instruction-
set computer) systems. In 1985, RISC technology was slowly
gaining ascendance, with the initiation of RISC development
projects such as Hewlett-Packard's Spectrum system, IBM's
RT computer, and the seeding of RISC-chip makers such as
MIPS Computer. These ventures were rare trial balloons of
technology. In the main, RISC was considered, frankly, a
risky business. And Sun's success—the entire workstation
and personal computer market's success, in fact—was based
on CISC. To stray from such a sure thing took a gambler's
heart.

Speed was essential, and CISC, Joy knew, was not the way
to crank up the processor's afterburners. RISC, for example,
executed one instruction for every ten needed in CISC. Staying married to CISC technology meant losing the critical race
for the fastest desktop machines on the market. Joy recognized that skeptics were justified in questioning how 100
MIPS could be milked from the tried-and-true silicon of
contemporary CPUs. But RISC was adaptable to media other
than silicon, such as gallium arsenide, and the world's most-
advanced microprocessor laboratories were beginning to develop even faster semiconductors out of new materials. Because "RISC chips can be made by almost any kind of semiconductor manufacturing method without being rede-
signed," these phenomenal performance leaps would not
include concomitant price hikes.

Memory was another issue. In order for RISC processors
to blaze along, they needed to be fed information at break-
neck speed. With a faster processor, programs could get
larger and more complex. Joy's RISC computers of the near
future demanded more memory to get the job done. Not to
worry, Joy assured the audience. Memory had almost become
a commodity, he believed at that time. More important,
projects employing Sun workstations and demonstrating the
feasibility of billion-byte memory systems for computers
were underway.

In his talk Joy suggested that the operating system for

RISC was UNIX. No one doubted him. Every RISC project
rumored at that time, even IBM's, used UNIX. Most RISC
development occurred under the aegis of the Department of
Defense, which was becoming quite partial to UNIX. The
DoD always wanted the latest and fastest of anything, which
meant RISC, and having a piece of the massive DoD pie
would be good for business. In Joy's mind, RISC and UNIX
had become inseparable.

He also mentioned that the DoD was looking for an operating system standard. The Pentagon's computers used many
different and incompatible operating systems. With so much
of the nation's defense tied up in a programmer's code,
whether a payroll program for four million people or the
microcode in a guided-missile nose cone, the military had to
streamline its computer expenditures, one of the fastest-
growing segments of its budget. Starting with an OS standard was important from two points of view. First, the OS
was critical to the availability of applications and knowledgeable users. UNIX had thousands of applications and was the
preferred OS in major universities, meaning there was a fresh
and constant supply of informed workers.

Second, virtually every computer company offered UNIX
in one flavor or another, allowing the DoD to distribute the
pain of standardization. Licensed liberally by AT&T, where
it was invented in the late 1960s, UNIX was everywhere—
Sun had SunOS; DEC had Ultrix; IBM had AIX; Microsoft
had Xenix; even Apollo had a version. The industry was full
of UNIX and its derivatives (see box, page 98). Choosing
UNIX as a standard operating system, then, made the most
sense from the DoD's perspective. Of course, existing installations and future ones would still include billions of dollars'
worth of non-UNIX equipment; even such a widely available
and diverse operating system as UNIX couldn't meet all the
DoD's computing requirements. (For more on why UNIX
was so popular, see chapter 4, "The Religion of UNIX.")

These standardization omens, however, were not to be
taken lightly. Universities were already entrenched UNIX
users. Larger, well-known, minicomputer-based applications
had started to appear on UNIX machines. Because so much

of the UNIX operating system and so many of its enhancements are in the public domain, UNIX-based products made
it to market with relatively low development costs, keeping
the computer's price tag and its applications highly competitive. Other market segments began turning to UNIX. Besides the DoD, other government agencies—as well as the
then newly independent Bell operating companies, and corporate giants such as General Motors and Ford—were
switching to UNIX. Only the hopelessly myopic missed the
momentum behind UNIX.

In 1985 the best and biggest development company devoted to the UNIX operating system was Sun Microsystems.
Sun had closed its fiscal 1985 books with more than $115
million in sales and, at the time of Joy's speech, was on track
for more than $240 million for the next fiscal year. (See
figure 2.3 for a year-by-year breakdown of Sun's annual
revenues.) Joy thought it natural to link Sun's UNIX expertise with the unlimited possibilities of RISC. Not only would
the task be fun, it would also be rewarding—quite profitable
to a roomful of engineers, all of whom held substantial stock
options in the then privately held company. The work needed
only to be done.

The audience loved the challenge. "So let's do it," someone cracked. People clapped, dreaming of 100 MIPS on their
desks. Joy spoke for them when he said, "You can never have
too many MIPS at your fingertips."

Industry observer Marc Stahlman noted, "Performance is
not a critical determinant of vendor or product selection. . . .
Raw performance [MIPS] has little relevance to market share
or revenue growth in established computer markets." He
pointed out that faster machines, such as Data General's MV
series minicomputers, were puny challengers to the more
sluggish DEC VAX line. Application fit was the critical factor
in a vendor's choice and in market share. As Stahlman put it,
"Reducing all the features and capabilities of a product to
MIPS numbers . . . is a great oversimplification. It ignores
the overriding significance of software, both at the applications and the systems level."

Despite observations like Stahlman's, Joy's audience

sought to put more MIPS on the desktop with the fervor of
a holy crusade. They needed power to get their job done—
power equal to that on big systems—but these men and
women were convinced that the centralized approach to computing, exemplified by mainframes and minicomputers, was
anachronistic. They craved the freedom to compute what
they wanted, when they wanted. This scenario was impossible in a centralized computer installation, where a computer's
cycles were doled out like precious stones. Joy's listeners were
engineers who appreciated the idea of personal computers
but decried PCs' laggard performance, which greatly reduced
their functions and usefulness. What they wanted was a
mainframe on their own desks—or at least the power of one.
That was the vision Joy unveiled for them. And they followed
in near rapture.

FIRST OUT OF THE CHUTE

As the 1970s came to a close, two trends in computing made
the birth of Apollo Computer possible. The first was the
near-instant popularity of personal computers and their woe-
ful inadequacy for scientists and engineers. PCs suited those
with relatively unsophisticated computing needs: word processing, bookkeeping, small-database management, and of
course, games, which many in the industry still associated
with the low-powered desktop machines. Atari and Commo-
dore, for example, were at a great disadvantage when they
broke into the PC market because they were already identified as game-machine manufacturers, even though some observers thought highly of their products' capabilities. As with
many industries, image supersedes reality. When PCs eventually sneaked into businesses, no one took these game-
makers' machines seriously. Even PCs acceptable to business
posed no threat to minicomputer makers such as Digital
Equipment Corporation, Prime, Data General, and others
that, with their powerful departmental (or work-group) systems, attracted the world's technologists.

The second major trend that cleared the passage for the

Chelmsford, Massachusetts–based Apollo was the local area network, the LAN. The advent of one computer "talking" to another—instead of being an exclusively self-referential box—caused computer scientists and users to reexamine the nature of computing. Although connecting compatible mainframes or minicomputers was nothing new, LANs portended the linking of disparate systems, and not merely those in the hallowed computer centers. Conceptually, LANs meant that every desktop could become a part of one integrated computing system, sharing resources such as printers and CPUs over the network. By the time Apollo shipped the industry's first workstation in 1981, these trends had become an emerging market.

Underlying these two trends were technology advances and standardization. Microprocessors were increasing dramatically in performance. Competition heated up, and that drove prices down. Similarly, in the early 1980s, computer memory (random-access memory, or RAM) dipped in cost and increased in quantity. Newly affordable 256K RAM chips were making possible tasks that their 64K RAM predecessors could not accomplish. Desktop systems and network devices fed on these advances and proliferated. On the software side, agreements on operating-system and network software led to widely incorporated standards, such as DOS and UNIX (operating systems), and Ethernet and TCP/IP (networking).

With its goal of feeding the computing needs of technical computer users, Apollo immediately embraced the latest processor technologies. Apollo was the first company that "took the latest microprocessor technology from chip makers and built high-performance, low-cost computers for the engineering desk." But the company refrained from going a step further and adopting software and networking standards. That latter decision quickly cost Apollo its preeminence in the market that it had virtually created.

Founded in 1979 by a cofounder of Prime Computer, John William Poduska, Apollo stated that its mission was to produce "a computer that would combine the high power of the shared minicomputer with the convenience of the personal

computer." To attain this goal, Apollo management instructed its engineers to build a machine that tweaked the
maximum in performance from the computer and its network. The engineers complied, and Apollo launched a wholly
proprietary product line. Although it was based on the same
Motorola 680x0 CPU that Sun and other competitors eventually adopted, everything else in the Apollo package was
Apollo's and Apollo's alone. The two primary elements of
Apollo's product strategy were the Aegis operating system
and the Domain LAN.

Developing proprietary computer technologies was standard practice up to that point. The rationale for this approach posited the advantages of performance: specialized
hardware and software for special people. This notion was
pitched to CPU-starved engineers. They, of course, accepted
the sagacity of the idea. Anything that got them more power
for their applications was right. The issue of compatibility
and integration paled before the crying need for more computing power. Besides, investing in extra minicomputer or
mainframe performance simply tightened another kind of
proprietary handcuff.

The prevailing business theory behind Apollo's DN (Domain Network) products, though, held that these users would
then be locked into using the company's products and would
even pay a premium price for the "privilege" of depending
on a single source. Such a plan seemed to guarantee a long-
term income stream. This belief was quite popular with
management and Wall Street. It made Apollo a bullish buy
on the market when Apollo went public in 1984. After all,
such business philosophies had worked for decades for IBM
and had solidified DEC's role in the computer industry in the
1970s. In fact, the concept of "open computing," so prevalent by the late 1980s, was considered a foolish business
approach, if not a heretical one, as the 1980s dawned.

Because of this mentality in the early part of the decade,
Apollo's DN products exploded onto the market. Even with
their forty-thousand-dollar price tag, the computers were
significantly cheaper than a minicomputer, normally priced

in the hundreds of thousands of dollars. Furthermore, the DN workstation offered significant advantages to a broad range of engineers and scientists. Bogged-down minicomputer users pleaded with their superiors to buy networks of workstations. Minicomputers demanded that numerous users share a CPU's time. Although this "timesharing" approach is ideal for many people—office workers, for example—engineers and scientists tend to process large, complex programs and data. Running them on a stand-alone system, even a slightly less powerful one, is far more expedient than vying for a CPU's attention.

With an Apollo computer and the right software, a mechanical engineer could speed the design and development of anything from an auto ignition switch to a booster rocket for the space shuttle. Electrical engineers could get new systems out the door even faster in their already frenetic industry. Saving time meant making money. Companies did not take long to be persuaded to buy these new and powerful machines. Apollo required even less time to become a *wunderkind* in the computer industry.

With Apollo's one-year head start on the competition, the DN computers refined the definition of a workstation. Reports in the early 1980s often lumped Apollo in with PC manufacturers or even network companies. There wasn't a category in the computer industry for workstations. The word itself engendered misunderstandings because a variety of companies called a host of different products a "workstation." Everything from a supercomputer terminal to modular office furniture bore the workstation rubric. It was on the verge of becoming a generic, almost meaningless word. (See the Glossary for the etymology of *workstation*.) By prefacing the term *workstation* with *engineering*, *technical*, or *high-performance*, Apollo led the way in distinguishing workstations from souped-up personal computers or networked minicomputers. That most people in the industry today understand the distinctiveness of workstation technology stems from Apollo's effective selling of itself and its products.

Apollo got the jump on everybody. It landed the premier

OEM contracts from 1981 through 1983, with the likes of
Mentor Graphics, Computervision, and Auto-Trol. Software
developers flocked to the company, sensing the importance of
breaking into the workstation market on a top-flight product.
In 1983 Apollo earned more than $13 million on $80.7 million in revenues. The next year, the numbers jumped to
$23.9 million in profits on sales of $215.9 million. *Business
Week* kicked off 1985 by charting Apollo as owning 60 percent of a $350 million market, which the magazine projected
would reach $3 billion in just three years. Industry prognos-
ticators were confident the Route 128 highflier would reach
the half-billion-dollar plateau in 1985.

THE HP WAY

Nestled in the foothills of the northwest corner of Silicon
Valley, Hewlett-Packard looked like a tranquil place in 1985.
But the region's preeminent corporation was in trouble. The
pace of the computer industry seemed to have run by HP.
Although it had a long and esteemed relationship with the
engineering and scientific community for its instrumentation
products and computers, it had missed significant opportunities, such as the personal computer and workstation
markets.

Missed opportunities is not the most accurate description.
Flubbed ones is closer to the truth. The touch-screen personal computer that HP delivered in 1984 was hardly a threat
to Apple, IBM, or Compaq. The touch screen was technology for its own sake. Using it was an annoying method for
manipulating elements on the computer display, the user
interface. It took the place of the mouse or the keyboard. The
HP 150, as it was called, used the DOS operating system—a
sound move because IBM PCs used DOS, and tens of thousands of applications had been written for DOS computers.
HP's PC, however, also used the 3.5-inch Sony disk drives
like those in the Apple Macintosh—an unsound move because none of the DOS software could work with them. DOS
products used the 5.25-inch disk drives. In view of the pro-

gramming complexity of the touch screen, its cumbersome user interface, and the disk-drive dilemma, the HP 150 was an unattractive machine for developers and users alike. This lapse in judgment was not surprising from the company that had blithely let one of its employees, Steve Wozniak, have the rights to build the first Apple computer because HP did not perceive Wozniak's design to be of any value.

The failure to establish a credible presence in the PC market, combined with a slowdown in other areas, hurt HP badly. Analysts and company officials had pinned their hopes on the PC industry's wild growth and set ambitious revenue and profit expectations. These expectations were not realized in 1985 or 1986. Although the company avoided layoffs, it mandated draconian pay cuts, encouraged early retirement, and froze most hiring. Morale slackened, and several key people left—some to go to Sun. Schedules for major product-development programs, such as that of the Spectrum computer, slipped.

When HP decisively launched its 9000 line of engineering computers into the workstation market in 1985, it was not necessarily the move of a giant into the territory of Hobbits. Apollo clearly ruled the realm, and Sun reigned as a lesser but unruly knight. HP was weakened internally by the diversity of its problems, while the workstation makers remained focused and grew stronger. HP's arrival, although not arrogantly dismissed, was regarded as that of a battered behemoth constantly looking over its shoulder for a sucker punch from its diminutive opponents.

HP did not, however, stumble in the workstation market as it had in the PC arena. The company's longstanding relationships with engineers paid off. Product loyalty won over some workstation buyers to the HP way of building workstations. Depending on how loosely one defined a workstation in 1986, HP had more sales than either Apollo or Sun had that year, at least according to one analyst at International Data Corporation. HP's products carved up market share because the company adroitly integrated the 9000 series with other popular HP computers and effectively linked its own systems to the competition's, especially those from IBM and DEC. Simultaneously, HP became an aggressive advocate for standards, particularly in the areas of operating system software and networking technology. HP's engineers were among the industry's leaders in standards committees such as IEEE 802 for LANs, and POSIX for the UNIX operating system. By the end of 1986, HP's presence in the market caused at least one analyst to hail HP as the market leader in certain workstation markets, such as factory automation.

HP entered the market with mid- to high-end machines and priced them accordingly. As such, the HP workstations did not touch the lower-priced end of the market that Sun was addressing with some of its systems. This strategy put HP head to head with Apollo and DEC more often than with Sun in 1985 and early 1986. As a rule, whenever Sun and HP clashed, Sun proved victorious, except in cases where HP's computers were already well established. But such was not always the case when HP battled Apollo—then the 9000 series did much better.

By 1988 HP had improved its position dramatically. Its RISC-based Spectrum minicomputers and workstations were selling well. Comforted with revenue growth in its instrumentation and medical-technology markets, HP was healthy and aggressive. It also cut prices in early 1989, making it more competitive with Sun. In 1988 and 1989, HP joined in some strategic alliances that repeatedly placed it in opposition to Sun, heating up an already scorching competitive market.

ENTER THE VAX

Digital Equipment Corporation astounded the industry with its growth in the 1960s and 1970s, during the heyday of the PDP series of minicomputers. The PDP machines made departmental computing for engineers an everyday expectation. The excitement of the 1960s and 1970s spilled over into the 1980s with immediate acceptance of the VAX line of powerful minicomputers, introduced in 1977. DEC's success with the PDP and VAX machines embarrassed IBM, which took more than a decade to respond to DEC's discovery of the minicomputer market. Even after IBM had muscled its way into the minicomputer arena with its System/38 class and Series 1 machines, DEC owned the engineering and scientific marketplace. DEC was a favorite among OEMs and was making major inroads into the business bailiwick that IBM thinks of as its own private playground.

The VAX minicomputer, which eventually supplanted the PDP line as DEC's main offering, gave customers an alternative to being locked into IBM's mainframe-oriented, data-processing, department-driven mentality. With a VAX, computing power could be distributed to those who needed it most. The VAX 780 astounded the computer cognoscenti of the time by cramming 1 MIPS of performance into a departmental minicomputer.

The VAX freed users from the single-vendor shackles of IBM. This freedom, though, was more ideological than real. Despite its dominance, IBM had its competitors; none of them, however, ventured beyond the computing strategies of IBM. Imitation was their sincerest form of flattery. Burroughs, CDC, NCR, Honeywell, and others garnered market share in the computing realm of the 1960s and 1970s. Their technology and marketing philosophy paralleled Big Blue's approach: sell mainframe computers to corporate MIS/DP (management information system/data processing) executives, maintain their loyalty through service, and keep out the competition by raising the specter of program incompatibility. With a major investment in mainframe software, in terms of both programs and trained personnel, DP managers were unlikely to jump from one mainframe technology to another. Once a mainframe system was installed and its inevitable inadequacies were revealed, MIS/DP managers were apt to stick to their guns. If departments need something else, fine. Just don't ask MIS/DPs for help.

DEC took another tack in selling its technology: Deliver a new hardware system and a computer architecture and devise a unique operating system (VMS, or Virtual Memory System) that takes maximum advantage of the hardware. Sell to the MIS chief, if possible. If not, penetrate the technical departments through personal contacts, technical and trade journals, and any other means.

The VAX/VMS buy did not lift the bonds of proprietary technology from the backs of users, but it gave them a choice of which closed path to follow. Plus, a fully configured VAX might run into the hundreds of thousands, a relatively affordable price compared to the million or more that a mainframe cost. Engineering departments did not need to exchange data with MIS-controlled manufacturing, planning, or accounting systems. But with the advent of local area networks, tying all of a company's computers into a single network was impossible because of the vast differences in these systems.

DEC's commitment to the VAX/VMS minicomputer method of computing made it miss the initial excitement of workstations. Like HP, DEC had ventured into the desktop market with its slow-selling Rainbow personal computer, which led to no pot of gold. The Rainbow used CP/M, a dying operating system that feebly competed with the DOS operating system of the IBM PC and its vast number of imitators, or clones. Underpowered, undermarketed, and incompatible with other DEC products, the DEC PC languished in obscurity until it quietly disappeared. Other DEC low-end computers, such as the DECmate II and the DEC Professional systems, could not even match the Rainbow's modest impression in the market. Besides carrying a heftier price than the other PCs available, the DEC personal computers were incompatible with each other. When they sold at all, fanatically loyal DEC customers were the buyers.

DEC's failure with personal computers soured the company's top management on the possibilities of selling desktop machines. Instead, DEC focused on lowering the costs of its minicomputers, networking them via DECnet, so more and smaller departments, not individual users, could have access to them. According to Michael Leibowitz, DEC had "the most to lose from an aggressive plunge into workstations. The performance of workstations tends to overlap . . . [the] tightly

woven line of VAX" systems. This reluctance to follow
Apollo and Sun into the workstation market gave the two
startup firms the time necessary to squeeze into DEC's traditional customer base of engineers and technologists and
build enough critical mass to prompt DEC's eventual foray
into the market.

When DEC finally unveiled its workstations, the VAXstation and MicroVAX series, everyone immediately viewed the
minicomputer maker as a viable competitor. Between the two
product lines, DEC believed it had the right blend of price
and performance, with the VAXstation being slower but
inexpensive and the MicroVax delivering higher performance
at a higher price. DEC's computers ran the VMS operating
system, meaning they could use the array of software already
running on the VAX minicomputers.

In early 1985, Bill Joy at Sun was more concerned with the
competition from DEC than that from Apollo, which Sun
then trailed in the workstation market. Important OEMs
such as Tektronix and Daisy Systems adopted the MicroVAX
as the underlying hardware for their specialty systems. In
1985 Apollo's director of marketing, Michael Gallup, was
quoted in *Electronics* magazine as saying that DEC would
"get upward of 20% of the market." Ironically, Gallup's
withering before DEC's entry came soon after L. F. Rothschild and *Business Week* had shown Apollo controlling 65
percent of the workstation market. In addition to making Sun
take notice of the VMS-based workstations, DEC was worry-
ing the smaller company with a UNIX-based computer, one
that Sun feared would woo those UNIX customers away.
Despite its tardy arrival, DEC found a receptive market and
respectful competitors.

In 1989 DEC added to its workstation arsenal. It introduced the DECstation 3100 and 2100 product lines. Using
the MIPS RISC chip, these computers were DEC's answer to
Sun's SPARC computers. Inexpensive and powerful, these
systems lacked the breadth of applications software ready on
Sun's RISC products. But those applications would come in
time. More important, however, both the 3100 and 2100

computers offered only the UNIX operating system at the time of their introduction. VMS was not available. This UNIX-only strategy was said to underscore DEC's commitment to the popular operating system. It also sent a clear message to Sun management that DEC was not about to concede the workstation market to Sun. The workstation wars were simply heating up.

The World Turned Upside Down

Historians have often pointed to the Battle of Yorktown as the last decisive conflict of the American Revolution. Fought in 1781 over a two-month period, the confrontation revolved around the British defense of the Virginia coastal port. The American rebels, led by George Washington, with French assistance, defeated their enemy. The victory earned the Americans control over a vast and strategic part of the fledgling nation, leading directly to Britain's total retreat two years later. The British commander at Yorktown, General Cornwallis, accepted his humiliation in the custom of the times and gave his sword to the Americans. His mortification was such, however, that Cornwallis sent an aide to deliver the symbol of his shame. During the surrender ceremony, a British band played a dirge called "The World Turned Upside Down," which aptly reflected the feelings of a great empire's general lying down in defeat to a hardscrabble band of American upstarts.

In the battle for workstation supremacy 205 years later, Apollo must have felt the same sinking sensation that Cornwallis had known. Although there was no public event at which Apollo's Poduska handed McNealy a symbol of the workstation kingdom, it was clear that Sun—not DEC, HP, or as some pundits suggested, IBM—had snatched the lead in the workstation industry. The workstation market that Apollo had created years before was overrun by Sun in 1986. By early 1987 Apollo was reeling from one setback after another, most of them delivered by Sun. Apollo was simply not able to hold its own against its California competitor.

Sun beat Apollo on several fronts, and Sun had an array of sophisticated products that matched Apollo's systems. The products were aggressively priced. Sun bested Apollo in every arena, winning key OEMs, major government contracts, and vital third-party products. Universities, the proving ground for tomorrow's computer users, joined automakers, Wall Street brokers, jet builders, and others in switching from Apollo equipment to Sun's. In increasingly greater numbers, new customers sided with Sun. When the computer industry suffered tough times in 1985 and 1986, Apollo stumbled with it. But Sun continued to advance at astounding rates.

The reasons for this rout are diverse. None, however, is more crucial than the way Sun anticipated customers' demand for standards, compatibility, and networks of different kinds of computers. Sun parlayed its identification with the idea of open computing into the top spot in its market. Woven into Sun's definition of open systems are Ethernet, a cable network for connecting computers and transferring data among them; VMEbus and Multibus, internal devices for transferring data within a computer; and other technologies. Fundamental, though, is the UNIX operating system, which oversees all the computer's operations.

In the 1980s, the top UNIX company was indisputably Sun. Despite AT&T's ownership of UNIX, it was Sun that delivered the major technological extensions to the operating system from 1982 to 1989. Sun designed the first window system for UNIX, which allowed users to have multiple screens of data on a computer display simultaneously. Sun's engineers created the Network File System, which vastly improved the way computers shared information. The computer languages available for Sun's version of UNIX were considered among the best in the industry, and Sun offered them free with the operating system—something Apollo did not do with its languages for its Aegis-based computers. When knowledgeable people thought about UNIX in the 1980s, Sun popped immediately into their minds. Sun, therefore, benefited not only from the boom in workstation sales

but also from the computer industry's overall recognition of
UNIX as an alternative to the proprietary operating systems
of IBM and DEC.

In the case of Apollo, it was losing so many sales to Sun
that it was forced to offer a version of UNIX for its workstations. Apollo's own Aegis operating system, though technically fine in many respects, carried the burden of being
proprietary. The savvy buyers of workstations were wary of
indulging in another fenced-in technology. Sun's emphasis
on open computing and UNIX made sense. Even with its
flavor of UNIX, the Domain/IX operating system, Apollo
was losing ground fast to Sun.

Sun indulged in another tried-and-true marketing ploy
that Apollo avoided: setting low prices. When all the numbers on an invoice were added, Sun's workstations consistently cost less than Apollo's. To desktop-computer clients,
price was an essential issue. Like minicomputers in the 1960s
and 1970s, workstations were liable to enter a company
through the back door—that is, without the knowledge or
support of the MIS/DP crew that ran herd over the company's mainframe users. Low cost carried value, but being
inexpensive did not guarantee success. Apollo hit hard on its
products' performance and networking, reminding customers
that it was computing power and local area networks that
made the workstation valuable, not just low price tags. Until
1985 this approach kept Sun a distant second. In September
1985, however, Sun introduced its Sun-3 series of workstations and rapidly took control of the market.

The first Sun-3, code-named Carrera, made a modest
public debut by traditional Silicon Valley standards. No one
descended from the heavens or appeared in a puff of smoke
or strolled onstage to the finale of some portentous music.
The announcement was held at Rickey's Hyatt in Palo Alto,
California. It was geared toward customers, although a few
trade-press editors sneaked in. Executives gave low-key presentations on the technical leaps that the Sun-3 made over
the previous-generation Sun-2 line and, more important,
demonstrated the performance advantages the Sun-3 had

over the competition. Slides were shown. Graphs were presented. Technical papers were alluded to. Then the audience was freed to play with the machines in the next room.

The three or four hundred attendees were obviously impressed, because the orders immediately streamed in to Sun's manufacturing facility. There were so many orders, in fact, that the company quickly outgrew its Mountain View plant and had to move its manufacturing operations across the San Francisco Bay to Milpitas. In their first three months on the market, Sun's second fiscal quarter of 1986, Sun-3 systems accounted for one-third of the $42 million in sales. In the next quarter, Sun-3 sales had jumped to more than two-thirds of the company's $57 million in revenue.

The Sun-3 workstations used the popular MC68020 32-bit microprocessor from Motorola—the same one Apollo and other workstation companies put into their machines. Sun had used earlier generations of Motorola CPUs, the MC68000 (Sun-1) and the MC68010 (Sun-2), as had Apollo and other competitors. On the face of it, then, Apollo and Sun were evenly matched. But in fact, Apollo had been outgunned technically, and in a market with such sophisticated customers, that was a grievous disadvantage.

Compared with the DN Series 3000, the Sun-3 packed much more performance and carried a lower price. As calculated by analysts at L. F. Rothschild, Unterberg, Towbin, Inc., the Sun-3/50 diskless workstation—a machine whose data storage occurs remotely on a server—touted 66 percent more performance than Apollo's diskless machine, measured in MIPS (2 MIPS versus 1.2 MIPS). The Sun computer cost 15 percent less, too. Of course, MIPS and money are not the only criteria for making a buy, but they are significant issues, ones understood by both technical and nontechnical people. Something that's faster and cheaper tends to be better.

In relationship to Sun, Apollo also suffered a blow to its reputation as a technical innovator and leader. Sun and Apollo started with the same ingredients, but in the fundamentals, Sun outdesigned and outimplemented Apollo. In a market segment that holds technical wizardry so dear, losing the reputation of being the leader can be devastating. And Apollo had been perceived as a technical pioneer. It was first with a workstation, no small accomplishment. Apollo had also developed a local-area-network scheme, Domain, that ran 20 percent faster than Ethernet. The Domain electronic-mail system was a model for the industry. Apollo's Aegis operating system was an impressive software package.

Keeping these achievements proprietary was what eventually hurt Apollo. Sun positioned itself as the purveyor of open systems. It talked up their low cost. Apollo, on the other hand, marketed itself as the workstation of choice for the technical elite. Users who demanded performance had bought Apollo because they wanted to get their job done as fast as possible. The Sun-3 undermined Apollo's marketing philosophy while overwhelming its technical advantage.

Apollo, seeing its fortunes slipping away, suddenly danced to the tune of standards. It even incorporated the word "open" into its marketing program, something it had studiously avoided before. It joined standards groups, sang the praises of its version of UNIX, and essentially reiterated the message Sun had sold the market for years. Just as Apollo was ready to throw its weight behind customers' demand for open computing, Sun made a subtle shift in its marketing, one that Apollo did not follow.

With the advent of its new Sun-3 workstation, Sun's ambitions changed. Sun transcended its status as a workstation company and became a general-purpose computer manufacturer. Its company literature, its slide shows, its attitude were altered to enter this new competitive realm. The faster it gained ground on Apollo, the less it considered Apollo a competitive threat. When Sun's vice president of finance, Bob Smith, rang in 1987 by announcing over Sun's worldwide computer network that Sun had passed Apollo in sales and profits, Sun's management was looking at larger and more dangerous opponents than Apollo. While Apollo was attempting to regain its role as the workstation leader, Sun was eyeing the entire computer market as its territory.

Sun's transition from a focused, niche player in the computer industry to a full-fledged computer supplier left Apollo further in the dust. It also illustrated a quality that tended to keep Sun ahead of its competitors: an ability to think and move faster, anticipating computing trends and the needs of users.

Although Apollo continued to grow, reaching $392 million in 1986, it also took a $14 million loss. In 1987 the company rebounded with $553 million in revenues and scored a modest 3.9 percent profit of $21 million. With its profits tumbling due to market share lost to Sun, Apollo cut prices and improved the performance of its machines to meet Sun's challenge, but it was too little, too late.

Sun continued to pour on the pressure. Soon after the first round of Sun-3 products was on the market, it unveiled the Sun-3/200 computer, which doubled raw workstation performance to 4 MIPS. It lowered the price of its Sun-3/50 to less than $7,000 and eventually to less than $5,000. With its expanded product line and low prices, Sun appealed to wider markets. Unlike Apollo, which was largely pigeonholed in the CAD/CAM market, Sun was a more successful competitor in other markets—electronic publishing, computer-aided software engineering, design automation, factory automation, mechanical engineering, finance, geophysics, and government, as well as CAD/CAM.

In 1986 Sun surpassed Apollo in the critical realm of third-party support. Key third-party suppliers formerly devoted to Apollo's technology, such as AutoCad and Auto-Trol, moved their wares to Sun's systems. Sun beat Apollo to market with RISC-based systems by nearly two years, an eon in computer-development chronology. Apollo also got trapped relying "on only three third-party resellers for more than half its revenue." When those few companies suffered setbacks in the computer industry's 1985–1986 economic pinch, Apollo felt the pain. By the end of 1985, Apollo had laid off 8 percent of its workers and had posted a $1.5 million loss, as compared with the $24 million in profits the year before.

Apollo has never fully recovered from its battering by Sun.

Its first quarter in 1988 showed promise, but it was hit again later in the year. As late as September 1988, it posted quarterly losses. Its market-share numbers dwindled compared with Sun's. Its revenues were less than half Sun's as the calendar year came to an end. One of the most promising companies at the outset of the 1980s looked to be a has-been as the 1990s opened. Apollo had become another reminder that the computer industry is one of the most volatile in the world. Further, it stood as an object lesson to Sun: avoid the stigma of being a proprietary-systems manufacturer (that was something only IBM and DEC could afford) and keep pushing the performance game.

By the beginning of 1987, Sun took complete ownership of the number-one rung on the workstation ladder. Apollo was no longer even in its strategic-planning picture. Sun's managers talked about the challenge from IBM and DEC and even Apple Computer, but Apollo had been relegated to a historical problem, something academic and interesting though not compelling to worry about. After all, Sun had used the workstation ladder to swing over to the towering general-purpose-computer ladder, which was fraught with danger. If Sun could scale those heights, though, the possibilities were awesome.

In 1989 Apollo's independent corporate existence came to an end when Hewlett-Packard purchased the one-time number-one workstation maker for $476 million in April. This buy catapulted HP into the premier slot of workstation vendors by virtue of combining the two companies' market-share numbers. Sun had to briefly accept being number two in the industry, after only a brief reign as the top dog. The acquisition underscored the maturing of the workstation market. HP, which along with Apollo had been losing market share to Sun and DEC, was unable to snatch a bigger slice of the workstation market through the success of its own products, so it resorted to buying a slice. HP deemed the purchase of Apollo to be a cheaper way to advance in an area HP managers were desperate to win.

HP was out to get Sun; that was clear. It even timed the

announcement of its purchase of Apollo to the day of Sun's new-product bash in San Francisco in April of that year. Had Sun's public relations staff not arranged for the stories to appear a day earlier in the major business, daily, and trade publications, the coverage of its new products would have been eclipsed by HP's blockbuster announcement.

HP's purchase made sense to many analysts, who held that it was time for more mergers and takeovers in the crowded workstation market. And the net loss of only a hundred Apollo workers after the completion of the merger between HP and Apollo indicated the complementary fit between the two organizations. But the merger would not be completely smooth. HP now had two competing product lines to sell. One had to go. Which direction would workstation product development head in the new deal? Apollo and HP users had to be confused. The two software systems the companies used were completely different. Would there ever be a convergence? How fast could the HP giant react to workstation users' needs? The bet was: not fast enough.

At Sun the agreement between HP and Apollo was not considered a major blow. The drop back to number-two position was considered a temporary aberration that resolved itself by early 1990, when Sun again became the leading workstation maker, according to DataQuest. Sun was able to capitalize on the confusion of corporate transition. Apollo customers unsure about HP jumped to Sun. HP users, in smaller numbers, reacted similarly. The HP-Apollo deal was a good way to grab market share, but it was not necessarily a good way to keep it.

WITH THE BIG DOGS

For most people a puppy is a cute, cuddly critter that gets extra attention. To a pack of dogs roaming a neighborhood, however, it's just another neglected runt. Between 1982 and 1985, Sun was a puppy in the computer industry. Customers were fond of its frisky nature, forgiving its occasional faux pas. The competition—especially DEC, HP, and IBM—

generally ignored it. In 1986, after Sun had snatched a series
of key OEMs and a major government contract from under
the noses of the big U.S. computer makers, a marketing
manager at Sun declared that the company "was pissing with
the big dogs now." What he meant was that no one would
think Sun was cute any longer and that the competition
would cease to overlook it.

Taking on Apollo—in effect, another youthful startup—
was one thing. Doing battle with established computer giants
was something else. As the "giant footsteps" of DEC and
IBM were heard in the workstation market, many analysts
and pundits were ready to hand the market over to them. In
such a rough and different competitive environment, most
companies' management would consider adopting a new selling strategy. A decision by Sun to emulate the big computer
dogs, the kind of choice a new neighborhood puppy would
make, would have been a natural response. But it was not the
one Sun made. Instead, Sun embarked on a radically different strategy, one that kept the computer establishment off
guard. As chapter 6 will explain, Sun offered its technical
achievements to the entire industry. It put its technology into
the public domain, licensing its wizardry and maintaining an
adherence to standards that appealed to customers.

Such a policy was anathema to other manufacturers. How
could you make a profit, they reasoned, if you "gave" everything away? The response from Sun's direct competitors was
more than skepticism. It was derision. Nowhere was the
scoffing more vocal than at Digital Equipment Corporation,
whose traditional customers—engineers, scientists, and technologists—were attracted to Sun's products and philosophy.
And nowhere was the about-face so evident as at DEC.

In *The Ultimate Entrepreneur: The Story of Ken Olsen and
Digital Equipment Corporation*, authors Glenn Rifkin and
George Harrar paint DEC's founder as an honest and
straightforward fellow, a dedicated and hardworking leader,
guided by the unshakable notion that he knows what is right.
Olsen is portrayed as intelligent, though not overly sophisticated in the ways of public relations and image. He had an

unshakable belief that he knew what was right for the market: deliver a solid, reliable product, and the future would be bright and profitable.

Olsen's convictions slowed DEC's response to Sun's invasion into his own backyard. He regarded the UNIX operating system embraced by Sun as "snake oil," despite its increasing use by his customers on his company's VAX and PDP machines. Equally important, DEC's CEO misconstrued the market's demand for the more attractive price/performance ratio Sun presented. This latter point is ironic because it was DEC's PDP system that offered computer users the first price/performance alternative to IBM and paved the way for DEC's spectacular growth in the 1960s and 1970s.

Olsen held a bias against workstations vis-à-vis the minicomputers that had made DEC's reputation, a bias that pervaded his company. As late as the summer of 1988, Olsen disdained the idea of putting high performance on the desktop. As he told one interviewer, "I once drove a 400-horsepower Mustang. Now these huge tractor/trailer combinations with 18 wheels on them go by out here with 300- or 400-horsepower engines. If I was to tell you that I have a Mustang with more horsepower than a big truck, and that your truck should be replaced by a Mustang, you'd laugh at me. It's the same thing to say three MIPS on the desk is going to replace the big machine." His scorn for desktop machines was fueled by DEC's misery in the personal computer market, which had led to one of DEC's most disastrous years. Finally, the continued success of DEC's minicomputers seemed to belie the value of workstations.

DEC's strategy was simple: build and support computers of various sizes and performance capabilities that used a single operating system, VMS. This operating system allowed users to run software on the different levels of computers. A VMS program was compatible across the DEC line. The computers could be networked effectively, and customers could continue to add VAX machines virtually indefinitely.

But the simplicity of the idea posed problems for custom-

ers in a complex world. Not all VAX computers, and certainly
not all VMS programs, addressed every problem at a customer site. Users demanded specific machines for the diverse
problems computers solved. Companies found themselves
living in a world of heterogeneous machines, while DEC was
offering a homogeneous product line. The problem that
Apollo faced, being proprietary, loomed before DEC. And
the company flinched.

As industry analyst Rich Edwards observed, "The typical
scientific/engineering computer environment today is not a
collection of systems from a single vendor, but a heterogeneous multi-vendor mix of systems ranging from high-performance systems (mainframes or supercomputers and/or
minisupercomputers) to superminis performing various functions (high-performance computing, network server, file/
database server), with workstations functioning as an individual user's 'window' into the computing environment." This
was the everyday world of the typical computer user. This
was the market in which Sun excelled. The competitors,
somehow, floundered.

Sun harped continuously on its "open architecture." The
company perpetuated technologies understood and used by
numerous companies and customers. For example, most
companies developed in-house software, which meant they
needed good programming tools. That need turned into a
massive potential market for UNIX-based systems, if only
for the computing elite that wrote programs. UNIX was
ideal for developing programs that ran on non-UNIX computers. Even at DEC, programmers developed, on UNIX,
software that ran on VMS-based systems. With its special
software-development tools, UNIX was also ideal for a wide
range of customers.

All of this is not to say that DEC's workstations did not
sell. In 1985, when the VAXstation II and the MicroVAX II
were introduced to the workstation market, DEC sold twelve-
thousand units, with a five-to-one ratio favoring the MicroVAX II. But DEC sold these systems to its existing customer base and almost exclusively to VMS users. Sun exec-

utives viewed the MicroVAX II as a major threat. McNealy never underestimated DEC and had the utmost respect for Olsen, but Sun recognized that the momentum of the market was toward UNIX systems, not VMS. And while VMS users were delighted with the new DEC workstations, the UNIX community was disappointed.

Key to Sun's success against DEC are price and performance, not only workstation to workstation, but workstation to minicomputer. Olsen himself is quoted as saying, "We will never compete on price." In the minds of many, DEC did not compete on performance, either.

Figure 3.1

SUN PERFORMANCE		
Sun-4/280 vs. DEC VAX 8800		
	Sun-4/280	**DEC VAX 8800**
MIPS	10	12
Dhrystone	19000	15000 (est.)
Linpack (SP/DP)	1600/1100	1400/970 (VMS)
Mass Storage Range	280MB to 2.3 GB	205 MB to 4.1 GB
Base Price (Diskless/48MB)	$62,900	$672,000
w/ 128MB Memory, 2.3 GB, ½" Tape	**$199,900**	**$979,000**
(Source: Sun)		

By 1986 Sun was delivering workstations that were faster than DEC's bestselling VAX 780 minicomputers. In 1987, Sun machines were challenging DEC's VAX 8800 superminicomputers and were dramatically lower in cost. As figure 3.1 shows, the Sun-4/280 workstation was slightly slower than the VAX 8800 but was a staggering one-tenth the price. Suddenly DEC had to justify to customers why they had to

pay ten times the price for only one-fifth more performance.
The rationale that VMS was a better operating system or that
more software packages ran on VAXes was beginning to ring
hollow in the minds of many DEC users. And it didn't ring at
all in the ears of those who were new to the computer market.

One other intangible element that Sun had was momentum. It had taken DEC seventeen years to reach the Fortune
500 and twenty years to top a billion dollars in sales. Sun did
these in five and six years, respectively. Sun was propelled by
a worldwide computing phenomenon caused by the personal
computer. The PC instilled the notion that everyone—not
just specialists—could have a computer at their fingertips.
DEC shied away from this idea, preferring the minicomputer
mentality.

By 1988 Sun had minimized DEC's role in the workstation
market, outside of DEC's captive VMS clients. In order to
expand its position, DEC capitulated completely to the Sun
approach. In January 1989 DEC introduced its so-called
Sun-killer machines, which ran only Ultrix, DEC's version of
the UNIX operating system, thereby leaving its VMS installed base in the lurch. To distinguish these computers
from the MicroVAX II and VAXstation products, DEC
dubbed the line the DECstation 3100 series and priced the
machines more aggressively than anything it had rolled out
before: between $10,000 and $90,000 per system. Many analysts concluded, much as they had in 1985, that Sun would
be buried by DEC's reentry into the market. The DECstation
3100 is a RISC-based system, sporting a performance of up
to 14 MIPS, 40 percent faster than Sun's fastest computer at
the time of the announcement.

Since, as Olsen had admitted, it takes DEC between three
and four years to develop a product, for the first time the
Maynard, Massachusetts, company had had to look elsewhere for assistance. Dropping its own RISC-development
project, DEC went to Silicon Valley and incorporated the
RISC microprocessor built by MIPS Computer, a startup
company dedicated exclusively to RISC systems. In the
minds of some, the DECstation 3100 established the first real

competition Sun had to face since it passed Apollo as the world leader in the workstation market.

Sun responded with its SPARCstation 1 machine, announced in April of the same year. Code-named Campus I, the 12.5-MIPS computer, though slower than the DECstation 3100, was priced far lower, starting at seven thousand dollars. It included 8 megabytes of memory, 100 megabytes of mass storage, and a sound system that rivaled some people's home stereo systems. Most important was UNIX. Unlike Ultrix, Sun's operating system was perceived as being "purer." Even on DEC's VAX systems, users preferred to run the 4.2 BSD version of UNIX from the University of California (on which the SunOS was based), instead of DEC's Ultrix. Furthermore, Sun's operating system and those compatible with it came to control more than 70 percent of the UNIX market. That meant that most of the UNIX applications software available worked with Sun's computers, not DEC's. This situation gave Sun a significant leg up on DEC as the two companies competed head to head.

DEC also suffered a credibility problem as it jumped into the UNIX market. It seemed to many that DEC's espousal of UNIX was a bit disingenuous, considering that it had built its multibillion-dollar fortunes on VMS, a proprietary product. But DEC attempted to hide these deficiencies and ignored its long history as a reluctant player in the UNIX market. It even joined the ranks of Sun's opposition, claiming that it was as "open" as anyone else.

OPEN FOR BUSINESS . . . AND WAR

In January 1989, almost three years to the day after Sun executives gathered in boardroom 2 to ponder their company's barriers to entry vis-à-vis the competition, Ed Zander, Sun's corporate marketing VP, called his managers to boardroom 2 for an update on the competition and Sun's response to it. Zander was on the other side of the fence now, having come to Sun from Apollo and taking over the vice presidency once held by Bartz.

On the day of the meeting, DEC was announcing its Sun-killer workstation and a host of other products. HP was introducing a new low-cost graphics workstation (one that specializes in replicating complex images on the screen); it was also cutting the prices of other computers, including its new RISC machines, making them much more attractive to customers.

Managers rushed in and out of boardroom 2 that day, carrying sheets of smooth facsimile paper with the latest information about the competition's moves. The consensus was that HP's price cuts were meant to counter Silicon Graphics of Mountain View, a $250 million maker of high-priced but very powerful 3-D-graphics computers. It was DEC's move that had the attention of everyone in the room.

"Don't discount HP," Zander warned, but it was clear he was provoked by DEC's new play in the market. Zander, Apollo's former marketing boss, who had been wooed to Sun by McNealy in 1987, paced the room, calling out details. "DEC says, 'up to fourteen MIPS,' and that it's only eleven thousand nine hundred dollars." People offered critical analysis of DEC's workstations, talking in the arcane language of computer technology, referring to "data byte order" and "Dhrystone MIPS versus Whetstone MIPS."

Zander noted that DEC's new RISC machine, using the CPU from MIPS Computer and running a version of UNIX exclusively, was a ringing endorsement of Sun's long-term strategy. Zander said DEC's action would undermine its credibility with DEC's traditional customers, suggesting that it "was now open season on VAX/VMS users." He was not, however, overconfident. DEC was a major player, and when it set out to invade new territory, something serious was going to happen. Previously, William Strecker, DEC's VP of product strategy, had been quoted as saying, "We intend to be the leader in workstations. We're tired of being annoyed by Sun." In the context of DEC's latest product blitz, Zander did not take such comments as idle threats.

"Ladies and gentlemen," he declared to the room, "Sun has never been in a real battle before. When Sun crushed

Apollo, that was a popgun skirmish. This, my friends, this is war. And we'd better be prepared."

Zander was also concerned because the opposing armies in the workstation business were not simply DEC and HP. Nor was it a free-for-all, with every group racing about the battle-field in a state of anarchy. They were organized and they were strategic. What's more, they had Sun in their gun sights. Their weapon was the Open Software Foundation.

4
The Religion of UNIX

UNIX is a computer operating system, but to many of its most avid advocates, it is much more. It represents a computing philosophy, a system of beliefs. For some, it is tantamount to a religion. If UNIX is a religion, the battle that eventually shaped up in the UNIX community between the Open Software Foundation (OSF) and UNIX International might well be thought of as a religious war started by the former group.

Originally dubbed the Hamilton Group because it first met in DEC's regional offices on Hamilton Avenue in Palo Alto, California, the OSF was a broad-based coalition of frightened computer makers scared enough to begin a pitched battle in the industry. They were frightened not just by Sun, which was a relatively small success story in a minor segment of the computer industry. They were unnerved by Sun's coalition with AT&T and the seemingly unstoppable momentum of the UNIX operating system, a technology owned and controlled by the former Ma Bell. Their fear stemmed from the assault UNIX was making on proprietary operating systems, such as VMS, Aegis, and the array of

IBM's system software. It was an anxiety so deep that for the first time in memory, Ken Olsen joined John Akers of IBM in a photo session, each declaring their sudden and abiding affection for "open" computing.

The companies that later were to form the OSF should have felt their first stirrings of paranoia when AT&T and Sun agreed in September 1985 to implement a three-phase plan to develop and distribute a single, unified UNIX operating system. UNIX had many flavors, and AT&T's licensing program freed it from any dominant developer's predilections. Its anarchistic capabilities gave UNIX its appeal and its limitations. But at its core, UNIX was a gregarious operating system, running on more CPUs than anything else on the market. With the exception of Microsoft's MS-DOS (for personal computers only), UNIX was the industry's standard operating system. When AT&T and Sun announced their agreement, it was said that an attempt to bring UNIX under control would benefit every company that used UNIX and every developer that worked with it. Although noted in the trade press and elsewhere, the notion of one flavor of UNIX did not raise a single eyebrow in the industry because UNIX had been fragmented for so long—no one believed that it could be successfully merged.

What finally unleashed their dread was the deal AT&T and Sun signed in 1988. As outlined in the second chapter, AT&T agreed to invest heavily in Sun at a premium price. That was because AT&T had lost its edge as the industry's leading UNIX house. But it had vast resources that could tremendously improve the position of UNIX; all it needed was the intellectual horsepower. Sun had the brains but not the brawn. With Sun and AT&T allied, UNIX might unseat huge numbers of users previously tied to proprietary systems. Alarmed by Sun's market-share mentality, the momentum for open systems and UNIX, and AT&T's deep pockets, industry executives forged an alliance in hopes of crushing the revolt against proprietary computing before it was too late.

The onslaught was directed at Sun more than at AT&T

because, competitors knew, customers perceived the smaller company as the UNIX leader. To undercut Sun's position with UNIX, the OSF held few weapons in check. As Kathleen K. Wiegner wrote in *Forbes* magazine, "Even in a highly competitive industry, Sun is unusually friendless. Its one good buddy, AT&T, is not exactly helping: Its relationship with Sun has drawn the fire of some of the biggest guns in the computer industry."

To most observers the appearance of DEC in the alliance against Sun and open systems was not unexpected. It was IBM's willingness to step into the fray that caught so many by surprise. IBM's early sorties into the workstation arena were pitiful. Although it was first in 1986 with a RISC-based desktop machine, the RT, the computer was nearly laughed out of the market. It ran IBM's AIX version of UNIX, one with too few attendant software applications to make it viable. The computer itself was slow and had no network capabilities to speak of. Most of the RTs the company built were delivered internally to IBM. That was about all anyone heard of IBM in the workstation market for two years. International Data Corporation, an industry tracker, reported that IBM won a meager 3.9 percent of the market in 1987, compared with Sun's nearly 30 percent share. Big Blue stuck to its vast commercial markets, selling to MIS/DP managers who abided by the industry adage that no DP executive ever got fired for buying IBM equipment.

It wasn't until late 1988 that IBM got serious about the workstation business. William Lowe, president of IBM's $7 billion entry systems division, asserted that his company's goal was "to be the leader in the workstation market." IBM did not manifest the "not-invented-here" syndrome so prevalent at DEC, which surprised some analysts when DEC dropped its own RISC project, Prism, in favor of adopting RISC technology from MIPS Computer.

IBM bought its first official PC-LAN technology, for example, from Sytek, Inc., of Mountain View. And in 1988 IBM shopped for high-end workstation technology from Silicon Graphics, just around the corner (literally) from Sun, investing in the company and signing a long-term purchase agreement. That was also the year IBM uncaged its UNIX hackers to man the company booth at UNIX Expo, a technology trade show in New York City. Until then, IBM hid its UNIX people from view, because they did not, by and large, conform to the staid IBM image.

IBM wasn't interested in UNIX, nor did Big Blue's embrace of the operating system represent a sudden liberalism in the company's marketing approach. IBM was motivated to aggressively corral the massive customer base that was tied to its SNA/SAA (System Network Architecture/System Application Architecture). Since the decontrol of AT&T, IBM saw the telecommunications giant as its potential major rival worldwide. Until the deal with Sun, AT&T posed only a minor threat to IBM's computer business. The phone giant, in fact, had had little success in the computer business. AT&T's computer efforts had generally been dismissed or ridiculed.

With Sun, IBM believed, AT&T finally had the strategic partner it needed to build a competing base of computer systems—potentially greater than that of DEC—which was why Akers was willing to stand before the world and link his giant firm with so many other computer companies it would normally have shunned.

Eventually, thirty-nine companies jumped onto the OSF bandwagon, proclaiming it had the leadership in open systems and UNIX. AT&T/Sun countered with a coalition of their own, counting nineteen members (see box) and eventually calling itself UNIX International, Inc. Although boasting twice as many members as UNIX International, in terms of market share OSF held less than 30 percent of the UNIX installed base. And that share was slipping to UNIX International.

OPEN FOR DEBATE

The debate about open versus proprietary systems has raged for a long time. Adhering to standards has always been considered akin to taking "the high road," particularly in the

The Opposing UNIX Armies

OPEN SOFTWARE FOUNDATION

Adobe Systems
Advanced Micro Devices
Altos Computer Systems
Apollo Computer
Booz, Allen, & Hamilton
Computer Consoles
Concurrent Computer
Cornell University
Data General
Data Logic
DEC
88open Consortium, Ltd.
Groupe Bull
Hewlett-Packard
IBM
Informix Software
Interactive Systems Corp
Intefirm Graphics Systems
Landmark Graphics

Locus Computing
Mentor Graphics
National Semiconductor
Micom Interlan
Nixdorf Computer
Norsk Data AS
Pacific Bell
Philips AV
Phoenix Technologies
Relational Technologies
Mitre
Siemens
Silicon Graphics
Stanford University
Stratus Computer
Swedish Telecom
Tecsiel SpA
Toshiba America
USC

Wang Laboratories

UNIX INTERNATIONAL, INC.

AT&T
Amdahl
Control Data
Fujitsu Ltd.
Gould
HCR
ICL, Ltd.
Informix
Intel

Lachman Associates
Micro Focus
Motorola Computer Systems
NCR
Olivetti
Prime Computer
Sun
Toshiba America
Unisoft

Unisys

computer industry. What qualifies as a standard is, of course, often determined by the marketplace. IBM's products are frequently viewed as standards simply because they belong to Big Blue. Companies that compete against the giant from Armonk, New York, have long held the idea that "IBM is not the competition; it is the environment." Still, standards do emerge from so-called disinterested organizations. In the area of LANs, for example, the Institute for Electrical and Electronic Engineers (IEEE, or "I triple E") defined the physical and electrical standards in its well-known 802 committees during the early 1980s. As a result, LANs proliferated throughout the rest of the decade. LAN companies, computer manufacturers, and software developers all conformed to the IEEE specifications in order to compete.

LANs were codified in their infancy, but UNIX had been around for nearly two decades by the time competing standards bodies were formed. Just as LANs involved technical minutiae of data communications, the haggling over UNIX has revolved around the bits and bytes of operating system technology. OSF proponents hold certain elements of UNIX dear, while UNIX International members adhere to their own variances. Although the distinctions might seem insignificant, even absurd, to laymen, they do make a difference. With one version, a third-party software package might run smoothly; on another, it could be troublesome or impossible to execute. Because the availability of applications software makes or breaks the value of an operating system and, hence, the computer it works with, the final ingredients of the "standard" developed by each group are critical to the companies that adopt the standard.

If the differences between the OSF and UNIX International were merely arcane points in a technically oriented philosophical discussion, few would notice. But real money—billions of dollars—is at stake. Taking a stand has become critical, particularly for IBM and DEC. Salomon Brothers analyst Marc Stahlman contends, "They have common interests because their dominant positions are threatened by the emergence of a Sun Microsystems- and AT&T-led alliance of vendors whose goal is to undermine their market share by popularizing computer systems based on the UNIX operating system." His assessment shows that "Sun and other UNIX vendors have rapidly penetrated IBM's and DEC's customer bases." As DEC's workstation manager, Joseph DiNucci, admitted to *Fortune* magazine's Stuart Gannes, "We knew we were losing big accounts right and left."

At this writing, neither body has released its final product. UNIX International has an edge, in that AT&T and Sun have already covered much of the ground necessary to accomplish the goal; also, AT&T's historical connection with UNIX and Sun's currently recognized leadership in the area have given UNIX International a leg up over the OSF. Because its members do not share a common purpose, the OSF has experienced some internal squabbles over how much of IBM's AIX to incorporate into its final offering. Few companies, particularly DEC and HP, want to give IBM any more advantages than it already owns. Both UNIX International and the OSF claim that they will democratically provide their UNIX soon enough to eliminate any claims of unfairness to other UNIX companies. The entire process has the industry waiting with anticipation—some with hope, others with dread.

THE RELIGION OF UNIX

Religious metaphors are often used to explain computer phenomena. For example, "The Programmer's Prayer" is a parody of "The Lord's Prayer"; a Silicon Valley stand-up comic who calls himself "St. Silicon" entertains at events by reading from the "Binary Bible"; Apple computer has staff positions called "evangelists," people whose efforts are dedicated solely to promoting a given technology or product; a computer trade journal refers to "the gospel of UNIX." One of the major conventions devoted to the UNIX operating system is Usenix. The call for papers for the 1986 gathering of the UNIX clans requested papers about, among other topics, the "theology of UNIX."

One religious metaphor that is particularly apt is a description of the evolution of computing. As this computer conceit has it, the world of digital computing was initially controlled by a "high priesthood" of computer cognoscenti—programmers, systems administrators, systems analysts—who oversaw the operations of mainframe computers. These priests held sway over their supplicants, who came to them, begging the priests to put the supplicants' punch cards into the stack and run them through the computer, or to fix the machine that had gone down. The former had control over the latter. They alone knew how to program and operate the arcane machines, which were locked away in climate-controlled sanctums open only to the priests.

But new developments threatened priestly power. After the mainframes came minicomputers and timesharing, both of which made computers more accessible to the supplicants. In the late 1970s, personal computers put computing power—albeit limited power—onto the desks of anyone who could afford to purchase a relatively inexpensive machine. Networking and distributed computing also helped undermine the priests' control.

In the late 1960s, as the minicomputer era ascended, there emerged in the East an agent that would one day begin to break down the hegemony of the priesthood. This agent was the UNIX operating system.

Computer operating systems are most often likened to traffic cops, controlling environmental activities around them: starting and stopping traffic, crossing pedestrians. In keeping with the religious metaphor, though, think of an operating system as a minister controlling the multifarious activities of the congregation. A computer's operating system controls many of the hardware and software activities that occur in a computer system. From the birth of digital computers until the emergence of UNIX, operating systems were designed to work with a specific kind of computer. In other words, the operating system for an IBM mainframe computer would not function on a minicomputer from DEC. Each operating system was, like the people who controlled the computers, a shrouded priesthood.

IN THE BEGINNING

The people who "invented" UNIX twenty years ago were two members of the aforementioned priesthood; some of their followers would come to think of them in almost godlike terms. Ken Thompson and Dennis Ritchie were cloistered at AT&T's Bell Laboratories in New Jersey. Although Thompson and Ritchie were part of the exclusive priesthood, they had a vision of an operating system that was open to more people. Thompson and Ritchie may have been high priests, but they were also hackers.

Their work represented a dissatisfaction and frustration with batch computing and the early timesharing system GE 645, which ran the Multics operating system. Thompson and Ritchie did their UNIX development work on a DEC PDP-7 minicomputer. Later, UNIX was ported through the C programming language, to DEC's newer PDP-11. The significance of this move was that C was a portable language—meaning that it could run on diverse hardware—which, in turn, meant that UNIX was a portable operating system that also could run on many different kinds of hardware. Moving the operating system to another computer required some time and effort; but at least it could be moved, which was not the case with other operating systems.

When it was first developed, though, UNIX was essentially still accessible only to the priests of computing—but so was the timeshared computer technology in those days. Those who could navigate through the labyrinth of UNIX, however, found a world of flexibility and power that was previously unreachable. UNIX users could, for example, customize the operating system for their own purposes; they could add tools and facilities that Thompson and Ritchie had neither incorporated nor envisioned.

The two heretics who developed UNIX were a reflection of the unusual environment in which they worked. Bell Labs was, in some ways, like a monastery. Essentially a research institute, it subsidized the work of some of the most brilliant minds in computing. If a commercial product emerged from the research, fine, but the underlying philosophy was research for research's sake. Under such circumstances, it is likely that Thompson and Ritchie never thought of their creation as a potentially successful commercial entity. Their patron, AT&T, certainly didn't think of it that way: for the first decade and more of UNIX's existence, AT&T was not in the computer business. In the days before deregulation, it was too busy running a quasi-monopolistic phone business, so its essential attitude was benign neglect—licensing UNIX to companies, universities, and research institutes. Acolytes were later necessary to spread the gospel.

UNIX: THE WORD

What does this word UNIX mean? It suggests unity, uniqueness. An ersatz UNIX credo is dubbed "Unixtarian" (see box). An etymological suggestion is that the term is a pun on *eunuchs*—UNIX being "castrated Multics"; Multics being a large timesharing operating system from Honeywell Bull. UNIX, on the other hand, was oriented more toward the needs of individual users—again, the idea of uniqueness and unity.

Yet the "name applies to a family of operating systems developed at Bell Laboratories." UNIX quickly fractured into several different versions. As with biblical families, feuding often broke out among the various versions of UNIX—among their apologists, rather, and Sun was in the thick of the feuding.

Because Bell Labs was not computer-product oriented, AT&T took no immediate steps to promote or sell the operating system developed under its auspices, other than licensing UNIX, primarily to universities. The task of promotion was left to the true believers, who comprised a small but devoted sect in UNIX's early days. UNIX adherents tended to come from the technical, scientific, and academic communities; a following also developed among military hackers at the Defense Advanced Research Projects Agency (DARPA). To many computer users who had been victims of the stranglehold of the priesthood, the UNIX experience was like a computing epiphany.

Unixtarian

I would like to discuss my own secular belief, being that this is a free network.

I would like to introduce a new religion, Unixtarian. This religion is founded on the belief that when you die you will enter a virtual address for eternity or until the scheduler crashes. In this case there is a rollback procedure that will place you in a spool queue where you will wait for a new virtual address. Now this religion is based on three great quotes:

"Let the command language be terse."
(Thompson 25:1)
"Let the programming language be terse."
(Ritchie 23:4)
"Let there be paging."
(Joy 45:1)

Now before any of you flame me, let me warn you that I am protected by the writings of my higher power: grep (1), mail (1), reboot (8).

(Source: posting to junkmail in 1987.)

With AT&T's lackluster support for UNIX, efforts of the operating system's devoted followers were required to propel UNIX into being a de facto standard in the computer business. One of these followers was Bill Joy, who was just an adolescent when UNIX emerged from Bell Labs.

Joy, who was to become a UNIX "guru"—as experts and leaders in any given field of computing are known—ended up as a graduate student at the University of California, Berkeley, which had become the leading university proponent of UNIX development. It was at Berkeley that the major variant of the operating system was developed and improved. This improved version of the operating system became known as UNIX 4.1 BSD (Berkeley Software Distribution). Subsequent versions were 4.2 and 4.3 BSD.

The prime contributor to the efforts at Berkeley—at both the conceptual and code-writing levels—was Joy. In fact, Joy's name was to become synonymous with "Berkeley UNIX." One of his professors was Dave Patterson, who recalls that Joy was quite a handful in class. "It wasn't always clear who was going to do the most talking—Bill or the professor."

Joy was working on his Ph.D. at UC Berkeley in 1982 when Sun cofounders Scott McNealy, Andy Bechtolsheim, and Vinod Khosla tapped him to be the fourth cofounder. Bringing on "Mr. Berkeley UNIX" as director—and later vice president—of research and development was a stroke of genius. The fledgling company planned to base its systems on established industry standards and to create and promote standards where needed. One of those standards was the UNIX operating system, and what better man to have behind the effort than the charismatic and quotable Joy?

When UNIX first emerged from Bell Labs, however, it was far from being a standard. Quite the opposite, it was a nearly unknown upstart in a world of proprietary mainframe and minicomputer operating systems. With the advent of decentralized computing, the number of its acolytes multiplied. Not trained in the ways of a cloistered priesthood, they espoused a new religious paradigm for computers, one heretical to the old religion. These heretics were hackers, mostly young men, whose lives revolved almost completely around computers. Many of them gravitated to the UNIX operating system because it held out the promise of liberation.

These liberation theologists of the digital world were free with their knowledge and expertise. They were willing— eager was more like it—to share knowledge and expertise with each other. For hard-core hackers, computer technology exists to be invented, challenged, modified, improved. In part, the "hacker ethic" read: "Access to computers—and anything that might teach you something about the way the world works—should be unlimited and total; all information should be free; mistrust authority—promote decentralization." This ethic sounds like the underpinning of what was to become a religion of the late 1980s and early 1990s: open systems. It was an idealized sentiment, one without much applicability to noncomputer users in the 1960s and 1970s.

Any new system of belief that emerges as a variant of some other creed, or in reaction to the existing order, faces obstacles. In the early days UNIX had a lot stacked against it, such as tepid endorsement from AT&T and the entrenched interests of proprietary mainframe and minicomputer operating systems. Much as Christianity subdivided into a multitude of denominations and sects, so did UNIX subdivide, with each branch staking out its own territory. By the 1980s three versions predominated: System V from AT&T; the Berkeley version; and XENIX from Microsoft Corporation, a company that had made much of its fortune by developing the operating systems for the IBM Personal Computer and PS/2 lines. System V saw its primary use in commercial applications, the Berkeley version was preferred in the technical and scientific communities, and XENIX ran on personal computers based on Intel's 80x86 chip.

But the differences did not stop there.

As the 1960s and 1970s gave way to the 1980s and more and more UNIX believers emerged, the diversity increased. IBM called its version of UNIX AIX (Advanced Interactive Executive). Apple Computer, sensing the burgeoning UNIX trend of the late 1980s, came up with a version, A/UX, for its Macintosh II line of computers. DEC's minicomputer version was dubbed Ultrix. Hewlett-Packard had a version of UNIX called HP/UX. The Aegis operating system for Apollo workstations, though proprietary, was a UNIX hybrid. In reaction to Sun's success with UNIX, Apollo came up with its own UNIX version: Domain/IX. Amdahl mainframe computers ran a version of UNIX called UTS. As a Paine Webber analyst archly put it, "There are currently more versions of UNIX than there are flavors of ice cream at Baskin Robbins." (See box for an overview of the major versions of the UNIX operating system as of mid-1988.)

In short, the "unique," "unifying" operating system had become a technological Tower of Babel with so many differences among the various versions that they could not completely intercommunicate. Sun Microsystems and Bill Joy made it their mission to standardize the fragmented operating system.

Major Versions of UNIX Other Than SunOS

NONPROPRIETARY VERSIONS OF UNIX

Berkeley 4.3 BSD. Berkeley UNIX is the basis for the Sun Operating System. This version added so many enhancements to AT&T's original that it became the UNIX of choice for scientific and technical users. Berkeley UNIX is largely the creation of Bill Joy.

System V. AT&T took a newfound interest in its creation in 1983, when the company announced System V and threw its support behind this version. Two years later, AT&T announced the System V Interface Definition (SVID), a formal document containing the specifications for System V. To test the compatibility of other companies' versions with System V, AT&T has the System V Verification Suite (SVVS).

XENIX. Microsoft's version of UNIX conforms to AT&T's SVID. Similar to Release 2 of AT&T's System V, it runs on Intel 80x86 processors. Microsoft also developed DOS and OS/2 for the IBM PC and PS/2 lines, respectively, and XENIX shares some compatibility with these two operating systems.

PROPRIETARY VERSIONS OF UNIX

AIX et al. IBM offers many versions of AIX for the different computers it makes. It runs on all 370 computers as well as on the PS/2 Model 80 and the RT PC (IBM's RISC-based workstation). AIX is quite similar to System V Release 2, and 4.3 BSD. Even though AIX is derived from System V, it has features not found on the latter version. XENIX is also available from IBM for the PC AT computer.

A/UX. Apple got into the UNIX game fairly late with its version of UNIX for the Macintosh II. A/UX looks like AT&T's System V and has some Berkeley features. In addition, Apple has enhanced the user interface and added such features as automatic recovery and system reconfiguration. A/UX also acknowledges various network input/output devices.

Domain/IX. Apollo's UNIX has a "split personality." It incorporates both System V and Berkeley UNIX, so users can choose which approach to take for their applications.

HP/UX. This version of UNIX, from Hewlett-Packard, runs on HP's HP9000 computers, Series 500 multi-user workstations, Series 300 workstations, and Series 800 RISC systems. It works with System V and has some Berkeley UNIX features. Unlike System V, it offers real-time capabilities and device, file, and memory locking—useful features for commercial applications.

Ultrix. DEC's version of UNIX is available on the VAX line of computers. Compatible with Berkeley UNIX, Ultrix also conforms to System V. Originally a UNIX detractor, DEC has changed its position to active support for the operating system.

One of the main reasons so many versions of UNIX came into being was that adopting the operating system for a company's product or products was relatively easy. The company had merely to license UNIX from AT&T and modify it to fit the company's needs—much less work than developing an operating system from scratch. The irony of this approach, though, was that each version of UNIX became, in some ways, a proprietary product. Because AT&T did not license the "binary code"—the digital essence of the operating system—but rather its source code, one company's version of UNIX most likely did not run on another UNIX company's products unless it was "tuned" for the other

machine. Until someone came up with a "binary-compati-
ble" UNIX, differences from version to version were destined to continue.

THE PATH TO ONE UNIX

By 1982, the year Sun Microsystems was founded, Bill Joy
was making himself known as the leading prophet of the
UNIX operating system. Not only was Joy a true believer in
the power and potential of UNIX, but he also proselytized
tirelessly for its adoption as a standard. His passions extended beyond propelling UNIX to predominance. Joy was a
high-tech visionary. Sun was a perfect place for his vision.

As vice president of research and development, he essentially reported to no one—as illustrated by McNealy's organization chart referred to in chapter 3. Amusing as
McNealy's little diagram was, it symbolized Joy's godlike
stature in the UNIX community. His prestige and charisma
were instrumental in drawing some of the best UNIX talent
to Sun: Sun became *the* place for UNIX experts to work.
Under Joy's tutelage and guidance, Sun's UNIX engineers
began the hard work of transforming UNIX into a standard
for the computer industry—a formidable task.

UNIX was not a standard when Sun opened its doors for
business in January 1982. It was fragmented among the
versions noted (see box, page 98–99). Industry pundits la-
mented the apparent chaos that reigned in the UNIX world.
How could UNIX ever become a standard, they wondered,
when so many different versions of it were in use?

Adding to the confusion was the sudden interest of the
progenitor of UNIX: AT&T. AT&T watched as UNIX increased in popularity. The giant company took notice of
Sun's work with the operating system; Sun continuously
added enhancements to UNIX and improved upon it. What
had been indifference on the part of AT&T turned into active
interest. Concurrently for Sun, compatibility with System V
became a high priority.

It was not surprising, then, when the two companies announced, in September 1985, that they would work together

to converge Sun's Berkeley 4.3-based UNIX operating system with System V, with the intention of developing a single version of UNIX. The 4.3 version tended to be favored for technical applications, and System V was most often the choice for commercial use. The convergence effort was an attempt to blend the best of both variants to come up with a unified system. As a Sun press release of August 5, 1986, noted: "The UNIX system is clearly established as a standard operating system, but in the past, applications developers were forced to choose between writing applications for the Berkeley 4.3 version . . . or AT&T's System V. . . . In addition to limitations on available applications software, each version of the UNIX system offered functionality not available in the other version. Some vendors have responded by offering a 'dual port' (both versions co-existing on one system) or a hybrid of the two versions."

Phase one of the convergence came with the announcement of version 3.2 of SunOS. This converged UNIX was based on the Berkeley 4.2 version, with added enhancements from the 4.3 version. What the merger of SunOS 3.2 and System V did was incorporate System V functions into SunOS. In the final unified version of UNIX, known as System V Release 4, Microsoft's XENIX, a UNIX derivative for PCs, would blend with Sun's and AT&T's systems (see figure 4.1).

Figure 4.1

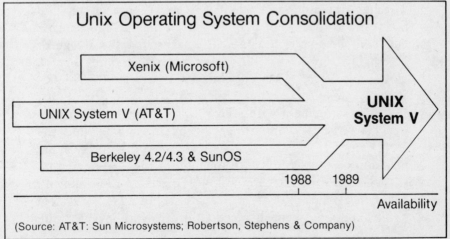

Unix Operating System Consolidation

Xenix (Microsoft)

UNIX System V (AT&T)

Berkeley 4.2/4.3 & SunOS

UNIX System V

1988 1989

Availability

(Source: AT&T: Sun Microsystems; Robertson, Stephens & Company)

This agreement between Sun and AT&T was yet another example of Sun's acumen in forming strategic alliances. The arrangement had all the earmarks of genius: a merger of the two dominant versions of UNIX, backed by the respective owners of the two major UNIX systems. Yet brilliant as the alliance with AT&T was, it was also controversial, destined to cause Sun problems as the decade waned.

In addition to cooperating with AT&T, Sun worked with other companies to help standardize UNIX. In February 1988 Sun and Amdahl Corporation announced an agreement under which the two companies would integrate various elements of their respective UNIX operating systems. Amdahl's UTS ran on Amdahl's mainframe computers, which were compatible with IBM System/370 mainframes, a mainstay of the computer industry. As was the case with so many Sun alliances and partnerships, Sun's objective was to make technology sharing easier—in this case to make mainframes more accessible to workstations, and vice versa. As with the Sun/AT&T deal, Sun wished to increase its penetration into commercial and financial markets, while, as a by-product, opening up technical markets to Amdahl.

With the increased compatibility between Sun and Amdahl systems afforded by the Sun/Amdahl alliance, Sun was in a stronger position to sell its workstations to companies once considered unlikely buyers of technical workstations. Through Amdahl, Sun made its first major product step into the realm of MIS/DP managers. The technology sharing between the two companies also improved the image of UNIX in the eyes of traditional corporate computer buyers.

A month later, in March, Unisys Corporation (the bland-sounding result of the merger of Sperry and Burroughs) signed an agreement with AT&T. "[The announcement] reflects a strategic commitment to open systems, and the UNIX operating system in particular," said Unisys Chairman and CEO W. Michael Blumenthal. The deal beefed up what Unisys called its Applications Operating Environment. The Unisys version of UNIX was based on AT&T's System V. The announcement involved a third player, however: Sun

Microsystems. Unisys had also licensed Sun's SPARC architecture as the foundation for Unisys' future high-performance computers running UNIX.

Spokespeople for all three members of this trinity were optimistic: "The UNIX operating system clearly has been established as the key industry standard for the 1990s," said Blumenthal. "The Unisys agreement validates the importance . . . of customers' demand for a single, unified UNIX system standard," said Sun's McNealy. "We are pleased that Unisys is willing to be a working partner in furthering the commercialization of the UNIX operating system," said Vittorio Cassoni, president of AT&T's data systems group.

Others were not so sanguine. Why, some analysts and Sun detractors wondered, would an aggressive, fast-moving company such as Sun team up with a couple of giant, stolid companies that were hardly known for their expertise or innovations in computer technology? Other UNIX players began to grumble that Sun's relationship with AT&T was getting too cozy.

GOVERNMENT PATRONAGE

Much as some politically left-leaning computer hackers—of which there are many—would like to overlook the fact, the computer industry would not exist on its current scale without the support of the U.S. Department of Defense. DoD funding has nurtured many high-tech companies, projects, and products, including UNIX. The DoD became interested in UNIX early in the operating system's existence, because of research ties between the defense establishment and many top-level universities, such as the Massachusetts Institute of Technology and the University of California at Berkeley, where DARPA subsidized some of the UNIX development work.

The DoD is an elephantine bureaucracy but not a monolithic one. Different groups have different needs and systems, but all of them have immense numbers of taxpayers' dollars sunk into computer systems—a welter of incompatible systems. Although mainframes still predominate in government computer installations, personal computers are well represented, as evidenced by the mission of an army procurement officer stationed in D.C. who moonlighted as a computer-product reviewer for *InfoWorld*, a weekly trade publication. In 1983 he paid a visit to the magazine's Palo Alto, California, office. He informed some of the staff that he had a multimillion-dollar check "burning a hole" in his pocket. The check was for personal-computer systems, and he was researching what would best fit his needs.

That was early on in the Reagan administration, one that gave carte blanche to the military and presided over a bloated Pentagon budget and defense-contractor scandals. Later in the Reagan administration, the Defense pork barrel was less liberally endowed. As the Reagan years drew to a close, it was obvious that government agencies would have to find a way to cut back. One such way might be to bring standardization and compatibility to the computing chaos that prevailed.

As is its wont, the government had been studying possible solutions to the problem for some time. One solution that looked attractive was to find an operating system to which all bidders for government business would be required to conform. The operating system that looked attractive was UNIX.

It was promising for several reasons. UNIX was growing in popularity and was available on many of the high-performance workstations that were so well suited for numerous government and military computing tasks. Because of long-time study and support of and research into UNIX by DARPA, the operating system was also uniquely suited to run on the DoD's Arpanet, a computer network developed by DARPA and tied into UNIX networks across the country. The UNIX community was already heavily networked, especially with Sun's productive efforts in the field, so plugging UNIX-based systems into Arpanet was relatively easy.

You know you've established a standard when the U.S. government requires the use of your product. In 1986 the government did just that for UNIX. From that point on, any

computer company that bid on government contracts had to
offer the UNIX operating system—at least as an option—for
the bid to be considered.

This requirement gave Sun an obvious advantage when it
went after half of a $500 million, five-year National Security
Agency contract in 1986. Sun eventually garnered a sizable
portion of the NSA pie and an impressive addition to the
company's bottom line over the years of the contract.

Not all computer companies were as enthusiastic about the
government's newfound UNIX religion. DEC, for example,
filed suit to block the Air Force's demand for compliance
with AT&T's System V Interface Definition in bids on a $4.5
billion contract because it could not comply. The Air Force
agreed to drop the SVID clause but held firm on its demand
for System V. Ultrix could not make the grade, so DEC
dropped out of the bidding in January 1988, leaving AT&T
to pick up a large share of the contract. This event did a great
deal to help solidify AT&T's and Sun's positions as UNIX
standard-bearers. It also irritated DEC and other companies,
including IBM, which felt disenfranchised because of
AT&T's relationship with UNIX—and with Sun.

That the government now requires UNIX in bid proposals
is one of the ironies of the "Era of Operating System *Glasnost*," or openness. Because UNIX is so "open," so malleable, it has demonstrated a certain technological vulnerability.
Because of its nurturing by hackers in open environments
such as universities, UNIX has not yet incorporated stringent security measures as salient features.

UNIX now comprises an integral part of the defense-
related computer networks that span the country. Two incidents that occurred in 1988 demonstrated the potential sus-
ceptibility of those networks—and of UNIX. In early November of that year, a grad student at Cornell is alleged to
have planted a "virus" that nearly wreaked havoc on the
DoD's Arpanet. "A virus is a program, or a set of instructions to a computer, that is either planted on a floppy disk
meant to be used with the computer or introduced when the
computer is communicating over telephone lines or data

networks with other computers. The virus was designed to
attack computers made by Sun Microsystems, Inc., and the
Digital Equipment Corporation that run the UNIX operating system."

The first victim of the virus was Lawrence Livermore
National Laboratories in Berkeley and Livermore, California.
The virus hopped onto Arpanet and quickly spread to Stan-
ford University in Palo Alto, to the National Aeronautics and
Space Administration's Ames Research Center in Mountain
View—not much more than a stone's throw from Sun's head-
quarters—and to UC Berkeley. The next day, it had infil-
trated computers at MIT in Cambridge, Massachusetts. Re-
ports indicated that it also hit several financial institutions in
Europe and research labs in Australia.

Although the virus apparently had no direct effect on
classified computer files, what made it particularly insidious
was the alacrity and efficiency with which it reproduced on
the network. Had it not been isolated and contained as relatively rapidly as it was, it might have spread to other institutions and companies, including Sun.

In mid-December, a hacker gained unauthorized access to
computers at the government's Lawrence Livermore Labs, a
home of secret nuclear research. This time, the hacker removed some password files from the Livermore system, making it impossible for some people to log onto their computer
until the prank had been discovered and rectified. Little
harm was done, and the hacker even left a message on the
Livermore system apologizing for his caper.

The Cornell incident was more destructive. As Chuck
Cole, deputy computer-security manager at Livermore Labs,
explained, "The big issue is that a relatively benign software
program can virtually bring our computing community to its
knees and keep it there for some time. The cost is going to be
staggering."

Both incidents reveal the potential vulnerability of such an
accessible and modifiable system as UNIX. Given the propensity of hackers to hand out information over the highly
networked UNIX environment, the government has reason

to worry about its increasing reliance on UNIX until better
security measures are incorporated. "Secure UNIX" is one
of Sun's goals.

BIBLES

Walk into any comprehensive bookstore, and you'll find hundreds of books and scores of magazines and journals devoted
to all aspects of computing. As overflowing as this computer
cornucopia is now, about six years ago it was a veritable glut.
More than three hundred magazines competed for scarce
shelf space. Book publishers smelled the gold in PC boards
and cranked out books in assembly-line fashion.

Many of these books and magazines, however, weren't
worth the paper they were printed on, and some less-astute
book publishers took a bath in their ill-founded decisions.
Today the computer-publishing industry has matured. Although many computer books are still being published, titles
are more carefully considered by publishers, and the days of
huge advances are over. Several dozen, rather than several
hundred, computer magazines vie for readers' attention on
magazine racks.

As you might expect, popular computers such as the IBM
PC and Apple Macintosh series each have several magazines
devoted to them. More striking, though, is the number of
magazines devoted not toward a computer and related phenomena but to a single operating system: UNIX. UNIX has
reached such a point of popularity and importance that it
supports the publication in the United States alone of *UNIX
World*, *UNIX Review*, both monthlies, and *UNIX Today*, a
weekly. At the 1988 UniForum—one of several trade shows
devoted to UNIX—at least two publishers, one British, offered charter subscriptions to UNIX journals. The sponsor
of UniForum, /usr/group, publishes the bimonthly *Comm-
UNIXations*. December 1988 saw the appearance of a new
tabloid: *UNIX Journal*. Japan has its own UNIX magazine.

In addition to these UNIX-specific magazines, other publications such as the *SunTech Journal*, *Sun Expert*, and *The*

Sun Observer carry, by definition, a lot of material about UNIX. Trade magazines for high-technology industries are full of stories about UNIX as it becomes a dominant force in the world of computers. Additionally, newsletters devoted to the operating system are available for people who can't get enough from magazines and books.

The number of books about UNIX is also impressive. Some have become bestsellers in the computer-book genre. Not surprisingly, Sun employees have authored some of them. Henry McGilton, a writer in Sun's technical publications department, says he has sold more than two hundred thousand copies of his two books on UNIX.

All these publications exist to spread the gospel of UNIX. They have contributed much to the operating system's success, but UNIX has nevertheless faced tribulations over the years. As history has demonstrated, the proponents of many of the world's major religions have had difficulties converting large numbers of people to their faith. UNIX was no exception. Although Sun did not do it single-handedly, the company played a major role in elevating UNIX from hacker cult following to the major player it now is.

Critics of UNIX pointed out its drawbacks: True, it was powerful, but its power made it a "memory hog." Far from being standardized, it had not only fragmented into its various sects, but it also offered users an often bewildering array of options and facilities. Sometimes there were multiple solutions to a problem or approaches to a task, some more complex than others. The critics had other complaints, but they, too, drifted into the UNIX camp over time. But before Sun even got around to advertising its UNIX leadership and its "open systems" philosophy, Apollo had jumped into the breach and not only attempted to co-opt the open-systems angle but also tried to lay claim to UNIX leadership. Having finally recognized the importance of UNIX, Apollo hastily added it to the product line in the guise of Domain/IX. Since Sun had overtaken Apollo in market share by 1986, the latter company decided to capitalize on Sun's reluctance to aggressively promote itself outside of the technical and scientific communities it so well understood.

It was not until nearly three years after Sun's birth that the company launched an ad campaign, a rather tepid and short-term one at that. Until that point, Sun had sold its products "solely on word of mouth," according to *Fortune* magazine. Customers were primarily engineers, and within the engineering community Sun's superiority was becoming recognized. Much as Apollo and other competitors dismissed UNIX, Sun's top managers doubted the value of advertising. The company was getting great press; who needed advertising?

Competitive moves such as Apollo's helped galvanize the marketing effort at Sun, which had customarily played second fiddle to engineering at this most engineering-driven of companies. Sun had the track record to demonstrate that it was the up-and-coming workstation company. It had to make sure this reality didn't get lost because of soft marketing.

Marketing alone would not necessarily convert nonusers to UNIX. To win over worlds other than the highly technical and scientific, Sun had to do something to make the interface to UNIX "user friendly," as the expression goes. The company had already greatly improved the interface with software tools such as SunView and SunWindows. This software enabled users of Sun systems to avoid some of the keyboard-command cosmos that prevailed in computer use until the early 1980s. Actually, pioneering work in so-called object- and window-oriented interfaces had occurred years earlier at Xerox's Palo Alto Research Corporation (PARC); but like AT&T with UNIX, Xerox had never done much beyond the lab with its advanced computer technology.

Apple, notably, licensed some of the Xerox technology, and the result was the object-oriented Macintosh computer, which debuted in 1984. The Macintosh gave a big boost to object-oriented interaction with computers and had a major influence on the computer industry, including Sun. To successfully turn UNIX into a standard, Sun had to make it easier to use. Two of the routes to greater ease of use were the Sun386i product line and the OPEN LOOK user interface.

In 1988 Sun introduced the Sun386i product line (code-named Roadrunner). Unlike Sun's Motorola- and SPARC-based machines at this point, the 386i was based on the Intel 80386 chip, which also powered IBM's PS/2 line—the successor to the PC family. The 386i products represented Sun's first forays into the PC realm, which was accustomed to more ease of use than UNIX was known for.

The *i* in Sun386i stood for *integrated*, a common buzzword in the computer industry. In this instance, what were integrated were two operating systems: DOS, the system in place in millions of PCs and clones, and UNIX. This was a scaled-down version of UNIX, however, because the full SunOS wouldn't fit into the amount of memory the 386i offered. Not only was this version of UNIX smaller, but it was also easier to use. It had to be easier, because PC users were accustomed to an interface more cordial than that of UNIX. Because the 386i products also ran DOS, users would be familiar with that interface.

In spite of its advances, however, this machine did not fulfill expectations of becoming the "Pizza Computer." Although some people at Sun had hoped the Sun386i would bring Sun into the retail market, the machine never reached dealer shelves. It was too expensive, and its technology was too complicated for all but the savviest dealers. Only a few VARs (value-added resellers) took on the machine, selling it with specialized software. By the end of fiscal year 1989, Sun had more than ten thousand 386i machines in stock—unsold and unwanted.

Even though the 386i turned out to be a disappointment for Sun, it did address a major aspect of computing that UNIX developers had not previously addressed in any significant manner: the user interface, or the manner in which a computer presents its operations to a user. As noted earlier in this chapter, the original UNIX user interface was something only a hacker could love: strings of cryptic commands that were effectively a low-level form of programming.

Later in the life of UNIX, companies such as Sun started to make the UNIX user interface graphical, or object oriented. Because of its malleable nature, UNIX was an ideal environment for uncontrolled innovation and development.

Not only did different versions of the operating system end up sporting different user interfaces, but these various interfaces did not necessarily bear any resemblance to those of other operating systems—not an auspicious situation for making UNIX a true standard. As Jon Kannegaard, Sun's director of tools and applications, put it:

> Your plane lands after a long flight. You rush to the car-rental counter, grab the keys, and jump into the car for the drive into town. Then you discover that this car has the brake pedal to the right of the accelerator instead of to the left. When you turn the steering wheel to the right, the car goes left. And there is no turn signal at all.
>
> Sound ridiculous? This is the state of affairs today with graphical user interfaces for computers. On some, the second mouse button means "display a window." On others, it means "extend the selection."

Kannegaard goes on to explain other inconsistencies of graphical user interfaces and points out that "this chaos is the impetus for the OPEN LOOK Graphical User Interface project at Sun."

In the 1980s the object-oriented user interfaces that had been developed at Xerox's PARC in the 1970s "moved out of the lab and into the market. In 1981, Xerox introduced the 8010 Star Information system, which had a graphical user interface." Because PARC, much like Bell Labs, was research oriented, the Star system never caught on. The Xerox technology, however, did move into the world. "The different and sometime conflicting ideas [that came out of PARC] found their way into the products from different vendors. This mixed heritage combined with continuous, uncoordinated innovation . . . got us to where we are today: interesting, sometimes wonderful, conflicting products and confused users. With the OPEN LOOK user interface, Sun, AT&T, and Xerox are bringing the best ideas from Xerox and Sun to users and standardizing them to end the confusion."

With an acknowledgment to Xerox, from whom it licensed

certain graphical user-interface technologies, Sun joined with
AT&T in 1986 to develop OPEN LOOK for AT&T. The
project got underway in 1987. Here was Sun, then, the brash
innovator, working with two behemoths whose research arms
had earlier developed two crucial computer technologies. Sun
had enhanced and driven one technology, UNIX, into the
vanguard and was about to embark on an effort to standardize the other, graphical user interfaces.

The move gave Xerox credibility and recognition it had
nearly lost because of companies such as Apple. It established Sun more firmly than ever as the leading UNIX
enhancer and developer. And it gave AT&T a better chance at
gaining control of the operating system that it had nearly
given away a couple of decades earlier.

Like firsthand and independent observers of UNIX's evolution, AT&T could not help but notice the divergent paths
the operating system was taking. Fragmentation was not
conducive to creation of the standard toward which Sun and
others were aiming. It was time to make some deals.

As chapter 2 shows, AT&T and Sun formed an alliance that
was to have cataclysmic effects on the UNIX community.
Perhaps in more ways than either party ever intended, their
alliance helped consolidate the fragmented UNIX world—or
further fragment it, depending on whom you listened to.

Sun is the acknowledged leader in UNIX and open systems development. The company has probably done more
than any other entity to proselytize on behalf of UNIX and
to back up its promotion with major development work. In
spite of all these efforts, though, Sun has helped spark a
major controversy within the UNIX community that may
have split it into different directions.

The controversy began to heat up in October 1987, when
AT&T announced that it would license Sun's SPARC architecture as the basis for AT&T computer systems. Furthermore, said AT&T, it was going to collaborate with Sun to
develop a UNIX "standard" that would eliminate deficiencies in the operating system—such as lack of features for
commercial applications—and be compatible at the binary
level across the entire SPARC architecture.

Not surprisingly, other companies in the UNIX community smelled incipient monopolistic practices that would give AT&T and Sun an unqualified advantage in the UNIX market. These moves would effectively make the Sun/ AT&T-developed System V and SPARC proprietary standards controlled by the two companies. This perception was bolstered in January 1988, when AT&T announced that it had agreed to purchase 20 percent of Sun by buying shares, in amounts and at times determined by Sun, at 25 percent above current market value.

According to Omri Serlin, publisher of the *Supermicro* newsletter, the October announcement by Sun and AT&T left out a "secret phase" in which the two companies would completely rewrite the core of UNIX to produce System V Release 5.0, to run initially on SPARC and scheduled for release in the 1990s. According to Serlin, the final straw, as far as the competitors were concerned, was a message Bill Joy wrote in response to a query about whether other companies could participate in the Release 5.0 rewrite. Joy's message said that only Sun and AT&T would be involved, with others being admitted to the project only as an exception.

The seeds of a new fragmentation were sown. The UNIX schism wrought by the OSF and UNIX International factions will eventually bring a New Testament to the UNIX religion, one that is more hospitable and appealing to the masses of computer users. The resolution will help the entire UNIX congregation, especially Sun, as its reputation as the prophet of UNIX remains unassailed.

5
Suits and Sandals:
The Business of Technologists

Most new employees who arrived at Sun Microsystems between the steamy growth years of 1984 and 1988 experienced the standard introduction to the company from its human resources (HR) department. Each Monday, an ever-larger herd of new employees ("new hires," in company parlance) would march into bigger and bigger conference rooms. These weekly gatherings were held in all major Sun offices throughout the world.

In these meetings HR representatives gave the standard corporate presentation of company benefits, vacation policy, and holidays allowed, and the new workers completed the required forms. The HR people handed out Sun T-shirts, coffee mugs, and brochures. They also showed a video.

In the video the company's executive vice president and general manager, Bernie Lacroute, explained a bit of the history of Sun. More important, he outlined Sun's vision. Sitting in his office with the pond outside his window as a backdrop, Lacroute described an engineer's playland. He talked about the generations of computing and the kind of hardware and software necessary to make the vision a reality.

Lacroute was not speaking in generalities. He named specific technologies, such as UNIX, Ethernet, and RISC. He delved into fine detail about the need for integrating those technologies into the vision. He did not stop there. He even warned his viewers that it was foolhardy to come to Sun if one did not understand this vision. There were, he told them, fundamental technologies you had to know to succeed at the company. At Sun, to see the future, you had to comprehend it as well.

For the engineers, computer scientists, and programmers who joined Sun in those years, such a message rang clear and true. After all, part of the motivation behind their flocking to Sun was its technology. Sun's products appealed to their technological affections.

HR did not, however, restrict the video screening to technologists alone. Each roomful of new employees included an array of nontechnologists, some of whose members were almost as far removed from UNIX hacking as they were from neurosurgery. Accountants, assemblers, truck drivers, mail deliverers, secretaries, telephone operators, everyone else not so technically astute was undoubtedly baffled by the jargon and the message of their new company's number-two executive. It probably inspired a few to think they'd blundered into a job that was over their head.

In certain meetings, the HR representatives, themselves confused by the message, may have toned down the importance of Lacroute's talk. As a rule, though, the videos were shown without such dilution. Lacroute's lecture exemplified the engineering imperative behind Sun's founding, something still well entrenched in the organization. Sun was a company established largely by and for engineers. The sooner new people understood that, the better.

ENGINEERING DRIVEN

An engineering-driven company is not merely run by engineers, although it does have them in the top echelons. It is not simply devoted to the pursuit of technology. A company

driven by engineering is motivated by it in the sense of
"contriving or planning out, guiding the course of." At Sun,
engineering is more than an activity—it's a philosophy.

This engineering ideology craves the latest in technology.
It aspires to the highest technical achievements. It sees tin-
kering with something, anything, and improving it as the
liveliest of pastimes. Changing the everyday into the extrav-
agant is an adventure; refining complexity into simplicity is
an obsession.

Engineering has a pragmatic side as well. It is a practical
profession. It deals with proven scientific laws. It doesn't
mess with the unknown, leaving that to science. Engineering
may take on an impossible task, but it will not shoulder an
undefined one.

This engineering pragmatism often instills a good deal of
common sense. The engineer-turned-businessperson recog-
nizes that no matter how much fun creating technical gim-
crackery can be, at some point, money must be made. Because Sun played the technology game at an advanced level,
its businesspeople needed a firm grasp of the technical
issues. With so much at stake in Sun's booming and lucrative
market, it was vital for many of Sun's engineers to slip out of
the lab and into corner offices. Instead of designing circuit
boards, they wrote organization charts; they eschewed de-
bugging software for revising budgets. Sun was lucky enough
to attract and promote some of the most competent engineering management in Silicon Valley. These men and women
shared, for the most part, the vision Lacroute outlined in the
new-employee video. They were the right blend of sharp-
minded technologists and hardheaded businesspeople.

ENGINEERS/EXECUTIVES

In their early stages, at least, most successful companies are
reflections of their founders and guiding spirits: Ford and
Ferrari, for example; IBM in the early days and, in some
respects, even to this day; the major Hollywood studios
before they were all bought out and run by M.B.A.s and/or

foreign conglomerates. These companies centered on individual personalities: Henry Ford; Enzio Ferrari; Thomas Watson; Samuel Goldwyn, Jack Warner, and others. Although Sun Microsystems is not an eponymous company named after Mr. or Ms. Sun, it is still very much a reflection of its founders and early guiding spirits. Most of these men were engineers by training, and those who weren't adhered to the primacy of the engineering ideology.

Andreas Bechtolsheim exemplifies the engineering spirit at Sun. Born in West Germany in the mid-1950s, he showed a technical inclination early. In 1975 he came to the United States to study computer science. He received his master's degree from Carnegie-Mellon University in 1976 and transferred to Stanford in 1977.

Stanford was an appropriate choice. Located on the northern fringe of California's famous Silicon Valley, Stanford was a hotbed of computer hacking. It was the primary educational font that gushed forth Silicon Valley's engineers and its management teams. Many of these young men and women worked through both Stanford's engineering school and its business school, giving an academic luster to the region's engineering ideology. Make gadgets that make profits was the clear message of a Stanford education.

Because he couldn't get his hands on the kind of computer he needed, Bechtolsheim decided to build his own. As his graduate project, he designed a computer workstation that could be networked across the already electronically well-connected Stanford campus. Largely out of frustration with the high cost and proprietary nature of existing workstations, Bechtolsheim chose industry-standard, relatively inexpensive, and readily available components for his workstation: the Motorola MC68000 microprocessor, Ethernet, and the Multibus—among others—and, eventually, the UNIX operating system. He gravitated to UNIX for the same reason many small startup companies had picked it. It already existed; it was available; and it was well-suited to Bechtolsheim's goal of creating a high-performance, networked, desktop workstation.

Stanford already had several intracampus computer and televison networks, so the university proved an effective testing ground for Bechtolsheim's creation. The hacker in Bechtolsheim was frustrated with the proprietary tendencies of existing networks; he wanted to make computer power more easily accessible. So he looked to the industry-standard Ethernet, invented at Xerox's PARC.

Bechtolsheim was not thinking specifically of a product while working on his project, but Vinod Khosla was. Their convergence was the start of Sun Microsystems, Inc.

In the early days of the company, Bechtolsheim's garb of choice was a pair of slacks, a casual shirt, and Birkenstock sandals. Five years later, when he was a millionaire several times over, his garb remained a pair of slacks, a casual shirt, and Birkenstock sandals. He is a slender, intense young man whose conversation tends to border on monomania when he is discussing technology, a subject that arises with great frequency. Discussions also tend to be one-sided, and Bechtolsheim often seems to be narrating or dictating. His face reveals that he is focusing his complete attention on the subject at hand.

As cofounder and one of the driving geniuses behind Sun Microsystems, Bechtolsheim has been accorded the position and freedom to continue pushing the company toward innovation. In 1987, for example, he was the inspiration for and a founding member of an "intrapreneurial" group that developed the SPARCstation 1, a small, fast, inexpensive desktop workstation based on Sun's RISC microprocessor. Bechtolsheim's team delivered a machine barely bigger than a Macintosh II but twenty times faster than a DEC minicomputer.

Bechtolsheim, who led the development effort, has a deep understanding of what technology sells to a technologist. He does not use market-research data to quantify his estimation. He knows what he would want. He knows what his team of engineers would want. Then he figures out what they would pay for it. Out of these calculations comes the machine of choice: the machine that engineers dream about having in their office.

Not surprisingly, Bechtolsheim, like the other young Sun cofounders, has been the subject of much media coverage, particularly in his native West Germany. Several articles about him have appeared in major German magazines and newspapers, and in 1987 a German TV crew roamed the corridors of Sun's Mountain View headquarters shooting footage of the local boy made good in Silicon Valley. The German media, like the U.S. press, highlight Bechtolsheim's engineering ideology, his mastery of producing clever technology, and his good fortune in business.

Of Sun's four cofounders—Bechtolsheim, Joy, Khosla, and McNealy—the first two are the "techies"; the other two exemplify the business end of the company.

Bechtolsheim's software counterpart is Bill Joy, the architect of Berkeley. Although his official title is vice president of research and development, as we've pointed out elsewhere and as others are fond of noting, "He reports to no one and no one reports to him in the corporate structure."

Joy grew up in Farmington, Michigan. He skipped a grade in public school and later became a National Merit scholar and a winner in a statewide math competition. He received a B.S. in electrical engineering at the University of Michigan, and in 1975 he made his way west to UC Berkeley, where he became the leading thinker in and developer of UNIX. In addition to designing the BSD version of UNIX while at Berkeley and later at Sun, he helped design the industry-standard Network File System and was a codesigner of SPARC.

True to his roots as a hacker, after rewriting UNIX "from the ground up," he all but gave his version away to universities and research centers for $150—planting the "UNIX seed like a high-tech Johnny Appleseed." According to industry experts, Joy's boundless enthusiasm and unfailing commitment to UNIX not only kept it alive but also drove it beyond its early reputation as a research curiosity and talisman to its small band of devoted followers.

In his early days at Sun, Joy sported a thin, wispy beard and baggy, casual clothes. Lately he has been clean shaven;

and at the April 1989 introduction of the SPARCstation 1, he was attired in a slick designer suit, which seemed to contrast with his taste in primitive art. He extended that taste in art to help establish a small gallery in San Francisco. For several years after Sun's founding, Joy and Bechtolsheim shared a rented house in Palo Alto.

Many early executives were cut from similar engineering cloth as were Bechtolsheim and Joy. Even more than Bechtolsheim or Joy, Bernie Lacroute personified the core traits of engineering ideology. He adhered to the engineering imperative that dominated Sun in its most successful years, 1984 through 1989. Lacroute, it can be argued, was the primary mover behind the business and engineering plans that established Sun as the number-one workstation company. In fact, as an anonymous Apple executive put it, "Sun would not be anything without Bernie Lacroute."

Lacroute, a native of France, and a graduate of the University of Grenoble and the University of Michigan, with degrees in engineering, was often described as Scott McNealy's mature counterpart. His apparent levelheadedness soothed many customers and investors put off by his boss's obvious youth and perceived impetuousness. Yet Lacroute, who was straightforward and unemotional in large gatherings, bubbled forth enthusiastically or angrily in smaller groups. His enthusiasm for Sun's technical triumphs was unbounded, particularly when new Sun products surpassed the competition's systems on obscure technical points.

His engineering savvy dictated much of his business thinking. He hated waste and always wanted to push a technology just a tad further, but never to the point of extravagance. He was not miserly, though, with his engineering staff, whether as Sun's manager of engineering or the company's only executive vice president. He oversaw one of the biggest research-and-development budgets in Silicon Valley, more than $250 million. As a percentage of revenues, Sun spends significantly more on research than most of its competitors do, and Sun's engineering staff enjoys well-equipped laboratories.

Lacroute held immense power and responsibility. All engineering departments reported to him, both software and hardware developers. Manufacturing looked to him for direction. He ran marketing for more than four years. He was also a member of Sun's board of directors. No other executive under McNealy carried Lacroute's clout. His influence on the CEO was the most telling.

Lacroute, who came to Sun from DEC, was said to be most proud of his role in the delivery of the VAX 780 minicomputer, the machine that made Digital Equipment Corporation the number-two computer company in the world. At Sun it was his managerial talents that were most in demand. But his intense, detailed technical knowledge guided his overall managerial approach and, more important, established at Sun's highest levels the primacy of an engineering ideology. So when he announced in April 1989 that he was leaving the company that he had helped to shape—to take a position with the venture-capital firm Kleiner Perkins—the company decided to throw him a going-away party.

The *au revoir* roast, attended by about two hundred people, was held in Sparcys, the company's Mountain View cafeteria, in June 1989. Eric Schmidt reminisced about his years of working for the departing executive vice president. Schmidt noted that at the time he arrived, he was one of three or so people in the embryonic engineering department at the time. At this writing, Schmidt is vice president of the General Systems group, which employs hundreds.

He rose through the ranks at Sun, having joined the company in 1983 as manager of software. Before being appointed VP in 1985, he was director of software engineering. Prior to coming to Sun, Schmidt was a member of the research staff at Xerox's PARC; he had also worked at Bell Labs and Zilog.

Schmidt and Joy both go back to Berkeley, where, after getting his B.S. in electrical engineering at Princeton, Schmidt picked up an M.S. in electrical engineering and a Ph.D. in computer science (PARC patented the results of his Ph.D. research). Although the two men studied and worked at Berkeley at the same time and both tool around the Valley in Ferraris, their personas differ. Whereas Joy appears flamboyant and hyperkinetic, Schmidt exudes an aura of rational cool. Unlike Joy, who is single, Schmidt is married and the father of two children. Both men do share a passion for software engineering, although Joy is the one still actively involved in it. Schmidt has translated his engineering expertise into overseeing the efforts of other engineers.

Arriving at Sun in 1985 were Wayne Rosing, VP of the Entry Systems Group, and Bob Garrow, VP of operations. The frequency of the word *engineering* in Rosing's biographical notes attests to his adherence to the engineering imperative: "He originally came to Sun as vice president of workstation engineering from Apple Computer, where he was director of engineering for the Apple II group. Before that, he supervised the LISA division at Apple, first as director of engineering for LISA development." Prior to joining Apple, Rosing held a variety of engineering positions at Digital Equipment Corporation and Data General Corporation. Rosing is also a Berkeley alumnus, holding degrees in mathematics and physics.

Garrow signed on later in the year as VP and general manager of the workstation division. He later became VP of operations. Garrow was a cofounder of Convergent Technologies, where he developed office-automation workstations. Before that, he had spent more than seven years at chip maker Intel, where he coinvented the Multibus, one of the bases for the workstation built at Stanford.

OF ENGINEERS, BY ENGINEERS, AND FOR ENGINEERS

Sun's charter was to build products for engineers. To implement that charter as successfully as it has, however, Sun needed more than a founding core of dedicated, ingenious engineers and software gurus.

The pervasive engineering ideology at Sun immediately became apparent. Not only was the company building desktop computers with engineers in mind, but it also infused the workplace with an ambience suitable to discriminating technologists. The reputations of Joy and Bechtolsheim were magnets to young computer scientists and electrical engineers. Sun's engineering management gained a reputation for promoting and rewarding its technical staff. In Silicon Valley and the worldwide UNIX community, the company was known as a place where an engineer could "do" something. Brilliant engineers gave up secure positions at established, mature companies such as DEC and HP to come work for this new company that treated its engineers like kings. Sun became known as an engineers' paradise. Some of the best and the brightest in the computer industry gravitated there.

Besides the atmosphere and glory, several emoluments attracted these budding technocrats. The pragmatic side of the engineering ideology was never overlooked just for the sake of playing with advanced technology. Money counts, too. Even in the first years, when salaries were not so generous, every member of Sun's technical staff received generous stock options at, in some cases, pennies a share. Some later formed spin-off companies with their vested fortunes.

Engineers were accorded great respect at Sun. They had relatively free rein to get their work done. Some projects started in an ad hoc, on-the-fly manner, and anyone who had the time and talent and wanted to work on a project could go for it. They could make the time because Sun encouraged the bizarre work habits of computer mavens. Sun was the antithesis of the 9:00-to-5:00 mentality. Engineers could come in at noon and stay until midnight, or they could come in at 9:00 A.M. and leave at 5:00 P.M.—three or four days later. The free-form approach to scheduling was generally encouraged by managers, many of whom had been marathon hackers at one time themselves. It was not without cause that the growing complex of Sun buildings was called a campus. In many ways, working at Sun was like being back at college and hacking at any and all hours of the day and night. The main difference was that now there were products to get out the door.

Within the company a special category of recognition was created for engineers. Traditional methods of advancement for technologists lead to engineering management, and Sun had no shortage of engineering managers. But it created a unique category, called distinguished engineer, which epitomized the engineering ideology: the freedom to pursue personal engineering goals while being rewarded with money and prestige.

Distinguished engineers, such as Warren Teitelman, Steve Muchnick, and James Gosling, contributed in major ways to Sun's influential and respected technology. In the case of Teitelman, recognition came for advancements in window systems development; for Muchnick, the acknowledgment came for Sun's estimable UNIX compilers. Both contributed to Sun's reputation as having the best software-development computer in the world. The Canada-born Gosling was a window systems "guru."

As the company preached and promoted a decentralized approach to computing, it also fostered a similar approach to product development. Although Sun added employees at a dizzying rate of two to three hundred per month, it initially managed to resist any temptation to impose a stultifying bureaucracy. Those tendencies were particularly repugnant to Sun's technical staff, most of whom craved the free-for-all atmosphere of creative engineering.

One such research-and-development effort exemplified Sun's engineering eccentricities. The creation and development of Sun's Network Software Environment (NSE) was, in part, a reaction to the company's getting caught with its technological pants down, a response to similar products that had appeared earlier from competitors.

Software engineering involves numerous tools, as they are called, that help developers produce a program. High-level languages, such as FORTRAN and Pascal, are only the beginning for a programmer. There are tools to trace the history of the program during development. Special software can search programs for repetitious and unnecessary code. Cross-compilers let programmers use parts of another program's functions, even if the program is written in a different high-level language. Most computer operating systems offer these tools, and Sun is considered to be among the better suppliers of these binary helpmates.

One of the biggest headaches facing users of a network of computers is developing large-scale software products. As a rule, single programmers do not have responsibility for the entire program, only their bit of it. That bit, however, must work with their colleagues' bits. When only two or three hackers are cranking out code, the problem is not so severe. But when five, ten, even a hundred individual software writers are building a program, the result can be a loss of coordination, with finger pointing and communication gaps occurring among the participants.

To address this situation, Apollo and HP offered tools to control the problems inherent in "programming in the large." Customers, as much as they appreciated Sun's workstations, warned the company that truly big projects required such software-management tools. Without them Sun would lose business to bigger (at that time) competitors. A crash program was quickly instigated, pushed by Lacroute and Schmidt.

The NSE development group was a microcosm of the best of engineering life at Sun. Of the twenty-plus members of the group, well over half were engineers. Although the ratio of engineers to nonengineers in the company overall may not have been as skewed as it was in this small, dedicated group, the engineering mentality outweighed that of others attached to the program. The NSE was a product for engineers—conceived, managed, and developed by engineers.

Launched in secret, the group was housed in a new three-story office building on the El Camino Real in Menlo Park, an upper-middle-class town on the northern edge of Stanford University, nearly ten miles from the main campus of Sun engineers. The building's directory gave no hint of its Sun occupants. Its most notable lease was held by a Charles Schwab discount brokerage, generally frequented by retired gentlemen from the community who watched the electronic ticker tape race across a screen while they bought and sold shares at the counter. Upstairs a few modest businesses

carried on, including one Earthtone PB, Ltd. The PB stood
for "peanut butter" and was the in-joke of the young and
generally shaggy group of Sun programmers who populated
Earthtone PB's offices. (Another in-joke was that they had
merely to go downstairs, to the Schwab office, to see how
their Sun stock was doing.)

Despite the Ping-Pong table, extensive online games, and
a freezer stuffed with Dove Bars, the NSE group delivered
their product in a blazing nine months. They worked long
and hard hours, spending their leisure time in the office, too.
The company simultaneously pampered and prodded them.
Lacroute and Schmidt constantly pushed the NSE's manager, Jon Feiber, to meet the aggressive schedule, which the
group beat by thirty days.

The Network Software Environment does not generate
significant revenue itself, costing around two thousand dollars. And it is often "thrown in" to a deal by a salesman more
interested in the commission from many machines than from
the sale of one or two programs. Still, the NSE came at a
critical time in Sun's product cycle. The fact that it exists
comforts large customers who are involved in massive programming activity. Yet the NSE, like Sun's UNIX, sells
workstations. It does so because it is targeted at technologists
by their peers: software by software experts for software
experts. It was an effective paradigm of the engineering
imperative at Sun.

TURNING TECHNOLOGY INTO PRODUCTS

Much as Sun was devoted to, even worshiped, technology, it
was no research institute developing technology for its own
sake. That task was better left to comfortable and mature
giants such as AT&T and Xerox. Better to ally with the
research houses—which Sun did with both of these companies—and concentrate on your own bottom line.

From the beginning Sun's bottom line was to beat its
competitors in the realm of price/performance. What this
meant was getting products out the door that were faster and

more versatile than those from the competition—for considerably less money than the competition's products. Sun was willing to sacrifice margins in order to gain volume.

Such a philosophy had two important implications for everyone at Sun. First, the company had to sell a lot more products than its higher-priced competitors did to garner the same amount of revenue. Second, that requirement meant beating competitors not only at the price/performance game but also in the time it took to get products to market.

Those imperatives led to an incredibly fast-paced environment—not only for engineers but also for all the support staff trying to keep up with them (see chapter 8, "Working in a Revved Engine"). It also necessitated an environment in which engineers could fulfill these imperatives—an environment, such as the one described earlier in this chapter, that fostered and rewarded an entrepreneurial spirit and accommodated behavioral quirks to get the job done.

Unlike the aforementioned research institutes, an engineering-driven company puts a premium on seeing products get out the door, and the engineers understand the value of seeing their work realized as products. A primary way of fostering the importance of products is a synergistic relationship among engineers and product managers.

Although an engineering company puts its primary focus on engineering personnel, it does not simply throw engineers at product-development projects. A relatively small and aggressive startup (or upstart, depending on the point of view) such as Sun—aiming to win market share at the expense of fat margins—can't afford a big-committee approach to product development. And Sun has been continually able to exploit the effectiveness of assigning a few hungry engineers to a project and giving them an "aggressive" schedule.

Just as the engineering-driven company cannot afford a committee to develop a product, it cannot afford features for features' sake, nor can it afford other impediments to the goals of price/performance and market share. This means an emphasis on minimalist engineering: squeezing the most out of the technology.

A minimalist approach keeps costs of the final product down. It makes the product faster and less likely to malfunction. It contributes to the development of more-advanced technology. Perhaps most important to the engineering-driven company, it challenges the creativity of engineers. Challenging engineers' creativity and making them feel like an integral part of a small, focused development team—both tend to give them a vested interest in the product on which they're working.

To further accentuate attention to excellent products, Sun encouraged a synergistic relationship among engineers, product-marketing people, and salesmen, and the majority of Sun product marketers and salespeople have a strong technical background themselves.

In the early days of its existence, Sun was top-heavy with technical personnel. The marketing-communications (marcom) and PR departments were minuscule, although *product*-marketing groups were more flush. To some people in marcom and PR, it seemed that they had to scratch and scrabble for everything they could get. A common joke among them was that if they changed their titles to "editorial engineer" or "marketing engineer," they would get more respect, attention, and resources.

This perception had some validity: engineers ruled the roost at Sun, and in light of the backgrounds of the company's principals, it was not hard to see why. Among nonengineers the argument was sometimes heard that technical top-heaviness produced marketing myopia in the engineers/managers at the upper levels of the company. "We can't sell to 'technical professionals' forever," went the argument. "Sooner or later, we're going to have to sell these workstations to nontechnical professionals who need to do jobs other than software development."

Top management moved slowly in that direction, however. Ultimately, management's strategy worked, as described in chapter 3. So as Sun moved slowly—almost imperceptibly—toward consumer markets, the company continued to bolster its reputation as an engineer's company. It attracted the best talent. It was doing some of the most exciting development work in the workstation arena.

SALESMEN/ENGINEERS

The ratio of members of the technical staff to others in Sun was large. It was even larger if salesmen were factored into the equation. Many members of the large Sun sales force had engineering or technical backgrounds. They almost had to: most potential accounts were technical companies, and the products being sold were suited for sophisticated technical tasks.

If we look at a profile of a composite Sun salesman, we find first that our representative is male (as in the industry at large, computer sales at Sun is decidedly male dominated—thus the use of the masculine pronoun here). Our salesman has some kind of technical or engineering undergraduate degree. On graduation, he goes to work in a technical capacity—say, as a programmer or technical-support staffer—for a computer company. (In the early days, that company was not Sun, because it was just getting started.) Later he may move into sales from within the company.

Next, he goes to graduate school and picks up an M.B.A. He then joins Sun as a junior-level product-marketing manager, where he labors while learning the workstation business and market. Then he works up to a senior level in product marketing, where he stays until he makes his move to sales. By this time, he is ready to exploit not only his early technical training and knowledge but also his intimate familiarity with Sun's products—or at least with a certain segment of them. He is also familiar with the needs and frustrations of his prospects. Many of them are engineers themselves, or if not, their buying decisions are heavily influenced by the engineering managers in their companies.

The description of the Sun sales force holds clues about the characteristics of the product-marketing staff. These people are chartered to sell products, but their initial training

is in the engineering realm. Business school has taught them
how to market the merchandise; technical training helps keep
them in touch with the needs of their potential customers.
Augmenting that link with prospects is continual interaction
with the engineers who developed the product they are trying
to sell.

THE BENIGHTED

Counterbalancing the preponderance of engineers were some
nontechnical groups: secretaries (called "administrators" in
the faux-egalitarian parlance of Silicon Valley); marketing-
communications types; some people in manufacturing; and
armies of personnel department staff and number crunchers.
All techno-neophytes were essentially on their own when it
came to comprehending the complexities of UNIX. If they
didn't opt for trying to slog through the voluminous "docubox," they could search out someone who had already gone
through the ordeal.

Many were lucky enough to have an assigned or a de facto
mentor called a "Sunvisor," but more were left to their own
devices. Some became converts to the gospel and plunged
into and mastered the complexities of UNIX. One project
coordinator in the marketing communications (marcom)
group came to Sun knowing virtually nothing about computers. He entered the campus, learned, and went forth to help
others with their technical dilemmas. Another young man
started off in shipping and learned enough on his own and
through mentors to become an accomplished technical-support representative. Yet another employee joined Sun as an
administrator and moved into the position of product manager.

This is not to imply that Sun's approach to engineering,
sales, and product marketing is unique in the computer industry at large. Product managers and salespeople at all computer companies have to interact continually with the engineering staff to do their jobs. No doubt the majority of
salespeople and product marketers at other companies have

technical backgrounds as well. And certainly other computer companies have their share of tyros turned techies.

So what was the difference between Sun and other companies? Sun was a company started by and for engineers. It made products essentially for engineers. It was not in "consumer markets." The few nontechies the company did hire were in many ways on their own to learn how to use Sun systems. Sun encouraged—in fact, demanded—that its employees use Sun tools. That meant—at least until 1989—no "user-friendly" spreadsheets and word-processing programs.

The Sun environment was so technical, so permeated with an engineering mentality, that it forced everyone to sink or swim. Not only was it obvious that the power in the company resided with technologists, but it was also clear that to succeed at Sun you had to speak the language. People who went into meetings having "discussions" and talking about "individual agendas" emerged "interfacing" and "talking about that off line." In addition to such buzzwords, which are rampant in the entire industry, Sun had its own lexicon with which new arrivals had to contend. They faced an alphabet soup of product names, such as the NSE and the SPE, to say nothing of UNIX commands such as *grep*, *awk*, and *biff*. Just as they had to become proficient in the technical tools they were given, they had to become familiar with the terms and expressions that distinguished Sun and its market. At Sun, words such as *open*, *platform*, *disconnect*, and *application* and phrases such as *heterogeneous network computing* and *graphical user interface* acquired special meanings (which is why a glossary has been included at the back of the book). Learning the language at Sun was just one more progressive step in a person's career.

ENGINEERING-DRIVEN MARKETING

Initially, the primary vehicle by which Sun marketed its products was word of mouth. Word spread through the technical community about what Sun was up to. Many technical professionals salivated to work there; many wanted to get their hands on the products—both to do their jobs better and to play with these great new desktop systems. This oral approach to marketing is common for technical products, whose users are by and large adherents to the engineering imperative. But at some point the spoken word must give way to the printed one. When that happens, marketing takes over.

The marketing coup at Sun was imperceptible. The steady stream of technical information poured out of Sun in rapid fashion. During the reign of Carol Bartz as vice president of marketing, she set a tone, under the guidance of Lacroute, that focused on the "technical professional," the power computer user—someone who used computers for tasks more complex than simple database searching, word processing, games, or spreadsheet analysis.

To be credible, Sun's marketing team initially took its cues from engineering. All marketing materials—from data sheets and brochures to graphics and videos for trade-show booths—reflected the engineering influence. In fact, engineering was the source for many of the more successful marketing programs. For example, the video described at the beginning of this chapter was produced by an in-house video team at Sun. The group's existence, however, was inspired by the creation of a video by Warren Teitelman. His group wanted to showcase the Network/extensible Window System (NeWS) product, demonstrating its impressive window-system functions. To get this video, being typical engineers at Sun, they simply did it. They rented video recording equipment, hacked out some notes, and focused the camera on the screen while a pair of hands took the product through its paces and Teitelman described the action. It was a boring bit of video, but it got the point across to marketing management: the company needed to have video demonstrations of its products. They were an excellent way to promote the technology. But they needed to have a more professional production crew than engineers with a Sony Camcorder.

In large part, that was the role of Sun's fledgling marketing organization—to take the promotional ideas of engineering and pretty them up. Sun's marketing organization created some of the best-looking brochures, newsletters, videos, magazines, and event graphics in the industry. The marcom hallways are littered with awards from national and international groups, recognizing the design and production values Sun puts into its marketing materials. Yet anyone who ventures past the gloss to the content encounters, in the majority of the material, a sea of technospeak mingled with marketing argot.

Part of this situation can be explained by the leadership of Bartz, an engineer by training, but much of it is the influence of Lacroute. He personally signed off on most marketing programs, down to the data sheets and press releases. He had a gut feeling about the technical nature of Sun's audience, and he did not deem it appropriate to talk down to them. He treated them as intellectual equals. After Bartz left marketing to preside over Sun Federal, the company's subsidiary, Lacroute took the reins of marketing directly into his hands for nearly two years, relinquishing them in late 1987 to Ed Zander, who came from Apollo and shared a similar view of Sun's customers.

ENGINEERING ENTERPRISES AND PROFITABLE PARTNERS

Selling computers to people who sell computers is more than half of Sun's business. And, in the early days, before Sun systems sported enough software to interest end users, that was virtually all of Sun's business. Although often compared with Apple Computer as an equivalent success story, Sun was in another world of marketing. This difference meant that Sun's marketing direction had to be thickly laced with engineering ideology. At Sun that was the credo of UNIX and open systems.

Even though most computer companies have built their successes on the basis of proprietary products, hard-core computer techies seem to have an almost visceral desire and need to share information and knowledge with one another. It's usually upper management, not the front-line engineering troops, who want to keep the companies closed and proprietary. In the case of Sun—to mix metaphors—the inmates were running the asylum. Here was a direct-sales computer company whose engineering management was eager to share its advances with select members of the engineering community.

Among the technology partners Sun pursued were original-equipment manufacturers. OEMs buy a company's computers and use them as a basis for their own products. For example, one of the first OEMs with which Sun signed a deal was Interleaf, one of the first companies to turn workstations into electronic publishing tools. A customer who bought a complete Sun-based Interleaf system got Interleaf's own page-composition software running on a Sun workstation. The system also included a laser printer from another manufacturer and a scanner from yet another manufacturer.

Interleaf already sold a system based on Apollo workstations, so it was a coup for Sun to pick up the Interleaf account as well. Shortly after opening for business, Sun had signed OEM agreements with some heavyweights in the computer business: for example, the multinational and multiproduct Schlumberger and photography giant Kodak, which was aiming for new technologies and markets such as newspaper composition systems. These deals were an extension of Sun's first OEM coup with Computervision and helped further solidify Sun's reputation as a major player in the OEM arena.

The majority of these OEM accounts resulted in products to increase the productivity and job performance of the customers Sun coveted—technical professionals.

Another engineering-driven strategy with which it bolstered its market penetration and presence was its Catalyst third-party program, involving companies that "ported" their software or configured their hardware so that it worked with Sun workstations. These products were nearly all targeted at other engineers, whether software developers who prized their Sun computers or CAD/CAM engineers who designed cars in Detroit.

The third-party software applications were highly technical, dealing with such arcane subjects as finite-element analysis, moldflow, and artificial intelligence. Obtuse descriptions of the products in the *Catalyst* catalog were virtually
incomprehensible to people outside the products' fields. The
catalog eventually became so huge that it was necessary to
hire a designer to revamp the format so that two product
descriptions, rather than a single one, could be squeezed onto
a page. As Sun gained stature, third parties clamored to be
affiliated with Sun. It was not until 1989, however, that a
simple word-processing program, WordPerfect, appeared for
Sun workstations. Convincing third-party developers to use
the Sun equipment as a platform often fell to Sun's engineers
more than its marketers.

REACHING THE MASSES

Although he was not blind to the benefits of marketing,
Lacroute was often a hard man to convince. For example,
during the introduction of the Sun-3 product line in mid-
1985—a crucial product introduction for the company—he
scrapped the brochure copy and most of the accompanying
photography, demanding that it be redone immediately. The
designer of the brochure had opted to put Sun-3 workstations inside late-nineteenth-century brick warehouses in San
Francisco and shoot the machines through a large, arched
window. Upon seeing a proof of one of the photos, Lacroute
exclaimed, "It looks like a fucking cathedral!"

He pointed, across a park built on a landfill, to an ultra-
modern building at the Moffet Naval Air Station. "That's
what I want," he explained. The literal-minded engineering
mentality could not envision these new, state-of-the-art
workstations sitting in an environment that suggested nineteenth-century technology: steam engines, spinning jennies,
textile mills, and the like.

Difficult as it may be to believe, in Sun's first three and a
half years, revenues went from zero to $250 million without
any significant advertising to propel that growth. Space sales-

people from magazines often repeated the industry rumor that Scott McNealy wanted to create the world's first billion-dollar computer company without any appreciable advertising. But the competition—especially Apollo, DEC, and HP—advertised heavily. Eventually, they argued, Sun would have to advertise also. Eventually, and briefly, Sun did.

In mid-1985 the company made a perfunctory attempt to mount a print-ad campaign. The resulting full-page ad was a tired cliché: a workstation suspended in midair with blue sky showing through the monitor. Swirling through the open monitor was a vortex of paper. The headline read, "Open Systems for Open Minds." This muddled message ran about three times in a couple of trade journals and vanished. If that was advertising, who needed it? Better to let word of mouth continue to sell our products, executive thinking went. For what Sun had spent on the ads, it could have hired another engineer or two.

The short-lived campaign withered even before the marketing-communications director who helped mount it left the company in late 1985. During Lacroute's nine-month tenure as de facto director, advertising remained nonexistent at Sun.

That situation began to change toward the end of 1986. In August of that year, Sun had hired as marketing-communications director Dee Cravens, a man who first thought Sun should direct its marketing efforts to everyone, technical or not. He referred to these common folk as "the butchers in Milwaukee." Cravens came from an advertising background, and he lobbied within the company to mount a campaign. His arrival roughly coincided with Sun's competitors'—notably Apollo—beginning to erode Sun's de facto ownership of the open systems message.

Cravens' influence, however, was minimal, and the advertising took on the flavor of the company's other marketing material—focused on technical features and laden with computer jargon. That was what pleased management. Cravens, seeing the light early, complied and instructed the ad agency to go the painless route and not fight the engineering-driven marketing at Sun. As a result, Sun's advertising has been turgid and uninteresting, except to the engineers who read it.

A New Wind?

From PR through manufacturing, marketing, sales, engineering (of course), and upper management, Sun is suffused with the engineering imperative. Without a doubt, Lacroute was the leader in this approach. He greatly influenced McNealy, who is wont to talk about the technical features of a Sun product as much as he is inclined to describe the company's finances. McNealy clearly believes that the technical aspects of the business cannot be understated. He once wrote, "To understand the future of the workstation business, you have to understand where the technology is going."

When Lacroute left in the summer of 1989 to become a venture capitalist, it was widely claimed that Sun was losing its mature operations master. Inside Sun, however, the concern was for its engineering leadership. Lacroute had infused all levels of the company with the preeminence of engineering. The new organization reporting to McNealy lacked as strong an engineering bias. A particular weakness was felt in the research-and-development arena. With the exception of Bill Joy, Lacroute was the only person who had a grasp of what a quarter-billion dollars in R-and-D funds was supposed to produce. In fact, Joy was forced to cancel a trip to the Soviet Union immediately after Lacroute's announced departure. He was said to be taking a more active operational role as the vice president of research and development, giving up his role as strictly the company's engineering intellectual.

Joy, however, was completely untutored in the realm of day-to-day business operations. His technical expertise, which even Lacroute acceded to, was unmatched, but his ability to negotiate his way through the maze of projects and their differing and sometimes conflicting priorities had never been tested. It was, on the other hand, Lacroute's playground.

Whether the engineering imperative will remain ascendent at Sun is hard to judge at this writing. The numbers of people who arrive at Sun every week are increasingly less technically inclined. The human resources department no longer shows the video of Lacroute extolling the virtues of Sun's engineering ideology to new employees. It may be that the change has occurred at the perfect moment, allowing the company to emerge as a more readily accessible marketing organization that preaches to the technically unconverted, vastly increasing its pool of potential customers.

The engineering imperative that suffuses the company might make such a change difficult. Already people inside and outside Sun are making unflattering comparisons to Apple's makeover after John Sculley replaced Steve Jobs. The company became more successful but a less interesting place to work. And if you're an engineer—especially a good one, who can pick and choose companies in sprawling Silicon Valley—a good work environment is as important as a financially stable organization. It is the careful balance between technical challenges and material rewards that attracts and holds top engineering talent.

If Sun can make the transition without losing its established market or witnessing a wholesale departure of its clever technical staff, the company should have no problem negotiating the new wind of management. If it cannot, the travails will have repercussions throughout the industry.

At its foundation, though, Sun looks strong. Lacroute is the first major player to leave the company since Vinod Khosla, who met his goal of retiring before age 30. Lacroute's penchant for engineering systems gave him a systematic approach to managing. The programs he introduced will not immediately unravel upon his departure. More important, the fundamental philosophy he helped articulate, the notions of open systems and distributed computing, are as solid as religious precepts at the company. They are key to the strategy that has helped propel Sun over the top in its market. They will not disintegrate because of one man's departure. When the final history of Sun is written, it will not be the lives of men that summon interest, but the engineering philosophy that gave away technology—the engineering imperative fueled by the eccentric UNIX attitudes. Few companies have carried it to such a degree as has Sun.

6

Giveaway Technology:
The Strategy of Standards
and Licensing

Emotions were running high at Sun for weeks following the announcement of the founding of the Open Software Foundation in May 1988. In the eyes of Bill Joy and Andy Bechtolsheim, the idea of the OSF's leading the development of UNIX standards was absurd. Here was a handful of companies that were, with the notable exception of Hewlett-Packard, decidedly anti-UNIX, and they were suddenly proclaiming themselves as its true spiritual force. To Joy and Bechtolsheim, the OSF was a political and public-relations pulpit to distract UNIX users from the lure of a UNIX standard. The surprising zeal of these new corporate converts to UNIX was suspicious at best, hypocritical and misleading at worst. It was against their own best business interests for UNIX to succeed. It was unlikely that the path they trod would be the way to computing salvation.

The impressive list of names on the roll call of the OSF, however, caught many at Sun off guard. The appearance of IBM's John Akers on the same dais with DEC's Ken Olsen and HP's John Young unnerved more than one Sun executive and indicated that the competition was lining up to play some

serious hardball against Sun's team. The "solidarity" of
IBM, DEC, and HP reaffirmed the nervousness with which
these newly organized competitors viewed the prospect of
Sun and AT&T's creating a single UNIX operating system.

Sun was no longer a bit player in the computer industry.
The people at Sun had turned the heads of the rest of the
market. Their strategy and its success had derailed the plans
of the biggest players in computerdom and had accomplished
what no standards body, no customer, no user group had
been able to do: it brought the major computer firms together to discuss technology standards.

Sun was already an active member of every major standards body. Its very success in the minds of the media and
customers was inextricably linked to fidelity to standards. In
1988 no standard was more revered in the computer industry
than UNIX was. Among analysts and the trade press, speculation was rampant: would Sun and AT&T swallow their
corporate pride and join OSF?

Joy and Bechtolsheim dismissed the notion out of hand,
and McNealy sided with them. "No way," he told Carol
Broadbent, Sun's public relations director. "There's no way
we'll give them money and then be ignored." Others at Sun
were not so certain. The perception of many outside Sun was
that with such huge companies throwing their weight behind
a UNIX standard, it was bound to succeed at some level,
possibly even superseding the Sun/AT&T efforts. Besides,
argued some, snubbing the OSF would undermine Sun's
tradition of being a leading proponent of standards.

AT&T's Vittorio Cassoni was surprised by the OSF's formation. His managers believed that joining the self-proclaimed standards group would diffuse the OSF's contention
that AT&T and Sun were turning UNIX into a proprietary
operating system, despite the two companies' constant assurance to the contrary. Cassoni and his team were pressuring
Sun executives to pay the $4 million ticket of admission to
the OSF in order to dispel any notion that Sun and AT&T
opposed the perceived noble efforts of the OSF.

Sun's engineers, who were used to the freewheeling development process in their own company, were already uncom-

fortable with the bureaucratic relationship they were encountering with AT&T while standardizing UNIX. The thought of linking their work with the slow-as-molasses mentality of IBM had them up in arms.

AT&T's pressure on Sun to volunteer for the OSF approach continued when Cassoni returned to Olivetti. Bob Kavner, AT&T's top man in the computer unit, came close to persuading Sun to change its position—a check for the OSF was even in preparation—but Joy, Bechtolsheim, and others prevailed upon McNealy not to give in. Sun had an opportunity to accomplish more on its own. Shored up by the support of Joy, Bechtolsheim, et al., McNealy abandoned the idea of tying his company to the OSF.

Instead, Sun and AT&T decided to beat the OSF at its own game. They announced the formation of UNIX International, and the war of UNIX standards began in earnest. There was still a possibility of linking with the OSF down the road. The arguments persisted. Join. Don't join. The advantages were weighed, reweighed. At this writing, the OSF continues to work without the creator of UNIX (AT&T) and the world's acknowledged leader in UNIX development (Sun). The volley of rhetoric is as fierce as ever, and everyone is claiming to hold the standard-bearer's flag.

TECHNOLOGIST AS PHILANTHROPIST: PHILANTHROPIST AS CAPITALIST

The religious metaphor used in chapter 4 to describe the UNIX operating system sheds light on the motivation behind Sun's business approach of giving away technology. Two of Sun's four founders, Bill Joy and Andy Bechtolsheim, were steeped in the UNIX milieu at Berkeley and Stanford. To get the company's first Sun-1 workstations out the door, the fledgling company added other young engineers, many of whom clung to the antiestablishment, hacker attitudes they'd learned in college. These attitudes prepared the company to adopt an unconventional strategy for distributing technology devised at Sun.

This strategy included the notion that UNIX belonged to

everyone at a modest price. This attitude of sharing UNIX was not a phenomenon of the early 1980s, nor was it restricted to Sun. It existed throughout most of the worldwide UNIX community and had emerged not long after Thompson and Ritchie devised their operating system. Yet for fifteen years, UNIX was sequestered in the laboratories and universities, gaining acolytes in a slow but steady manner. From the late 1960s into the early 1980s, a set of computer mores different from Sun's giveaway approach prevailed, one that seemed to satisfy customers and contributed to the overall boom in the computer industry. As with all things, however, change reared its troublesome head.

The grass-roots philosophy of inexpensively distributing Sun's extensions and enhancements to UNIX coincided nicely with a change in the market, one that only Sun noticed and took advantage of initially. In 1987 Jonathan Fram, then a vice president of technology at the Wall Street investment house Bear Stearns, observed that "major market shifts can occur on a regular basis. Two ingredients are required for such a shift. First, a major change in purchasing demographics and customer preference must evolve, thereby rendering established vendors' marketing strategies and barriers obsolete. Second, a new vendor must deliver dramatically better price/performance on a sustained basis when compared with incumbent suppliers. . . . Sun has both such ingredients."

Bob Herwick of Hambrecht & Quist echoed Fram's conclusions in 1988, stating that Sun's "strategy makes it the principal beneficiary of the shift in end-user purchasing to distributed computing with open architectures and support of standards." Other analysts came to similar conclusions. "Sun Microsystems," wrote one Wall Street prognosticator, "was founded in 1982 to ride the third wave in the computer era."

Whether Sun is riding a wave or not is debatable, but from the beginning the company has adhered to a strategy based on standards. Under the guidance of McNealy, Joy, Lacroute, and Bechtolsheim, the use of standards grew into an advocacy of open systems.

Open systems is a term that has been around the computer industry since the early 1980s. In the 1990s, references to open systems are everywhere in the industry.

What exactly is an open system? *The Random House Unabridged Dictionary* places "open system" in the category of thermodynamics and describes it as "a region separated from its surroundings by a boundary that admits a transfer of matter or energy across it. Cf. closed system." The same dictionary defines "closed system" (also in the realm of thermodynamics) as "a region that is isolated from its surroundings by a boundary that admits no transfer of matter or energy across it."

In thermodynamics, as in the computer industry, closed systems preceded open ones. According to *Random House*, *closed system* dates from 1895–1900, whereas *open system* did not come into use until about forty years later.

Since these two terms were coined and gained enough use to be admitted into the lexicon, they have taken on different meanings in the computer cosmos. In a computer context the gist of the two terms is the same, but *open systems* and *closed systems* have come to mean, respectively, nonproprietary and proprietary.

Computer systems have become increasingly more open or increasingly less closed, depending on your point of view. The conventional computer wisdom was once to keep computer users as remote and as far removed from the computer as possible, leaving actual interaction with it to a priesthood of system administrators and programmers. That philosophy evolved into the business of proprietary systems: keeping customers tied to a single vendor's products.

The closed approach meant not only that users rarely had any firsthand contact with the computer they were using, but it also meant that a company purchasing, say, IBM mainframes had to pay IBM's price and was at the mercy of IBM's new-product-release schedules. Compensating for these limitations was security. IBM—and other big, established companies, for that matter—would always be there for support and service.

The term *open systems*, it can be argued, has degenerated

into a trendy techno-marketing slogan. A more meaningful
and comprehensive explanation of what Sun meant by open
systems was provided by the man who was a primary shaper
of Sun's computing philosophy, former executive vice president and general manager Bernie Lacroute. Although Lacroute never made it as a flashy spokesperson for the company, he labored to mold Sun's direction and success.

In an essay in the spring 1988 edition of *SunTechnology*,
Lacroute explained how computing had evolved through four
generations, from the batch processing of computing's early
days to "distributed computing," which Lacroute portrayed
as one of the underpinnings of Sun's philosophy and the basis
for open systems.

Another underpinning was Sun's aggressive use and promotion of standards, which has helped moved the industry
away from its longstanding fixation on proprietary systems.
Although the computer industry has standards-making bodies that put the stamp of approval on certain standards developed within the industry, the tendency had too often been to
"make your own." The make-your-own approach was most
noticeable in the area of operating systems.

Sun's tireless, almost fanatical enhancement and promotion
of UNIX was primarily responsible for pushing this operating system into the position it enjoys today. Even Apollo, the
company that gave birth to the workstation industry, had to
swallow its proprietary pride and eventually offer UNIX on
its machines. As chapter 4 notes, the federal government's
demand for UNIX in contract bidding underscores the necessity of computer companies' offering UNIX, at least as an
option, on their machines.

Sun was not content simply to adopt and enhance existing
standards, however. Nor should it be assumed that the company was purely an eleemosynary missionary bent on dis-
pensing computing bounty to a technologically impoverished
world. As a technology-driven company and technological
innovator, Sun was ambitious enough to want to develop
standards that the computing world would adopt and that
would bring in revenue from licensing fees. Customers could

become "locked" into standard systems as well as proprietary ones. They had more options, but these were not limitless.

This technically oriented business philosophy has helped put Sun in the forefront of a new customer buying pattern in the computer industry. Big, diversified companies are joining the transition from disparate networks of incompatible machines to "integration." According to an analyst at Morgan Stanley, the markets for technical workstations and UNIX "have grown in response to the trends toward distributed computing and open, as opposed to proprietary, systems. The rising popularity of UNIX reflects the push for open systems worldwide. Users have embraced UNIX because it improves the portability of applications software, enables users to run software on other vendors' systems without a major effort, and allows multi-vendor networking." Even Marc Schulman of Salomon Brothers, who generally dismisses the success of Sun in favor of more established outfits such as DEC, HP, and IBM, concedes that proprietary systems are no longer in favor. He understates the situation when he writes that "incompatibility has become a major problem" and that there "is the widespread desire of computer users to create multi-vendor computer networks."

Most computer companies claim to be standard-bearers, too. As noted in earlier chapters, virtually all of them offer a UNIX operating system of some sort; each of these companies is thereby able to bask in the glow of UNIX's recognized status as a world standard. Nearly every company has adopted Sun's Network File System as the primary method for file sharing over a network. IBM, of course, is so large that whatever product direction it takes becomes a standard. Few in the industry dispute the adage that IBM is not the competition; it is the environment. Still, IBM has begun to chime the bell of standards with the rest, signing onto the OSF and buying Sun's NFS.

That standards are de rigueur for computer companies in the workstation industry these days is a direct result of the success of Sun. If Sun had plodded along in its growth, standards would be just another item on a Christmas list of

good wishes, like peace on earth and goodwill toward men.
But Sun did not plod. It accelerated its growth so quickly as
to turn the head of every computer maker. Not wanting to
miss the standards rocket that Sun flew on, they scrambled to
get on board. Whether they will succeed in displacing Sun
cannot be determined at this writing, but they are turning on
their own afterburners in hopes of gaining on Sun as the
industry-standards king.

Understanding how Sun established this reputation reveals
how it achieved its success in the market. More important is
understanding why Sun chose to gamble its entire future on
this policy, with the strategy for its SPARC microprocessor.
It's the reason why Sun may become one of the three or four
major computer companies as the twentieth century comes to
a close—or just a blip on the time line of computer history.
Sun's successes and failures as a standards maker are the key
to its strategy with SPARC. From the lessons it learned in
giving away its technology, Sun was prepared to risk the
company on its RISC chip.

THE NETWORK WAS THE COMPUTER

In November 1984, when the company was just over two and
a half years old, Sun unveiled its Network File System
(NFS), the first in a series of products it wanted the industry
to adopt as a standard. Designed by a team of engineers led
by Bob Lyon, NFS represented a major leap in the direction
of distributed computing and, in a short time, was licensed
by virtually the entire industry, becoming a recognized de
facto standard not just for workstations, but also for the
entire computer industry, from PCs to mainframes.

The reason for the success of NFS was its necessity. Companies were leaving the timeshared world of minicomputers
and mainframes, leaping headlong into the realm of desktop
computers linked over local area networks. Machines
cropped up in every nook and cranny in the world's businesses, all of them eventually needing to share data easily
with other systems. Network administrators were constantly

fighting resource battles because employees of companies large and small had to transfer massive files across the increasingly networked corporate landscape, replicating the files on one machine after another. File sharing became a critical need.

With Sun's NFS software, individuals could "mount" their file system—all or some of it—so that other users on the network could work with their files as if the files were their own. Other users accessed the distant file system without having to know that they were doing so. The files in use appeared to be located on their own computers, to the extent that they were actually listed in their file system directories. In the parlance of the industry, those files were *transparent* to those users.

Today this technique is common, primarily because of the widespread use of NFS, but its appearance was widely hailed as a major step toward distributed computing because it occurred independently of the operating system. That is, it ran on computers that used UNIX, VMS, DOS, and other operating systems. Operating-system disparity was the norm in the world's organizations from small businesses to juggernauts such as the DoD. Lyon and his group used technical tricks to further Sun's goal of distributed computing. NFS helped cut through the Babel of disparate systems that had prevailed.

These technological tricks were clearly demonstrated at the 1986 Uniforum trade show in Anaheim, California, where sixteen manufacturers, including DEC and Data General, demonstrated the capabilities of NFS. From that point the popularity of NFS zoomed.

Although NFS technology convinced the organizational world of its value, the Sun marketing strategy for NFS was what made it an unqualified success. Instead of treating NFS like any other product, Sun licensed it to the industry. Licensees received the source code of the program, which they could then integrate with their own systems, instantly making their computers more accessible in the increasingly networked user environment. Equally important, Sun placed the specification for NFS on a public computer network called *usenet*, which was predominantly an electronic bulletin board and information-exchange medium for UNIX users worldwide. From that specification, it was possible to construct an NFS program that worked with other NFS software. The advantage for other companies, of course, was that they did not have to pay Sun the relatively nominal license fee. At least one company, Southern California–based Network Resources Corporation, saved the license costs and developed its own NFS from the specification, proving the veracity of Sun's claim that NFS was "free" to the world. Most other firms saved the time and expense, however, and simply bought a tape of the software from Sun.

NFS was critical to the acceptance of Sun as a creator of something more than "just another workstation system," or JAWS, as newcomers to the industry and their products were derisively nicknamed. NFS gave Sun distinction among the gaggle of competitors. The NFS licensing program gave a luster to Sun's strategy as a promoter and provider of standards. Finally, although Sun had used the tag line of "open systems" virtually from its inception, prior to NFS the only beneficiary of open technology was Sun, which had incorporated industry standards into its workstation products. With NFS, Sun returned the favor to the market.

The ovation NFS received from users, analysts, and even competitors prompted Sun to focus its development and marketing energies on networking technology. Sun purchased Centram Systems, the maker of TOPS, a software product for linking IBM PCs and Apple Macintoshes. TOPS accelerated the release of Sun's SunLink data-communication software, allowing users of Sun workstations to have windows on their display that looked and functioned just like the displays on IBM-mainframe and DEC-minicomputer terminals. The SunLink products—such as those for the GM-sponsored MAP/TOP protocol for manufacturing networks—were Sun's entrée into the massive and potentially lucrative factory-automation market.

With the initial success of NFS under its belt, Sun fostered the expansion of NFS to work with increasing numbers of operating systems. It adopted the international X.400 messaging protocol for sending electronic missives over public data networks such as Tymnet and Telenet. Most important, Sun evolved a networking philosophy that permeated the company.

Under the direction of John Hime and Bernie Lacroute—and inspired, perhaps, by a fetish for TLAs (three-letter abbreviations)—Sun packaged its networking products in two related programs: Open Systems Networking (OSN) and Open Network Computing (ONC). OSN emerged as the overall strategy and catch phrase for Sun's entire product line. OSN was a philosophy (or "positioning statement," in Sun marketing language) that emphasized the role of network technology and workstations. ONC, on the other hand, denoted actual products—in this case, the network software, including NFS, that came with the operating system Sun users got when they purchased a Sun computer. Both OSN and ONC coincided with the promotional rubric "The Network Is the Computer." A press release describing the promotional campaign quotes Scott McNealy: "We designed our architecture so that ultimately a user can get to all of his company's computer resources from his desktop system, without having to know the idiosyncrasies of every machine on the network. 'The Network Is the Computer' means all the systems work together like one big resource."

The emphasis on network technology for a workstation company might seem strange, even confusing, but Sun was never content to remain merely a "hot box" company. The terms and themes employed by Sun to describe itself and its products were applicable to the thriving local-area-network industry's players such as 3Com and Novell. In fact, in a later study of outsider perceptions of Sun commissioned by Sun itself, only one Sun customer was able to identify the theme "The Network Is the Computer" with Sun—and he got it backward, saying, "The Computer Is the Network." But in 1986 and 1987 the competition was challenging Sun's networking story. Despite the success of NFS, Apollo and even

AT&T began to offer credible alternatives to it.

The issues involved were excruciatingly technical. In the case of Apollo, it claimed its network software was superior to NFS because of arcane differences in the way its networking product, the Network Computing System (NCS), kept track of the network addresses and updated tables for use by workstations. It was admittedly an improvement on Sun's Yellow Pages program, which was separate from NFS itself. Sun's NFS managers, Bill Keating and Eric Schmidt, helped position Sun's OSN and ONC stories as a "complete response" to the NCS program from Apollo.

Apollo fired another salvo at Sun when it launched the Network Computing Forum (NCF), which was billed as a standards organization. Apollo convinced workstation makers and customers that everyone should get together and debate the issues that Sun believed NFS had solved through its de facto status. Late in the process, Sun saw the momentum for NCF building, and because the company labeled itself an open company that supported the use of standards, it signed up. At the organization's initial meeting, discussions revolved around the details of file transfer, network security, remote execution of programs, network management, the development of distributed programs—all elements that were at various stages of maturity at Sun and elsewhere.

These extraneous debates cast doubt on the strength and position of NFS, if not in the minds of customers, who still used it and appreciated its value, then at least in the attitudes of some people at Sun. When Sun's team of networking-products managers, including Bill Keating and Larry Garlick, heard some criticism of NFS and praise for NCS, alarms went off. The NCS-versus-NFS saga underscored one of Sun's deepest weaknesses: self-doubt.

Because Sun had expanded so quickly, it often lacked an understanding of its own strength and power. Individuals at the company were too close to the days of being a small upstart. Claiming to be a leader was one thing, acting like one was something else. The public face of confidence often belied a worried soul. If NCS, which was new, untested, and being offered by a company on the decline, could catch fire in the market, then the viability of NFS should never be taken for granted. A standard was standard only as long as customers accepted it. And customers were a fickle lot.

Apollo's ploy to displace NFS with NCS continued into 1989 but with much less attention. The creation of the Open Software Foundation a year earlier had increased the level of confusion in Apollo's position. Although the OSF discussed making NCS part of the operating system the group eventually espoused, the nascent standards body was years away from delivering anything, and that undercut Apollo's attempt to thrust its network software into territory previously ruled by Sun's NFS.

Companies outside of Sun were being created around NFS-based products. In 1989, for example, two NFS designers who had left Sun the previous year founded Legato. This Palo Alto, California, startup offered NFS-based server software to anyone already using the network software. The small company figured the NFS market was big enough to deliver lucrative spin-off revenues. Larger companies, such as Network Research Corporation, added NFS-based products to their product line. Many of Sun's numerous OEMs designed their customer networks wholly on NFS. Sun's network software was widely entrenched, while the NCS remained intangible and negligible in the marketplace.

While Sun sustained a consistent and easily understood network story, Apollo had to straddle the fence between two standards groups, the OSF and NCF, both of which it had helped create. The world perceived differences between the two organizations, each of which had a slightly different angle on network software, making it difficult to keep Apollo's position straight.

Although Apollo kept pounding on Sun's network software, its blows were less destructive than those of the OSF and NCF. At one point, Sun felt secure enough that it could simply adopt NCS and offer it as an option to those customers who desired it, and retain its role as the leading purveyor of standards among workstation vendors. Then HP acquired

Apollo and breathed new life into the NCS alternative. Although it was unclear what Apollo technology HP would incorporate into its own extensive product line and which ones it would discard, Lou Delzompo, a product manager for NFS, thought it wise to assume HP would throw its considerable influence behind NCS. HP continued to act bitter about being snubbed by Sun and AT&T in their efforts to standardize UNIX. There was no reason to believe HP would sidestep an opportunity to hurt Sun's position with NFS. Sun, once again, felt under attack by a company that would "outstandardize" the "open" company.

Delzompo recommended that Sun redefine NFS to counter HP's claims of its inadequacy. Sun did offer other software that had the functions of NCS, but this software consisted of separate programs that ran with, but were not a part of, NFS. To Delzompo and others, the difference was merely semantic; but to some, the situation signaled significant software-integration problems. To make a legitimate claim that, for example, Yellow Pages was a part of NFS, Sun's engineers had to erase the boundaries that separated the software. Although not a daunting task, it required man-hours that were currently not budgeted.

If that integration was not possible, Delzompo and others entertained the option of scrapping Sun's own enhancements to NFS and incorporating those of NCS. Delzompo believed these "alphabet debates" were meaningless to customers who only wanted to buy machines that met certain criteria. He articulated a growing point of view inside Sun: perceived technical leadership on such arcane issues meant little when compared with the loss of stature the company would endure if it refused to adopt a rapidly accepted industry standard.

Delzompo exemplified the new pragmatists inside Sun— those who wanted the company to capitalize on its position as the leading standards company. The pragmatists did not care whether Sun owned those standards or not. They did not even care if Sun relinquished its own established standards for newer, non-Sun ones. The point, in their minds, was that customers want standards and don't give a damn where they originate.

In the spring and summer of 1989, when the network-software maneuvering was at its height, Sun played a cagier game than the competition expected. The natural reaction should have been for Sun to gather its marketing wagons around its endangered NFS product. But it did not. It left its established network software to stand on its own merits, adding marginal value to it but essentially keeping it whole. A standard, according to this view, was standard because it did not fluctuate with the current fad. It was stable. If the market's demand for functions changed, there should be a new standard.

Such a cold-eyed view of one's own products does not come naturally. It's learned. Sun management apprehended this bit of wisdom from its experiences with different software—the second product the company developed and released in hopes that it would emerge as a standard. This product followed the same path NFS had blazed in 1985, but when Sun set it in motion publicly in 1986, the product's managers immediately discovered the destination would be quite different.

Now You See It, Now You Don't

Computer window systems are beginning to be taken for granted. Developed during the 1970s at Xerox's PARC, window systems invest a computer with the capacity to put more than one screen of information onto a display simultaneously. The best-known window system is the one that runs on the Apple Macintosh personal computer.

The problem with window systems in the 1980s was the absence of standards. Nearly every computer maker built its own window system. Besides the Macintosh version, the industry had SunWindows, MSWindows from Microsoft, and DECwindows, as well as varieties from Apollo, HP, Silicon Graphics, and others. For software developers the situation was confining. Applications—for example, a spreadsheet program that used windows—had to be written for a specific window system in order to run on a given computer. That meant software writers had to re-create their program for every window system for every computer, even if those systems all ran with the UNIX operating system. Or as was often the case, the developers simply bypassed the window system and "took over" the entire display, thereby avoiding the hassle, but also missing the benefits. Such an approach showcased programming expediency, but customers, as usual, were the losers.

To alleviate the incompatibilities, a movement toward window-system standards caught on in the early 1980s. Companies in the computer industry funded efforts at Carnegie-Mellon and MIT. The work at MIT, part of Project Athena, resulted in the X Window System, which emerged as superior to the Andrew Window System produced at the Pittsburgh university. If for no other reason, this superiority developed because the MIT work was made available to the public, while the Andrew window system remained the property of its benefactor, IBM, with distribution limited, by agreement, to universities.

Concurrent with window-system development was the arrival of the PostScript page-description programming language (a page-description language encodes the attributes of pages—column width, fonts, leading, etc.—into software that can then be dispatched to a laser printer, typesetting machine, or other output device). Designed and owned by Adobe Systems of Mountain View, PostScript "describes" type fonts and pages that are "device independent." Pages composed in PostScript can be sent to any PostScript-compatible output device—a relatively low-resolution laser printer or a high-resolution typesetting machine, for example. One of the major benefits of PostScript is that it frees customers from being bound to a dedicated (read *expensive*) publishing system. When used with a Linotronic typesetting system, the PostScript language gives the huge worldwide publishing industry greater flexibility and cost savings for printing books, magazines, and other materials. Without Adobe's PostScript or a similar product, the desktop publishing industry would not exist.

These technical challenges were well established when Sun

surveyed the window-system dilemma in the mid-1980s. Although SunWindows was an excellent product, it ran only on Sun workstations, limiting its impact in the marketplace as well as its interest to major software houses. So the company threw its resources behind the development of the Network/extensible Window System. What the NeWS creators wanted, and what some say they got, was the most advanced, technically exciting window system available.

NeWS combines the page-description technology of PostScript with the distributed nature of NFS. NeWS windows can be any shape a user wants them to be: circles, squares, triangles, polygons. NeWS represents the first use of PostScript for applications other than composing and printing pages. Because NeWS incorporates the Network File System, programs written in PostScript can exist anywhere on the network and show up on any other NeWS machine on that network. NeWS removed PostScript from the limitations of printed hard copy and put PostScript page descriptions directly onto any computer screen on the network.

The kickoff of NeWS was greeted enthusiastically by software developers. When the product was launched at Sun's 1986 user-group meeting in Washington, D.C., software writers crowded into Sun's booth at the show, virtually ignoring other new and recently announced products. NeWS was something hot. The development team, which included James Gosling, David Rosenthal (both had worked on window-system projects at MIT and Carnegie-Mellon), Michelle Arden, and Tony Hoeber, among others, was ecstatic.

The idea of NeWS was so clever that Sun initially contemplated marketing NeWS as a proprietary product. There was money to be made with it. Some at Sun saw NeWS as an ideal barrier to entry for the competition. Making it a standard, on the other hand, would undercut that possibility. The prevailing notion, the nearly religious dogma of Sun's hacker community, opted against taking the proprietary route. Debate was short-lived anyway because of the machinations of the X Windows proponents, primarily DEC, the major funder of Project Athena. MIT was going to announce a

licensing program for X.11, the final release of the X program. Because it came from a university, X had the aura of a
nonproprietary, beneficial technology, one that could quickly
become a standard.

This development put Sun's NeWS team in a bind. Even
though X was not ready for the market, prototype versions
ran on multiple systems; the first one, ironically, was a Sun
workstation. NeWS, on the other hand, was not as close to
release, and it ran only on Sun's computers that used the
Motorola MC68000 family of chips, an inauspicious coming-
out party for a self-proclaimed industry standard. With the
goal of having NeWS run on multiple operating systems as
well as a variety of hardware, everyone at Sun knew that
demonstrating the window system exclusively on a Sun workstation would have limited effect. A crash effort went into
preparing NeWS for other computers. The first non-Sun
system was the Atari ST personal computer, another
MC680x0 machine. It worked. In fact, it was this limited
success that emboldened the NeWS team and Sun management to preannounce NeWS at the user-group meeting in the
nation's capital. And it was the MIT distribution plan for X
that persuaded Sun to take NeWS down the path of NFS.
License it freely. Put the specifications in the public domain.
Make it a standard.

Following on the heels of the user-group event, the spring
1987 Comdex trade show in Atlanta gave the NeWS team
members another opportunity to show off their product on
the then-spanking-new Intel 80386 microprocessor. NeWS
so impressed Intel's management that one vice president
jumped on the window system's bandwagon, hailing it as
"the window system of choice for many OEMs in the upcoming generation of 386-based technical workstations." Bill Joy
went to the UNIX Expo trade show in New York in December and explained to his audience that NeWS was "a
replacement for ASCII in a bitmapped world," meaning that
NeWS was destined to change the way people interacted with
computers as far as what they saw on the screen.

The possibilities for NeWS did not go unnoticed outside of

Sun. The respected trade journal *Computer Graphics World* summed up the potential for Sun's proposed standard at the time of its introduction:

> *CGW* is keeping a close eye on NeWS and its implications: If hardware and software vendors, particularly those providing windowing systems, adopt the NeWS architecture (which has already been two years in the making) widely, they would no longer have to convince developers and customers to adopt their proprietary standard—that race would be over. Who would win? Applications developers could write one NeWS-based system. End users could choose an interface based on its particular look and feel rather than on its ability to attract third-party software developers. A large organization with "islands" of uncommunicative computers would at least become an archipelago. And Sun, of course, would prosper.

Sun's strategy of giveaway technology lit a fire in the workstation industry. Only this time it wasn't the blaze of glory that NFS had experienced; it was a wildfire that Sun's competitors desperately wanted to extinguish as soon as possible. When NFS first glowed, there was nothing quite like it that worked as well. The elegance of NFS from a software developer's perspective appealed to virtually everyone. NeWS had those same characteristics. The integration of PostScript with a network-based window system was sheer genius, much as the development of the RPC/XDR (remote procedure call/external data representation) protocols of NFS revealed simple programming brilliance. But one critical difference existed between the two software products: time.

When Sun introduced NFS in 1984, it was a modest-size company that lagged behind Apollo and HP in the nascent workstation market, an arena so small that DEC was barely pursuing it at the time. No one cared strongly if NFS belonged to Sun because the company was not such a force in the market. NFS worked and it was needed. The intervening success of Sun in those two years unnerved the competition.

They were not about to let the Mountain View upstart claim yet another technical victory by establishing a second major industry standard. It can be said that the announcement of NeWS drove more companies into the camp of X supporters than the technical merits of X itself.

The force with which the competition reacted to NeWS caused some moments of paranoia at Sun. NeWS team members muttered that "they are out to get us." Although NeWS licensees did appear, they were not nearly as numerous as those knocking on the door for NFS. Many of those that did buy NeWS did so with the proviso that Sun not announce their agreement. These companies feared that others would think they were taking sides in a standards war that had clearly not been decided, and no one wanted to be associated with a possible loser.

DEC jumped on Sun with both feet by telling customers, analysts, and the press that NeWS was not a standard because Sun controlled it. Bernie Toth, DEC's workstation leader, told *Datamation* magazine, "Users want a set of industrywide standards. It's hard to see how users and vendors would accept anything like NeWS that is being pushed by one company." The veneer of respectability that X carried by being a product from the premier engineering school in the United States was not without its influence.

It was the increasing support for X that caused Sun to unveil NeWS prematurely in October 1986, when it was not nearly ready for delivery to developers. At the announcement, the NeWS development team's Arden told her listeners that the window system would be ready in March of the next year and not bundled with the Sun operating system until six months after that. Even with that much lead time, something Sun had never before allowed for a product, NeWS was late for delivery.

The combination of a viable alternative to NeWS, the unified competition, and a prematurely announced product caused Sun to change its strategy on NeWS. In April 1987, Sun unveiled its window-system strategy: support X *and* NeWS. The idea was to give customers a choice between standards, thereby keeping Sun's position as an advocate of industry standards yet offering superior technology. This strategy devolved into a product called X/NeWS, diminishing even further Sun's own advanced window system.

Although NeWS experienced a rougher road than NFS had, it did establish itself as an alternative to X as a window system. Technical cognoscenti have a lively interest in NeWS, but even if Sun had waited until the product was ready, the competition would likely not have let Sun get away with another coup, as had happened with the network software. The success of the strategy that Sun revealed with NFS was impossible to repeat, because the competition knew the game plan too well and had their backup in X. This assault on NeWS was yet another indicator of the competition's determination to give Sun no quarter in its rise to the top of the workstation market.

Although NeWS cannot be considered a failure, it was not destined to become a standard. NeWS was the technological equal of—and perhaps superior to—the MIT-developed X Window System, but it arrived too late on the heels of X. So Sun owned up to its "where standards exist, use them; where they don't, invent them" credo and admitted that X was the standard. Not wanting to discard NeWS, however, Sun offered an "X/NeWS" hybrid: "X is the standard we support; if you want NeWS, we'll give you that too."

To establish more standards in the industry, Sun would have to catch the competition completely off guard, do something grand and unexpected. It did. It introduced SPARC and caught the competition with their collective pants down.

OF RISC AND REWARDS

The Wall Street Journal is not often given to excess. Its reputation rests on accurate, staid prose. Even its look is reserved, reflecting more the conservative days of yore than the razzle and dazzle of today's financial markets. Yet, in a page-1 story about Sun Microsystems, the newspaper kicked off a generally balanced article with this tantalizing head: "The Revolutionary: Computer Maker Aims to Transform Industry and Become a Giant." Although the report discussed many aspects of the company, its salient thesis described Sun's dramatic moves with its SPARC technology, a computer architecture that was strategically presented to the market in such a way that it upset the profitable applecarts of the world's computer makers.

SPARC, a reduced-instruction-set computer (RISC), stands for Scalable Processor Architecture. Designed at Sun with the help of computer scientists from the University of California at Berkeley, SPARC is noted technically because it is ideally suited to adopt new microprocessor media as they are developed, such as gallium arsenide, custom CMOS, and even the newer, more-exotic ceramic semiconductor materials. These new technologies will eventually replace the traditional silicon wafers associated with today's computers. What these new media offer is speed—lots and lots of speed—and computer speed is increasingly important as computer software becomes more and more sophisticated and demanding of the hardware.

The ever-increasing performance of SPARC computers and RISC processors is not what got *The Wall Street Journal* so excited. Technology comes and goes, and through the years that newspaper has seen many technological revolutions—so many, in fact, that editors seem to be somewhat jaded. But business revolutions are less frequent and much more exciting. Business writers at America's largest financial daily and elsewhere saw something unique in Sun's presentation of its product, enough to bestow on the company the uncharacteristically positive sobriquet of "revolutionary."

With SPARC, Sun, in effect, created its own competitors, not something currently advised in today's business schools but often touted as one of the new ways of doing business. It did so by offering licenses to its SPARC technology in July 1987. The press release carrying this news began: "In keeping with its open systems philosophy. . . ."

Open systems, some thought, was taken a bit too far with the SPARC program. It would become the Achilles' heel by which the competition would unseat Sun. Never before had a computer manufacturer unveiled its CPU architecture to the industry for the price of a license and a royalty. It caught the competition by surprise. It was one thing to make software available, since competitors invariably offered some alternative. Making your own software an industry-wide product, even at the loss of differentiation, was smart, especially for a company grabbing for increased market share. It was another thing to let go of hardware advantages, to establish, in effect, clone companies to beat you on price since they would not have to recoup the massive development costs involved in bringing SPARC to market.

The long-term goal was not to make money directly through the license program. Rather it was to expand the overall demand for SPARC products. This expansion was possible because more than a simple CPU was licensed. The licensee got a complete product: chip, board, and the entire Sun operating system. It was like going to a department store and buying a stereo component system. The package was complete, with only some setup required. And as with any stereo component system, the licensing program meant lots of manufacturers would be offering a variety of price and performance ranges. With every component based on SPARC technology, all software would play on every computer, just as audiophiles can listen to Vivaldi or Waylon Jennings on anything from a low-priced Fisher stereo to an exotic Denon system.

To UNIX software developers, SPARC was music to the ears and money in the pocket. Increasing the SPARC market by giving away, in effect, its binary secrets meant more machines in additional vertical markets. New application areas opened up for UNIX with SPARC, as the price and performance spectrum yawned wider. This diversity also pleased the DOS and Macintosh developer communities. With so many markets working on SPARC-based systems, the horizontal, general-interest software customers, such as word-processing and spreadsheet users, would emerge in droves in untapped areas.

An added benefit of the SPARC strategy was that it disso-
ciated Sun from the hardware sales. Sun was to be only one
of many SPARC vendors that competed with every other
SPARC system maker. One of the stumbling blocks for
NeWS, after all, had been the inextricable link between it
and Sun. The unmitigated success of NeWS would have
given Sun an obvious and commanding role in the industry,
but a successful SPARC program fueled more than one company, both established ones and startups. In effect, the
SPARC strategy created the possibility for a market of
shrink-wrapped software for the workstation industry.

SPARC vendors went so far as to incorporate as a separate
organization, the SPARC Vendor Council (SVC), which soon
became SPARC International, in November 1988. The
group's intent was to ensure that Sun would not sway from
its adherence to openness. The SVC pushed the idea of
SPARC as a RISC standard. It attracted software developers
and systems integrators. To assist SVC members, it established guidelines for implementations and created tests and
verifications for SPARC-based hardware and applications
software.

Although clearly an organization that brought advantages
to Sun, it was not a pawn of the company. It battled Sun on
licensing points. It established its own operating board, with
Sun having only one representative. Sun's member sat across
the table from representatives of direct competitors such as
Solbourne and Toshiba. To emphasize its independence, the
group devised its own logo. Its first press release listed public
relations contacts at six companies, not one of which was
Sun.

Inside and outside Sun, this plan had no shortage of doubt-
ing Thomases. In an industry strewn with once-stellar has-
beens, the idea of handing out inventions to the competition
seemed outrageous. Yet it was the outrageousness of the
concept that was likely to make it work. McNealy, Joy, Lacroute, and others believed that the market's feeding frenzy
on standards was only beginning. If they had a true clonelike
environment, such as the one that exists for the IBM PC,

customer appetites would be ravenous, enough for Sun and many other vendors (McNealy, in fact, praised the concept of "clonability" at the introduction of the SPARCstation 1, as well as on other occasions).

The concern that a larger company with more resources might outsell Sun in the SPARC arena was, to some, "exactly what Sun should want to happen." That is, Sun still received royalties, gaining profit without the operations overhead. More important, with an increase in the number and size of players in the SPARC industry, the reality of a world of shrink-wrapped software would finally emerge in the high-performance workstation market, just as it did in the PC environment. It was the licensing of SPARC that compelled major PC software firms to develop SPARC versions of their software. In the summer of 1989, for example, Lotus Development Corporation and Ashton-Tate, two of the biggest players in the PC software market, announced their commitment to SPARC technology—each company's first endeavor in the high-performance RISC systems arena—and perhaps the beginning of the partial validation of some people's vision of Sun in the consumer computer marketplace.

The number and diversity of SPARC players is impressive. On the microprocessor side are Texas Instruments, Philips NV, Cypress, Bipolar, Fujitsu, and LSI. Each company designs and manufactures SPARC for different markets. Not all of these SPARC implementations will sit inside desktop computers and run programs for CAD/CAM engineers. They can work in various and curious environments—everything from spy satellites to advanced copy machines.

These chip makers were buoyed by the increasing number of computer-system makers that had adopted the SPARC RISC approach. In the non-chip arena—in addition to Sun—AT&T, Xerox, Unisys, ICL, Solbourne, Metaflow, and Toshiba were behind SPARC. These companies shipped products to virtually every class of computer user. Solbourne, for example, was intent on beating Sun with a workstation clone, robbing Sun of its marketing and service advantages primarily through price. Metaflow was operating in the supercomputer class. Toshiba was taking SPARC into the laptop-computer market, where Toshiba was already an established leader. AT&T, Xerox, and Unisys brought SPARC technology into the general-purpose and office-computing realms. Sun continued the SPARC penetration into the workstation market. And, of course, there was the link between SPARC and UNIX.

The deal with AT&T caused the most fuss initially because of the tie with UNIX, bringing both an operating system and a CPU standard to play in the market. The combination was the equivalent of the DOS/Intel alignment in the personal computer arena, but with a much greater number and variety of price and performance choices. As noted in the section on the Open Software Foundation, it was not until AT&T actually poured money into Sun that competitors felt the dire threat of SPARC. With its resources alone, Sun was not deemed capable of leveraging SPARC as a standard. None of the systems companies that first bellied up to the SPARC bar struck the likes of DEC, IBM, Apollo, and HP as significant, long-term competitors in the computer market; the proprietary trough seemed safe to drink from for quite a while.

Then the $300 million capital infusion from AT&T changed the situation. Suddenly, more than hardware, software, and a few inefficient competitors were at stake. There was money, big money, with which to deluge the industry with SPARC programs.

Timing was also a critical factor. Sun's pervasive belief in time-to-market worked again. The unveiling of SPARC occurred when the jury on RISC technology was still out. True, lots of development projects were underway, but few products had emerged. The Sun-4 workstations were the first in their class. They, along with HP's Spectrum RISC minicomputers, proved the viability of RISC. Every computer maker had to have RISC or be considered a technological troglodyte. Long after SPARC vendors were shipping RISC systems, DEC and Apollo finally got around to offering the advanced hardware. DEC knew that its own RISC development project was late and going to be later, so it hastily abandoned it in favor of the MIPS RISC processor, which was more readily available. Even IBM, which qualifies as the first maker of a desktop RISC computer, the inconsequential RT, did not offer anything that came close to the price and performance of SPARC products until February 1990.

SPARC products did not immediately take over the market. It took months, even years, for members of SPARC International to start getting their equipment out the door. Initially, Sun was the largest seller of SPARC systems. The Motorola and Intel CISC chips continued to dominate the market, including, in 1988, the products that gave Sun most of its impressive revenue stream. But the trend was clear, especially at Sun. If it wasn't a SPARC product, it was almost a leper. Marketing and engineering programs at Sun were heavily slanted in favor of SPARC. Hiring RISC specialists became an obsession with recruiters. For months in 1988, speculation swirled around the company that the Sun-3/80 workstation, which used Motorola's MC68030 CPU, would be scrapped. The Intel-based computer, the Sun386i, was also said to be in jeopardy. But the company continued to build these two machines, as well as the SPARC, and to support all three technologies under the guise of "one architecture, three instruction sets." Sun executives wanted to cut a deal with Intel or Motorola to license SPARC, but both companies declined, in favor of their own RISC ventures.

The first SPARC systems were based on the gate-array technology of Fujitsu, giving the Japanese a distinct edge in the emerging worldwide RISC-systems market. To Bill Joy's mind, this delay seemed typical "with a lot of American companies. They spend so much time making up their minds that they miss good opportunities. They don't act quickly enough"—an imperative with which Sun was familiar both in philosophy and practice.

Whatever large American semiconductor manufacturers initially missed about the implications of SPARC was not unnoticed by their Japanese counterparts. Along with Fujitsu, Matsushita, one of Japan's biggest chip makers, latched on to SPARC. Unlike Fujitsu, which licensed the technology directly for the purpose of expanding its microprocessor offerings, Matsushita used SPARC to elbow into the U.S. workstation market through its investment in Solbourne Computer of Boulder, Colorado.

The next big Japanese outfit to bet on SPARC was Toshiba. Over the 1989 Memorial Day weekend, Sun announced a key deal in the process to legitimize SPARC and make it the number-one RISC CPU. Toshiba agreed to build low-cost desktop and portable systems using the SPARC chip. Hailed as "the biggest boost yet in Sun's controversial strategy to create a new breed of computer clones," the pact was also heavily criticized by protectionists as being anti-American. Likened to the selling of F-16 technology to the Japanese, the Toshiba agreement even provoked name calling; one pundit resorted to calling Sun's young CEO "Scott McGreedy."

Less-provincial observers thought it was a watershed achievement and believed that Sun and the entire SPARC market, including U.S. firms, would benefit. As much as AT&T's investment in Sun, Toshiba's acceptance of SPARC legitimized the aspirations of the RISC chip's designers. Innovative SPARC products would pour off assembly lines, related technological advances would buttress it, the market would grow, software would emerge, and royalties would accumulate in the bank.

It was absurd to contend that Sun's strategy was pitting Japan against the United States. Sun's executives were not anti-American by any means. They simply endorsed the philosophy of free trade at an extreme level. McNealy believed that the shibboleth that American companies could not compete in production costs was a dead issue. In an interview with *Manufacturing Systems* editors in 1989, he claimed that "the U.S. is not that tough a place to be building cost-effective computers. We're building all of our products today in Mountain View and Milpitas, California, as well as Westford, Massachusetts. We've found [that] we've been able to maintain very good cost-competitiveness."

More important, McNealy and others at Sun believed that

their company's own products, those on the market and on the drawing boards, were impressive enough to hold their own against any competitor's, no matter what its national origin. Its SPARCstation workstation, for example, was so fast and cheap that some took to calling it the "SPARCin-tosh." The Yankee Group, a Boston-based consulting firm, thought so highly of the notion that it held a seminar called "SPARCintosh: The Imminent Collision Between Lower-Cost Workstations and the Next Generation PCs." The July 1989 conclave included speakers from NeXT, Computer-Land, Intel, Motorola, Businessland, and Sun.

In the summer of 1989, Sun was on track as a $2 billion organization. Although it remained committed to the customer base that used its Motorola- and Intel-based CPUs, the company's future lay with SPARC technology. Its revenues were primarily coming from SPARC products. In the first quarter after its introduction, after being available for only two months of shipments, the SPARCstation 1 accounted for nearly 20 percent of the record revenues. Perhaps more significantly, the margins on the SPARCstation computers were quite healthy compared with those on the MC68030 workstations, which gave Sun managers a lot of room to negotiate prices when the competition finally delivered comparable products.

Sun's expansion of the RISC market was only the beginning of the SPARC success. Like NFS, the SPARC licensing program caught the competition in mid-1987 without a response. The HP, MIPS Computer, and Motorola RISC technologies represented the only likely competition to SPARC, but each had its own disadvantages. HP's was purely proprietary: nothing got Spectrum chips but HP machines. MIPS had an extremely limited and tight licensing program, and it was incapable of pushing the market through its own system sales. Motorola built and sold the chips themselves, not the technology that created them.

Sun's long-standing posturing about open systems was finally put to the ultimate test with SPARC. Sun passed the exam brilliantly. The company had learned through its NFS program that establishing standards made you popular with customers. That made you money. Investors liked that. Sun also learned from its experience with NeWS that being king of the standards was a way to gain too many enemies too quickly. Being a fast-growing upstart was one thing; being a fast-growing Fortune 500 company was something else. You weren't cute any longer when you got big. No one rooted for billion-dollar underdogs.

Sun's licensing plan for SPARC has remained unique in the industry. This strategy's success or failure in the long run can be measured only by the rise and/or fall of Sun Microsystems. SPARC itself may go on for years, with SPARC International being wholly independent to develop and expand the SPARC market. Sun is not necessary for the RISC architecture to be a winner. Other players can make that happen.

Sun's management is betting that its SPARC program will sustain the dizzying growth it has enjoyed since the company's founding. The company continues to focus on a two-pronged global strategy: create an expanding market through standard systems and acquire the biggest possible share of it. Devotion to this overall plan, with its occasional pitfalls and miscues, made Sun's management an instant success, the ideal cover story for business journalism (and the reason for this book). But the best, most innovative plan is only as good as the people who execute it, and keeping such a free-flying rocket ship of a company on target has not been the easiest of assignments.

7
Managing Hypergrowth

The hiring of Bob Lux as Sun's vice president of customer service in late 1985 can be interpreted as the moment when Sun had "made it" in the computer business. The company was desperate to address its customer service problems, which were quite serious at the time. Initially, Sun was not overly concerned about service problems, primarily because the technical sophistication of the users equaled or surpassed that of Sun's engineers and programmers. But as the company's products worked their way into varying market segments, the need for an effective customer-service program emerged as Sun's biggest problem. McNealy, in fact, kept a simple ten-item list of Sun's hottest issues. For nearly two years customer service held the top spot, like some phenomenal blockbuster on the *New York Times* bestseller chart. It was not, however, a place of honor.

New customers were crying for service. Vice President of Sales Joe Roebuck was hearing of lost sales to DEC and Apollo because new buyers required a more extensive service program than that offered by Sun. Without a heavily revamped customer-service group, it was inevitable that Sun

would stumble, possibly stagnate. Sun executives knew no
one on board had either the experience or the time to handle
the task. The company had to import the best talent—and
quickly.

Sun's search for a customer service executive led to Lux.
An accomplished veteran in the minicomputer market, he
knew the computer industry. He understood technical users'
needs. He had significant experience in the workstation
market. He was also from the competition, Apollo Computer,
where he was the customer service chief. Luring Lux away
from the workstation market's number-one company at that
time was quite a coup. It was one of the key intangible
indicators that Sun was about to leapfrog into the number-
one slot.

Lux came to Sun from Apollo without ever having worked
for a California company. Although high-tech outfits along
Massachusetts Route 128 are casual by comparison with
their downtown-Boston neighbors, Lux was unprepared for
the informal style of Sun's management team. On Route 128,
executives, even engineering managers, regularly wore suits
and ties. Not so at Sun. Top-level meetings at Sun often were
gatherings of scruffy-looking men and women who, to an
outside observer, would never pass as business leaders. Scott
McNealy donned a suit only when he had a meeting with
people from outside Sun. Bill Joy, Eric Schmidt, Wayne
Rosing, and Andy Bechtolsheim—all technologists by inclination—rarely cinched their collars with a knotted tie. Bernie
Lacroute, a European and an East Coast–trained manager
from DEC, had long ago adopted the less formal attire of his
cohorts at Sun whenever his schedule allowed.

In his first few months Lux insisted on maintaining his
conservative East Coast image. A handsome man with an
extensive wardrobe, Lux graced Sun's halls with sartorial
luxe. As a result, he constantly fielded good-natured ribbing
from his peers. Lux was not stuffy or pretentious, however,
and handled the comments well. But no matter how impressive his example to others, sandals and T-shirts prevailed
during executive sessions.

During one meeting of McNealy's managers, though, Lux had had enough. The barbs about his being overdressed got to him. "Alright. Alright," he screamed, "I surrender!" He jumped onto the table and proceeded to perform a highly animated striptease, taking off his coat, vest, and tie to the laughter and applause of the others. Rarely after that meeting was Lux seen in his conservative attire. He had succumbed to the management style of Sun.

PARADIGMS OF HYPERGROWTH

Like a national economy, the strength of a company is measured by its expansion from year to year. In most U.S. businesses an annual growth rate of about 5 percent per year is considered decent. In the volatile high-tech segment, an astounding 20 percent annual increase is considered acceptable. Through 1988, with one exception, Sun Microsystems doubled its size in nearly every area during each quarter of the first six years.

Most successful startup companies enjoy a period of initial hypergrowth. After all, when an organization comes out of the starting gate, it has nothing. The first sale for such a company begins the tale of hypergrowth. The overwhelming majority of these companies, however, quickly lose that momentum. Perhaps the dizzying expansion continues for a year or two—some even stretch the phenomenal period out for three or four years—but eventually, as the company becomes bigger, the rate of growth slows down.

Hypergrowth is endemic to small companies that tend to be ranked below the Fortune 1000 or 2000 list. They spurt from $500,000 in sales to $1 million, then to $2 million, possibly going from $2 million to $4 million, to $10 million, then to $20 million. Then the reality of such expansion takes its toll, and the slowdown begins. Such doubling causes enormous strain on organizations, and policies to control that strain inevitably lead to the contraction of the growth. To paraphrase consummate businessman Ned Beatty in the film *Network*, it is the normal process of things.

In Silicon Valley, where hypergrowth is virtually the norm, firms have jumped from nearly nothing to a $100 million dollars in a handful of years. Adam Osborne, for example, was an entrepreneur who started publishing books about microcomputers in the mid-1970s, when these little machines first made their shaky debut. As microcomputers caught on, so did Osborne's publishing venture. Then, in 1980, he sold the business to media giant McGraw-Hill. With the money from the sale of his publishing company in his pocket, he turned his entrepreneurial eyes elsewhere: to the microcomputer market itself.

In 1981 he unveiled Osborne Computer Corporation, maker of the world's first "portable" computer. By today's standards the word *portable* was a misnomer. Osborne's clunky machine weighed nearly thirty pounds. It featured the sleek industrial design of a World War II field telephone, and it had a CRT screen less than five inches wide.

It sold like hotcakes. Today a quaint relic, it was state of the art for portable computers at the time, and Osborne's company took off like a shot. Osborne's business plan called for selling ten thousand units total, but soon after starting, the company was selling that many computers per month. Although the fledgling company located in the East Bay city of Hayward, California—away from the high rents of Silicon Valley—Osborne Computer seemed to exhibit no cost controls. It added employees at a furious pace. It hired corps of contractors, sometimes overpaying them by mistake.

While this anarchy was occurring, the "field telephone" was quickly replaced by a sleeker-looking box, which accounted for the unit sales listed above. It was still a relic—a gimmick, almost—with which technology was rapidly catching up. For success to continue, Osborne had to upgrade the machine and expand into other product lines.

The company did have another machine under development, but Osborne's fatal error was whetting its customers' appetite for this new product, which it couldn't deliver on time. Potential customers, not wanting to be stuck with an antiquated box on their hands, stopped buying existing computers, waiting for the announced but undeliverable new model.

Inventory of the old machine piled up. Cash flow became a trickle. Less than two years after it opened for business, Osborne Computer Corporation filed for bankruptcy. Other companies—Gavilan and Eagle, for example—joined the failed fraternity, but none took off so fast or crashed and burned more spectacularly than Osborne. An object lesson in how not to run a business, Osborne represented the dark side of hypergrowth: too much too soon and the inability to handle it.

More-successful hypergrowth companies adopt ambitious but manageable paths of expansion. One of the most successful hypergrowth companies in Silicon Valley, 3Com Corporation, was located just down the road from Sun. It was founded by one of the inventors of the Ethernet local area network, Bob Metcalf. In 1979 Ethernet was used to connect minicomputers, such as DEC VAXes, so that users of one machine could work on another. The biggest advantage was the sharing of resources such as printers, plotters, and data-storage media. Ethernet was one of many LANs at the time.

After the successful introduction of the IBM PC into the business market, 3Com, under its CEO, Bill Krause, saw an opportunity to apply the minicomputer resource-sharing benefit of LANs to PCs. Why buy a printer for every desktop machine? Just add a LAN and save a bundle. Since IBM did not initially offer a Big Blue–sanctioned LAN, 3Com and a few other companies jumped into the market first, gobbling market share quickly.

LAN prices began to drop as the competition intensified. Weaker LAN companies began to evaporate in the more combative market. 3Com emerged as the biggest of all LAN-only manufacturers. It topped $100 million before any of its competitors reached that milestone. But by 1987, hypergrowth expansion started to slow. To keep the momentum going, 3Com purchased competitors, fended off a suitor, and slowed its hiring and acquisition of buildings. It reached $385 million dollars in mid-1989, after eleven years of operation. It had passed through hypergrowth successfully and was now looking for reasonable and manageable expansion rates.

Such was not the case at Sun Microsystems. At Sun, hypergrowth was the central part of the plan. It was the bedrock on which the company engineered its success. Sun did not balk when the tension mounted. When the frenzy and the confusion seemed overwhelming, the company did not flinch. Hypergrowth, like UNIX, was part of Sun's religion.

THE HEADACHES OF HEAVENLY HYPERGROWTH

As Sun ended its first year of business, the infant company had pulled in $6 million in revenues. Revenue figures more than doubled every year, until after six years in business, Sun topped the $1 billion mark in revenues. This feat is unequaled in American business, with one exception: Compaq Computer of Houston, Texas.

Compaq made its first billion dollars by selling hundreds of thousands of inexpensive but relatively powerful personal computers in hundreds of preestablished retail computer stores. Sun, on the other hand, sold a much smaller number of units at higher prices, through a direct-sales force, to computer-power-hungry engineers and scientists in universities and other high-tech meccas.

Building a direct-sales organization is fraught with much more danger to a company than using existing retail outlets. If every new food product on the market had to develop its own Safeway and A & P grocery chains, Americans would probably starve. Things would be worse if salespeople in the food business had to sell directly to customers. Big-ticket computer sellers, of course, do not have it so rough: they don't have to sell to everyone. They do, however, have to identify the likely candidates. That takes time, all while they are expending the finite resources of the company.

Sun went after customers aggressively through its sales force. Because the strategy of hypergrowth necessitated a large direct-sales force, Sun added salespeople at a furious rate. After all, the little company was competing in the markets of IBM and DEC, where direct sales and service were givens. Such a policy, however, "places substantial stress on operations and the field organization to deliver without glitches while growth continues at breakneck speeds."

The company hired highly qualified sales engineers who could understand the technical problems of customers and could configure workstations that would best perform in their environment. All direct-sales companies, including IBM and DEC, covet these talented salespeople. So Sun introduced an attractive commission program that ramped upward as the individual brought in more sales, occasionally taking a bigger bite out of the quarterly numbers than had been planned.

Initially run by Vice President of Sales Joe Roebuck, the sales organization enjoyed significant success, adding players regularly. According to Carol Bartz, when she was marketing vice president in 1985–86, Sun's number-one priority in the years after the engineering and manufacturing elements had been put in place was "to expand our sales force." Sun doubled its sales group under Roebuck during two six-month periods: June–November 1985 and February–July 1986. In Europe, 1987 was the year of rapid growth. Darryl Barbé, Sun's vice president for European operations, managed a region that contributed 25 percent of Sun's revenues. In that year Sun opened three European subsidiaries, for a total of seven. In early 1987, Nihon Sun Microsystems opened its doors in Tokyo. By mid-1989, Japan alone was contributing nearly as many dollars to the company's coffers as was all of Europe.

In mid-1988 the company reorganized its sales force to better reflect its international stature. Dennis Ohryn, formerly vice president of international operations, became VP of Sun's worldwide field operations, streamlining all sales and field-engineering activities into one office. Roebuck remained the head of North American sales. The expansion of the direct-sales group, however, continued under Ohryn's aegis, with a particular concentration in Asia, Europe, and South America.

This ongoing expansion of the field sales force was augmented by a value-added resellers program that caused significant "turf wars" between Sun's direct-sales group and the VARs. Excruciating meetings took place between representatives of the two sales teams in order to determine which organization could sell to what customers. Sales naturally felt that the VARs were encroaching on their territories, while the VARs considered the restrictions on where and to whom they could sell unreasonable. As a result, the VAR program emerged slowly. Still, it was critical in areas in which Sun salespeople faltered, particularly with smaller customers, who purchased fewer workstations, or those that wanted a special hardware/software package that only a VAR offered. Complaints persisted, and many have yet to be resolved.

The rapid growth of sales led to explosive revenue, but the costs of the expansion kept Sun's profits to a minimum. In fiscal 1988, for example, the year Sun vaulted from a $500 million to a $1 billion company, revenues grew by more than 95 percent, while operating margins decreased from nearly 13 percent in 1987 to just over 10 percent. The trade-offs for revenue over profits were consciously accepted as the occasional pitfall of management's strategic vision of achieving dominant market share. Without market share, in the long run, good short-term profits would be meaningless.

Sun's overall vision and its execution of policy to fulfill that vision were generally greeted as positive. Plaudits for Sun's strategy came from all directions but particularly from financial analysts who were charged with being the most concerned about Sun's bottom line. S. G. Warburg researchers commented, "Sun has pursued a correct strategy of focusing on the long term and growing market share at the expense of margins." Dillon Reed noted, "While skeptics are complaining about profit margins, it is our view that gains in market share and growth are really what count today." At Prudential-Bache, analysts were "impressed by the degree and the scope of the long-term strategic planning that takes place at Sun, particularly in light of the heady growth that might justifiably occupy all of the company's time." These observations were not restricted to the limited review of those who pay for Wall Street advice. The general media were awash in praise for Sun.

One factor that cannot be overlooked in Sun's phenomenal growth is the role of the media—not merely the trade magazines, which tend to be rhapsodic about technological advances, but much of the mainstream press as well. Sun was a media darling—from trade magazine to business journals to major daily newspapers.

The relationship between Sun and the media was synergistic. Sun's success story was a natural for the press, particularly in the era of seeming Japanese ascendancy in high technology. Here was a high-tech Horatio Alger story, complete with a melting pot: Sun was conceived and made in America, and half of the cofounders were foreign born, as was the executive VP and general manager.

Sun was the upstart, the underdog, a revered American archetype. Within three to four years of the company's founding, it had usurped the number-one position in the workstation world from the progenitor of the industry, Apollo. Sun did not wait for the press to beat down its door, however. The company helped interest the press and assisted it in the placement of stories. At first under the management of Jackie Rae, followed by Carol Broadbent, Sun's public relations team doted on the press with efficient regularity. They groomed long-term relationships with bright, key writers. For example, John Markoff began covering Sun while working for *InfoWorld*, a weekly trade magazine based in Silicon Valley. A quasi hacker, Markoff appreciated the technology Sun produced. When he moved to the more influential *Byte* magazine and then to the *San Francisco Examiner* business section, he took his in-depth knowledge and appreciation for Sun with him. Markoff eventually jumped to the *New York Times* as one of its premier technology writers, bringing his interest and understanding of Sun along. In each of his incarnations, upbeat stories about Sun appeared in his publication's pages with his byline. Esther Dyson, now a columnist at *Forbes*, took an early interest in Sun in her influential *Release 1.0* newsletter and carries it in her columns today. Paul Freiberger did likewise as he moved from *Info-World* to *Personal Computing* to the *San Francisco Examiner*, where he replaced Markoff, and helped keep the understanding of Sun's position strong in the local business press.

Good ink in the press does not automatically beget more good ink, though. There must be some substance behind the words. Sun had a good product line in a hot market. But it was the overall quality of the management team that most impressed the analysts and reporters.

NOT JUST HYPE—PEOPLE, TOO

Sun is noted for its youthful leadership, managers, and employees. The youth of its founders did not necessarily bring impetuousness and indiscretion, but it did carry enthusiasm, energy, and endurance—all essential ingredients building a billion-dollar company from scratch.

Young as the founders were, they were wise enough to know they could not go it alone. They quickly found assistance from experienced hands who understood the value of good product matched with a hardworking team. From the outset, Sun's board of directors was populated by experienced men. Three of them—L. John Doerr, Robert Sackman, and David F. Marquardt—had advised other successful Silicon Valley startups, including Apple, Tandem, and Rolm. These three have an extended tenure on the board, having served since 1982, Sun's first year. The board members' longevity has given Sun consistent and stable advice and oversight.

One of Sun's early investors, the Eastman Kodak Company, has had a regular board member since 1983. Another corporate investor, AT&T, added its president of the Data Systems Group, Robert Kavner, to Sun's board in 1988. That same year, Kenneth Oshman, a cofounder of Rolm, and

William R. Hearst III, publisher of the *San Francisco Examiner*, joined the company's chief advisory group.

Beyond the board of directors, Sun hired tough and accomplished managers. Perhaps the most significant addition to Sun was Bernie Lacroute in 1983. After thirteen years at DEC, where he ruled over the successful development, introduction, and marketing of the VAX 780 computer, Lacroute came to lead Sun's engineering department. In May 1985, he rose to be Sun's only executive vice president. Between then and late 1987, Lacroute stood as the single most influential person inside the corporation.

Lacroute and McNealy became an exceptional team. Known to everyone in the company as Bernie, Lacroute embraced his CEO's strategy for snapping up market share in the workstation arena. Likewise, McNealy acceded to Lacroute's notion of what that market wanted in terms of both the technology and its marketing. They complemented one another. Lacroute, said *Business Week*, was "the levelheaded alter ego to McNealy."

Although both were exceptionally self-confident men, neither intruded too deeply into the affairs of their vice presidents. For example, despite McNealy's previous experience in manufacturing at both Onyx and Sun, he let Sun's managers make long-term strategic decisions once he became CEO. James Bean, Sun's manufacturing vice president, led the effort for factory automation, eschewing management's temptation to use Sun workstations to drive the factory-automation system. The company's own product was not capable of such a task in 1986 when the changeover began, so Bean opted for HP equipment and IBM PCs. Bean also avoided trapping Sun into becoming a vertically integrated manufacturer, something that hurt Apollo when it ran into tough times.

Despite Lacroute's reputation as a technically astute, detail-oriented manager, he did not use his knowledge of minutiae to derail the decisions of his engineering managers. Rather, his relentless queries forced those reporting to him to stay on top of their own choices. It was embarrassing when

Lacroute seemed to know more than those directly involved
about a given product in development, an experience of more
than one engineering vice president at Sun.

Outsiders' views of Sun's managers were decidedly positive. The combination of seasoned veterans and fiery young
newcomers especially impressed the investment community.
Analysts referred to Sun's brass as "deceptively good despite
the youth," "savvy," and having "an excellent record of tight
expense control."

Most people were particularly laudatory about management's nimble handling of the tremendous expansionist pressures the company experienced. Integrating hordes of newcomers into the organization was no small feat, as anyone who
has worked in a hypergrowth atmosphere can attest. Sun
management never let chaos prevail, although confusion
about where to put everyone did emerge from time to time.

SPACE WARS

By locating primarily in the northern fringes of Silicon Valley—away from the traffic, congestion, and other such hassles
of San Jose and the Valley's core—Sun doomed itself to pay
premium rents. As the number of employees ballooned, so
did the number of buildings Sun had to occupy. So fast was
the company acquiring buildings that a developer who was
tilting them up like mushrooms erected a building shell near
the headquarters building without properly filing an environmental impact report. The vacant shell of Building 8 sat
for months, presiding over a landscape strewn with the detri-
tus of a construction project halted midway through completion. Rumors abounded that the developer would have to tear
down the building and restore the site to its original condition. The hulking shell seemed to symbolize Sun's real-estate
dilemmas. As the building remained unoccupied, Sun had to
scout around for alternative sites for the influx of new employees.

Proposals to move most Mountain View employees to
either Milpitas or San Jose met such strong employee resis-

tance that they were abandoned. Instead, Sun bought a large nearby building from Ford Aerospace and eighty-seven vacant acres in Newark, California, a few miles north of Milpitas. Later the company announced plans to explore the prospects of developing a site in East Palo Alto, just north of Mountain View.

About the same time that Sun announced purchase of the Ford building, the company also revealed plans to take some of its manufacturing operations offshore—to the "Silicon Glen" area of Scotland. This move may have seemed odd, coming as it did from a company that boasted a "made in America" way of doing business. As Sun grew, however, an increasing amount of its business came from foreign markets. By 1989 more than 50 percent of Sun sales were outside the United States, with the Pacific Rim countries representing the fastest-growing segment of the non-U.S. market.

Sun was fast becoming a large international corporation, for which a manufacturing facility outside the United States made sense, particularly with the advent of a unified European market in 1992. The European market for Sun products was voracious enough to warrant the Scottish plant, and growth in the Pacific Rim suggested that a plant in that part of the world might be in the offing.

Closely related to Sun's need for corporate real estate was its unrelenting need for personal real estate. Even engineers, those highly prized individuals of a technology-driven company such as Sun, were sometimes forced to double up in small—drab, in the case of some of the older buildings—offices. Managerial dictums attempted to keep people as happy as possible under the cramped conditions, but as often as not, creative anarchy was the method by which people found solutions to the lack of space.

Managers bartered, made back-room deals with each other, and employed a form of eminent domain to get and retain office space for their people. Cubicles appeared where boulevard corridors once ran. Conference rooms disappeared, cut up into small offices. For the most part, McNealy and Lacroute allowed their vice presidents to outmaneuver each other in acquiring real estate for their workers. Sometimes one manager might cry foul over another's "stealing" of a suite of offices, but mostly managers plotted new ploys of their own to gain floor space.

Everyone expected relief when the Ford building metamorphosed into a Sun structure, but no one expected the relief to be long-lived. Space wars are a fact of life in startups and companies experiencing hypergrowth. Perhaps when Sun has settled into a stable, mature corporate existence, all employees will have their own office. Until then, resourcefulness is almost as important as rank in determining who gets the plum spots.

PREVENTING THE "OSBORNE SYNDROME"

Sun took a lesson from Osborne. After two years of existence, Sun was exhibiting controlled hypergrowth. Its second generation of products was well established, and a third was well under development. Cost controls were strict—cofounder Khosla was jokingly reputed to have to sign off on the purchase of even a box of pencils. The pace of hiring was fast, but not frantic; whereas Osborne had staffed up almost reflexively, most Sun managers spent a lot of time looking for the best and the brightest, as well as those willing to work incredible numbers of hours to make the company—and themselves—successful. Hiring freezes were not uncommon when management was the least bit concerned that the revenue stream might abate. One side effect of hiring freezes was that existing staff had to work all the harder to get more accomplished. Having people who worked extremely hard— to say nothing of smart—was one of the factors behind the singular success of Sun's hypergrowth.

Successful startups are particularly susceptible to the problem of cost control. Flush with venture capital and initially successful, a company can easily become overconfident—even cocky—and squander its resources and early advantages. Sun established a strategy for internal management that any fast-growing company can adopt.

Capitalization. Sun was never an undercapitalized venture. From the beginning its investors understood the importance of keeping Sun's economic engine roaring. The acquiring market share strategy meant the rapid incorporation of manufacturing space, which necessitated huge capital outlays. Over the years, Sun received various infusions of cash. In January 1984, for example, First National Bank of Boston extended an $11.5 million credit line, adding to the $4.2 million equity financing Sun had received at its founding in 1982. Later that year, when Sun had used up that money, the Bank of Boston added another $27 million to the growing company's capital pie.

These occasional placements continued through the years, growing each time to reflect Sun's need for cash. The biggest cash deal, of course, was the January 1988 agreement with AT&T, which totaled $300 million over a three-year period. In the summer of 1989, Sun picked up another $140 million in credit for developing real estate. Seldom did Sun suffer for lack of an ample bank account despite its ravenous need for cash. This meant that the company could adhere to a growth strategy that would pay off handsomely down the road.

Hiring. Out-of-control hiring brings with it the possibility of layoffs in the event of a slowdown, and layoffs are endemic in the volatile computer industry. Layoffs are demoralizing to a company. Key people get worried and leave along with those of less importance. Even avoiding layoffs can be debilitating to employees. Hewlett-Packard, a huge, mature company, boasts a no-layoff policy; but when the company was experiencing tough times in 1986–87, the no-layoff solution was to encourage early retirements and enforce a company-wide 10 percent pay cut and an unpaid-vacation policy.

To a company in the throes of hypergrowth, hiring smart is crucial. Hypergrowth companies, unlike established giants, can ill afford deadwood and inertia in the ranks. Even with good hiring controls, a hypergrowth company has to add people at a furious rate to keep up with its own success. The volume of work always surpasses the number of new bodies, however, thus introducing the possibility of job burnout.

Sun withstood its various cash-flow crises by keeping its staff to a minimum. Sun had the highest revenue-per-employee statistic in Silicon Valley, better than that of any of the competition. To accomplish this feat, management brought on contractors and temporary employees to handle specific projects. At times, these projects would become full-time programs, and the contractors or temporaries would be offered full employment—but only after Sun had determined the importance of the work involved and those doing it. This technique saved the company millions of dollars as it avoided investing in programs that could have backfired and people who failed to measure up. The hiring pace got out of control in the first half of 1989, but the sobering view of the company's first quarterly loss in the middle of the year put the brakes on hiring for several months.

Physical plant. A growing company needs increasing amounts of space. As mentioned above, Sun distributed its operations. By doing so, it was able to save money by expanding rapidly in less expensive areas and to attract top talent that demanded a better, more costly environment.

Security and leaks. Laxity about security is a risk among startups and rising-star companies. Hours tend to be flexible, and people are constantly coming and going, so security violations are a risk. Add to this an open, "hacker" mentality, and Sun had to be on guard against leaks of confidential information. Yet Sun was able to maintain a good balance between freedom of information and employee paranoia. By and large, employees were stockholders, which meant it was consistently in their own best interest to protect Sun's proprietary information. At the same time, Sun's own managers were most often the guilty parties in spilling the beans.

Vaporware. All computer companies preannounce products; preannouncement is SOP. Announcing products before they are actually ready—whetting your customers' appetites and then leaving them unfulfilled for too long—can have consequences that range from the problematic to the catastrophic.

The extreme case results in a crash-and-burn, as happened with Osborne. The effects need not be cataclysmic, but they can be costly.

Some fairly recent examples of premature product announcements were the latest revision of Lotus Development Corporation's famous 1-2-3 spreadsheet, the latest update of Ashton-Tate's equally well-known dBASE database program, and revisions of word-processsing programs from software giant Microsoft. Lotus missed its product-delivery deadline by eighteen months. Ashton-Tate had to announce two delays for dBASE IV, and Microsoft got behind schedule on its programs. In just one day, Microsoft's founder, Bill Gates—who holds 35 percent of the company's stock—lost $174 million on paper.

Bureaucracy. Given Sun's freewheeling and open nature, the company was able to maintain fairly good control of people and operations without degenerating into dreary authoritarian bureaucracy. Even as revenues grew into the hundreds of millions and the employee roster increased to the tens of hundreds, Sun managed to rocket ahead without creating a morass of middle management to interfere with the expansion. (By 1989 that situation had begun to change somewhat. See chapter 9 for details.)

Entrepreneurs. Although increasing bureaucracy in day-to-day operations is an inevitable by-product of growth, one of Sun's most important qualities, entrepreneurism (or strictly speaking, intrapreneurism), has continued to play a part. Frequently, innovation has little place in a Fortune 500 corporate juggernaut, where stasis and inertia may have become part of the corporate culture. In the mid to late 1980s, though hardly in the juggernaut category, Sun was growing at an incredible rate—yet it nonetheless managed to keep innovation and alacrity in the vanguard.

An example of entrepreneurial fruition was the SPARCstation 1 computer, the brainchild of Sun cofounder Andy Bechtolsheim. Five or so years after Sun's birth, Bechtolsheim was looking for a new challenge. His idea was to develop a small, fast, inexpensive computer targeted at the education market. Bechtolsheim and others knew that the secretive NeXT, Inc.—started by Apple cofounder Steve Jobs—was working on an "education machine," and that was doubtless part of Bechtolsheim's motivation.

Initially, he planned to spin off a separate company, largely subsidized by Sun, to develop the machine. But after Sun formed its Education Products Division, the merger of Bechtolsheim's project with the division made sense. The machine's developer, however, worked autonomously, relatively unencumbered by divisional imperatives; with his small team he rolled out a 12.5-MIPS desktop workstation about a year and a half after the project was first conceived.

Outside the company, Sun encouraged entrepreneurism among third-party software and hardware vendors. It underwrote some of the costs an established and successful vendor incurred when porting its products to Sun workstations. It promoted third-party products tirelessly to Sun workstation users by funding a magazine, publishing an extensive third-party catalog, producing mutual data sheets, and developing co-op advertising in vertical as well as horizontal markets.

Sun's steady, diverse, and well-managed third-party program is an unqualified success. It encompasses a broad spectrum of groups within the company, so support for it is widespread. Two third-party groups in marketing are Strategic Industry Partners Program (SIPP) and Catalyst. Other departments also contribute heavily to third-party success. The online *Software Technical Bulletin*, for example, gives software developers quick and easy access to operating system patches and software bug fixes. Engineering holds regular brainstorming sessions for third-party vendors at no cost. Two-way communication between software companies and Sun persists throughout a workstation's development. Many of these programs are controlled directly by their managers, with virtually no interference by upper management—a condition that encourages a sense of autonomy and responsibility among the project's principals.

Sun's executives did not take on these expenses because

they saw themselves as part-time venture capitalists, seeding the creativity of others. They did so because, as Paul Freiberger wrote, "Software is crucial for a new computer. Lack of it dooms it." They understood that to succeed, their products needed the ingenuity of more minds than their own.

This kind of "creative anarchy" is in line with McNealy's dictum: "To ask permission is to seek denial." This is not to suggest, however, that upper management took a laissez-faire attitude to every proposed project that fell outside official company plans. Some were conducted, until their widespread discovery, virtually in secret. At the point management did learn of them, it had to perceive a benefit to the bottom line, and most, if not all, of these projects were conservatively underwritten.

Search for quality. In Sun's early days it shipped an uncomfortably large number of systems that were DOA (dead on arrival). Understandably, product quality became a key concern of management. Before long, though, that concern transcended the assembly line. Sun formed a company-wide quality department, complete with a vice president reporting to McNealy. Soon, quality was an obsession in search of a definition. Every employee was required to take a "quality class" to attain some vaguely defined certification. The work paid off mostly in manufacturing. Sun instituted an extensive supplier-qualification program before signing any new vendors. It invested heavily in automated test equipment and dramatically increased the number and regularity of employee-training hours.

Diversification of products. Even though Sun was clearly a maker of systems for technical professionals, it offered a variety of products to its users. This diversity gave it a good balance and mix of technology for the engineers, scientists, and others who depended on high-powered desktop machines. It gave the company multiple revenue streams and margins, making the organization more flexible in handling differing computer requirements. It also made Sun's products appealing to a broader range of customers.

Despite Sun's incorporation of these and other techniques

for managing hypergrowth, it stumbled into an occasional wall. Most of these problems, however, did not affect growth or the bottom line. But in the fourth quarter of fiscal 1989, Sun ran up against its greatest crisis immediately after unveiling its latest and most extensive product line, one that would eventually supersede everything else Sun had offered the workstation market.

THE NEW WORLD OF PROBLEMS

"Welcome to the New World," proclaimed the banner on the vaulted entrance to San Francisco's Civic Auditorium. Aside from the banners, the auditorium's exterior presented its usual municipal-monolith charm. Inside, however, the drab institutional paint that could as well have graced a city detox center had been replaced by trendy pastels; potted palms dotted once-neglected alcoves. It was indeed a new world.

Sun was putting on its biggest, splashiest, most expensive product introduction to date. Company honchos Scott McNealy, Andy Bechtolsheim, Bill Joy, and Bernie Lacroute made the presentations in front of a crowd of press people, analysts, customers, and employees. Five hundred people filled the large room.

McNealy was "on," self-assured and cracking jokes. He pointed out that magazine and newspaper columnist John C. Dvorak had once likened Sun intros to product rollouts by vacuum cleaner companies. "We hope this will be different," McNealy quipped. He also hoped that all the real-time demos that flashed onto huge video screens behind him would work.

A question-and-answer session with press and analysts produced an attendance of about a hundred. When asked by a reporter about the HP purchase of Apollo, McNealy responded, "I guess it's a merger of one company that couldn't make it [in the workstation business] with one that's trying to." The brash, boyish president also made his obligatory reference to "insurmountable opportunities."

With its ever-broadening and diversified product lines,

Sun signaled that it was not content to remain strictly a workstation vendor. At the splashy 1989 product announcement, McNealy reiterated this position. "With this announcement," he stated, "Sun is showing that it's more than just a workstation company." McNealy noted that Sun saw SPARC and RISC as the computing wave of the future. The company, he believed, had to continue to grow in order to enter the 1990s as a major computer company—which it had every intention of doing.

Any institution develops an outlook, a culture. The group culture in, say, the classics department of a university is bound to be different from that in a new computer company. One is cerebral, methodical, steeped in tradition. The other, riding the waves in what is a mercurial business under any circumstances, is virtually inventing itself as it goes along. A company that invents itself as it grows exponentially is subject to a great deal of stress. As a piece of Sun marketing material once put it, "the Silicon Valley landscape is littered with success stories" that failed.

Although not coming close to failure, Sun faced its biggest hurdle ever immediately after the "Welcome to the New World" introduction. The culture of hypergrowth suddenly faced the incredible: a period *without* a minimum 20 to 30 percent growth from quarter to quarter.

The upheaval in the spring and summer of 1989 did not shake McNealy's belief in the primacy of acquiring market share. He still maintained that hypergrowth was a prerequisite for a computer company's survival in the 1990s. Amid the flurry in the press about Sun's possible financial loss and executive departures (most recently, Executive Vice President Bernie Lacroute and Chief Financial Officer Joe Graziano), Sun underscored its growth-at-all-costs philosophy by announcing a major agreement between itself and two Taiwan-based computer manufacturers.

According to the agreement, Datatech Enterprises and Tatung Company promised to build SPARC-based clones of Sun workstations. The deal was significant because it meant dramatically less expensive systems would soon be flooding the workstation market, creating significant opportunities for software companies, which, in the "software sells computers" cycle, would unleash the pent-up demand for high-performance workstations among general business users. This scenario scared the likes of MS-DOS- and PC-dependent vendors—so much so, that Bill Gates, Microsoft's top executive, flew to Taiwan to plead with another clone maker to stick with Microsoft's DOS-based products and shun Sun's UNIX systems. Two days before its Taiwan announcement, Sun revealed that it had established a distribution agreement with a ComputerLand franchise in Phoenix. Despite this franchise's predominant focus on direct sales to corporate clients, the simple fact that a retail outlet would consider selling UNIX-based workstations gave observers pause.

The *hyper* in *hypergrowth* can mean excess or exaggeration in a negative as well as a positive sense. In the case of Osborne, the negative prevailed. With Sun, so far, it has been overwhelmingly positive.

It was clear that even while struggling with the biggest dilemma of Sun's young corporate life, its managers were intent on following the same strategic path that had led it to its current position. The ingrained fiscal conservatism that McNealy imbued in his officers caused a ripple effect throughout the company. Everyone was charged with shaving pennies from their individual bottom lines.

8
Working in a Revved Engine

Dennis Wolf began at Sun in the financial department in late 1987, initiating the company's first formal forecasting group, and he reported to Joe Graziano, the chief financial officer at that time. As with many new "groups" at Sun, Wolf comprised the entire staff and management team.

Wolf's charter was to predict the sales of Sun's complex product line by units and revenues. Working with market research reports, competitive analyses, and common sense, he was to anticipate trends, shifts, and possible disasters. His task was further complicated by the constant introduction of new systems, the phasing out of old ones, and the company's baroque pricing and discount policies. He was responsible for getting accurate historical revenue information by discrete product line so management could predict such things as manufacturing requirements, gross sales, and profits. When he found time, Wolf had to interview, hire, and train his as-yet fictitious support staff. In the process, the new Sun employee needed to learn where the information resided, who managed it, how valid it was, and what analytical tools the company provided—as well as uncover the secrets of

UNIX in order to write simple reports and to communicate
via electronic mail with his managers and his peers. And by
the way, he was asked, when did he think he could deliver his
first report?

Wolf, a good-humored individual who takes his work seriously, flinched at the size of his assignment, but he did not
hesitate to throw himself into the work. As the days passed,
he understood that the data he needed to build an accurate
forecast for the company was dispersed and unreliable. New
data-collection systems were crucial to meet management's
demand for a more refined forecasting model. He knew what
the company had to do to get there. That information, in fact,
made up his first report, which he completed in two weeks.
In the meantime, Wolf hired one other member for the forecasting department, which soon moved from the financial
department to corporate marketing, under Ed Zander.

In the spring of 1988, Zander's Tuesday-morning staff
meetings were noisy affairs. Everyone was demanding increased headcount and more money for their projects, while
management was complaining to Zander that he had too
many people and spent more than his budget called for. Still,
Zander pushed his people to hire talented individuals in
severely understaffed areas, such as Wolf's, while juggling
headcount with temps and contractors elsewhere and regularly pleading with management to loosen their strict control
on the budget and manpower limits.

One Tuesday that spring, Wolf announced that a new
forecast analyst, his second, had started the day before. The
fellow was a highly qualified individual from a Fortune 500
company. He held an M.B.A. and an undergraduate degree
in financial planning. He was experienced, bright, and ready
to work. This was good news to Zander, because Wolf's
analyses were seen as increasingly noteworthy in executive
staff conclaves. The next Tuesday, Wolf brought a hiring
requisition form to the staff meeting for Zander to sign.

"What's this?" Zander asked, his voice raised a decibel or
two above normal conversational tones. "You just got some-
body."

Wolf said, "It's a replacement. The new guy left."

"What?"

Wolf was almost laughing. He explained that the new employee had arrived a week ago Monday and spent most of the day in employee orientation, a half-day affair that Sun's human resources department requires of all rookies on staff. The rest of the afternoon, Wolf familiarized the man with his office and the Sun campus and explained, as best he could, the UNIX system. It was a typical, relaxed first day on the job. After Zander's staff meeting the past Tuesday, at which Wolf had announced his new hire, Wolf spent the afternoon with his new employee, describing in detail the work that lay ahead. Nothing had actually been done, but the scale of the job had been fully delineated.

The next day, Wednesday, the man resigned. He told Wolf that never in his career had he seen so much work before him with so little staff to accomplish it. He complained about the utter lack of support tools, the difficulties of UNIX, and the unbelievable absence of administrative staff. He pointed out that other Fortune 500 firms had lots of help below analysts: secretaries, clerks, and such. Sun had none of these. He could not understand how Wolf expected him to accomplish what he had been assigned to do. He told Wolf that working in such a frantic place was tantamount to suicide.

When Wolf explained this to Zander and his staff, everyone laughed. It reaffirmed what they already knew: Sun was not just a job but, as the U.S. Navy recruitment advertising puts it, an adventure.

"This company is not for the faint of heart," Zander said as he signed Wolf's requisition for a replacement.

SWEATSHOP IN A HOUSING PROJECT?

White-collar working conditions hardly bring tears to the eyes of even the most empathetic person. Highly paid, well-fed, nicely coiffed and dressed, today's professional works in an environment far different from the workplace of the Industrial Revolution's factory, or even the nineteenth-century office sweatshops described by Herman Melville in his classic story "Bartleby the Scrivener." By the standards of most Fortune 500 companies, however, Sun's office workers, especially managers, are driven to extremes while deprived of many amenities. In his parody of work life inside Silicon Valley companies, Michael Malone ribbed Sun as one of the firms that had, among other things, "80-hour workweeks. . . . Full parking lots at lunchtime. Sunday morning meetings." One Valley wag observed that Sun is such an intense place to work that "you lose weight just standing in the lobby."

Any fast-growing company always confronts more things to do than there are people to do them. Job descriptions become almost meaningless as tasks cannot wait for the "right" person. Department switching is not uncommon. Longer-term employees may have had four or five different jobs and worked in as many or more different buildings or offices. Volunteering is often the sole qualification necessary for taking on a job. At Sun, where fast growth is an understatement, this situation holds true from top to bottom. An extreme example, but only one, is Chief Financial Officer Bob Smith's decision to join workers on the loading dock to help ship Sun-2 workstations at the end of a quarter in late 1982. Since Sun counts only shipped units as revenue, the portly CFO's action was an important contribution to the bottom line. Almost every small company, as Sun was at that time, has such "executive in action" stories. But Sun adds something else that is rare even in small companies and virtually nonexistent in billion-dollar ones: management self-reliance.

The man who lasted three days in Dennis Wolf's forecasting group was unnerved by the colossal scope of his assignment, and more important, he was also aghast at the lack of even the prospect of any support from clerical or administrative staff. At Sun, clerks, secretaries, and administrators are nearly as scarce as tennis shoes and sweatshirts at an IBM executive meeting. Your workstation is your administrator. And if you lack experience in UNIX or are reluctant to learn, your "administrator" can be your worst enemy.

In many big companies, executive secretaries have their own staff to assist in the work that flows from the CEO's or the chairman's office. Very often this is true for vice presidents as well. Directors usually have a secretary and a clerk at their disposal, and managers are given an administrator to help them with their jobs. Such staff support is common, even expected.

At Sun, until 1987, McNealy and Lacroute, who held the combined offices of CEO, chairman, president, company general manager, and executive vice president, shared one good-humored administrator. The two men wrote most of their own memos, communicated directly with their line officers via electronic mail, and took many of their own calls directly. This approach did not go unnoticed by the rest of management and permeated the company. At best, vice presidents each have one administrator dedicated to them, and some have none at all. Directors usually have administrative help assigned to them, but they generally share that person's time with others on their staff. Each department at Sun is staffed with an administrator, and managers must share that person's time, which is next to impossible in view of the number of people each administrator assists. Managers who are used to buzzing a secretary for every little whim had better get used to getting their own coffee, opening their own mail, and standing in line at the photocopier, or they will founder at Sun.

Many executive perks that are commonplace in companies the size of Sun and smaller do not exist. Executives have no special parking places; they have to look for a spot along with everyone else in the increasingly cramped lots that symbolize a growing company. (Frequently they don't have to look too hard, though, because they often arrive at work before the majority of their troops pull in—and often stay later.) Sun has no executive washrooms. Although their offices are relatively spacious, executives get no polished mahogany desks and other such trappings.

Another aspect of working in an expanding organization is

cramped quarters. Sun cannot occupy buildings fast enough.
Of course it can pay near-extortionist rents to local realtors
who are well aware of Sun's space problems, but the fiscal
conservatism of management shuns that kind of solution. As
a result, "space wars" is an ongoing feature of life in Sun
Microsystems.

Sun is spread throughout Silicon Valley, with most of it
centered around its corporate headquarters near Shoreline
Park in Mountain View, at the southern end of the San
Francisco Bay. It leases twenty or so buildings in the area.
The next-largest concentration of buildings is in Milpitas,
just around the terminus of the bay, about fifteen miles to the
southeast.

In Milpitas the rents are considerably lower, so in 1987,
with space at a premium and a minimum in Mountain View,
management concluded that a move to Milpitas was logical.
To inform their decision, they commissioned studies to determine the driving patterns of employees. Rumors scampered
through the Mountain View campus for weeks as management studied the possibilities, and the consensus in the
rumor mill was that the majority of the people wanted to stay
in Mountain View. Some departments officially petitioned
their vice president to express their displeasure at the
thought of changing locations. There was even a meeting in
the cafeteria between McNealy and the entire engineering
department on the matter. Eventually, management dropped
the idea of a wholesale move to Milpitas and began moving
only those departments whose tasks were suited for groups
already located there, such as customer support, manufacturing, and the Sun federal division.

Another story making the rounds was that management
wanted to move a major portion of the company to a giant
building in north San Jose—one of the most gridlocked areas
of the Valley—that had once housed the phenomenally successful computer-game company Atari. A move to San Jose
would have been about as popular as one to Milpitas, and
neither happened.

Meanwhile, Sun continued to pay a premium for its leases,

but it deemed the monetary sacrifice worth it to retain its
Mountain View–based engineers and marketers. The cost of
leases, though, was putting serious pressure on Sun's already
tight margins. The solution to paying big rents for lots of real
estate was for Sun to buy its own. So the company purchased
a five-story, 232,800-square-foot building from Ford Aerospace. The Ford complex was located in Palo Alto, less than
a mile from the Mountain View hub and accessible from the
same exit ramp off Highway 101.

Sun paid $35 million for the building; remodeling it to
specifications would cost more. In buying the building,
though, the company was able to extract two thousand employees from rented space. Furthermore, with no apparent
end to the escalating real-estate prices in the Bay Area, Sun
had made itself a fairly sound investment that was sure to
appreciate each year. In February 1989, Sun announced that
it had entered into an agreement for the purchase of eighty-
seven acres of land in an embryonic technical park in Newark—just across the bay but far enough away from the
clogged Milpitas area to make a sane commute conceivable.
Sun also proposed to the East Palo Alto City Council that the
company buy property there, possibly establishing the corporate headquarters in the city just up the road from its current
location. In June the East Palo Alto City Council gave Sun
first rights to develop a 170-acre site in the city if the city
decided to go ahead with development of the area.

These moves were long-term strategic actions and did not
solve immediate requirements. The Ford building needed
major renovation and would not be occupied until at least a
year after its acquisition. The Newark land was just that: a
flat, empty expanse of dirt. The company was still adding
staff, sometimes more than two hundred people a month.
Space wars persisted as a problem and, so some claimed, hurt
employee productivity and morale. Vice presidents staked out
their territory and were reluctant to give up their share to
other departments.

In one executive staff meeting, run by Lacroute, Facilities
Director Klaus Kramer (now a vice president) and his team

came under fire for the space plan they had submitted, which
proposed that the company adopt cubicles instead of the
widely used walled offices. Wayne Rosing, vice president of
Sun's entry systems group, doubted the advantages of cubicles over walled spaces. "People would rather double up in an
office than be in the wide-open spaces," he grumbled. The
graphics division vice president, Bernard Peuto, added his
protest against partitions. Marketing, sales, and other departments chimed in with their objections to breaking down the
walls. And then Eric Schmidt, the executive in charge of the
general systems group, discovered an error in the report's
math, invalidating the proposal's claim that it would alleviate
overcrowding. The facilities group was sent back to its drawing boards.

By mid-1989 office space was at a premium. In Building 6,
the corporate headquarters, half the conference rooms were
turned into offices, forcing many executives to hold meetings
in the cafeteria when the few other rooms were booked. In
blind hallways temporary workers and contractors were given
tables and chairs at which to work. Engineers worked two,
sometimes three to an office originally designed for one
person.

It was little wonder, then, that employees complained. Not
only were they expected to do their own administrative and
clerical work, but they were also forced to do it in crowded,
hectic conditions. In Malone's satire of the Silicon Valley
workplace, he sketches a futuristic exchange between a
teacher and a student. The student is bewildered by the
austerity and the rigor of life in high-technology companies
like Sun. "But why," he asks, "did people stay?"

There are innumerable reasons why people work, why they
remain at a company, and why they leave one. All the moti-
vations of money, security, opportunity, success, dependence,
inertia, routine, and good or bad fortune affected Sun's staff,
just as they do in any other organization. But they were by no
means the most important reasons why people put in marathon hours. They did not account for the tolerance of the lack
of amenities. The majority of Sun's employees were not

lackluster people, no-talents happy to have any job. These were some of the best people available in Silicon Valley and the entire computer industry. Outsiders, especially those with comfortable positions in other Fortune 500 firms, questioned why such bright people put up with the pressures of such a fast-growing company in such relative austerity. They could get better treatment elsewhere. What did Sun have that attracted them and kept them? they wondered.

To say, as the *Los Angeles Times* did, that "Sun is generally an intense company populated by workaholics who routinely spend 75 hours or more a week on the job" does not make the company seem attractive to prospective employees. Yet, as the Southern California newspaper grudgingly admitted, "Sun is considered one of the glamorous places to work in Silicon Valley." The company did, of course, offer generous stock options to its employees before it became a publicly held concern. Its salaries, although not at the top of the region's scale, were competitive. It was a stable company, with consistent, though not spectacular, profits. Sun appeared to be in for the long haul, a place where people could build a career. But again, these considerations were mere basics and not exclusive to Sun. Something else kept intelligent, overworked people laboring close to the bone and spurred thousands of others to clamor at Sun's door to join in the frenzy.

Sun tapped more than the human impulse of greed or the need for security. Working there was inspired by less-prosaic, hard-to-measure influences. It was the "senses" of Sun that infused its staff with enthusiasm. Sun engendered a sense of mission among its people. It was on a technological crusade. Sun projected a sense of urgency. Things were happening now; immediacy was paramount. Sun reeked of ambition. Nothing was too tough, too outlandish to try. It fostered a sense of self-control. Individuals had more than a voice; they had influence. Underscoring everything was a sense of humor. Sun's people discovered that success, even occasional failure, can be fun.

These senses permeated the entire organization, if not each

individual. They made it possible for Sun to sustain break-neck growth rates and become a major force in the computer industry—not simply from a revenue perspective, but also as a viable leader in the intellectual ferment of computer science and technology. Without these influences Sun would be an interesting story; with them it is a compelling one.

THE SENSE OF MISSION

As discussed in earlier chapters, Sun is an engineering-driven, technology-obsessed company. Underpinning this technology in the minds of its engineers and their disciples is the UNIX operating system. UNIX, as noted in chapter 4, carries religious, almost cultlike qualities with it. People at Sun believe in the value of UNIX, its superior and liberating qualities for computer users. Even the most cynical at Sun see UNIX as a powerful underdog with decades of potential. Its modest share of the installed base of operating systems notwithstanding, UNIX "has become a standard, despite squabbling"—a fact that underscores the fervor with which its supporters, particularly those at Sun, have proselytized in the industry.

Sun's position as the leading UNIX company in the indus-try gave it a unique identity early on. Its founders spoke confidently of their operating system's being an industry standard when hardly anyone else used it; when only special-ized applications software existed for it; when there were so many versions of it that it was impossible to tell which UNIX was the real UNIX.

This obscurity and confusion did not daunt Sun's sense of mission. If anything, it fueled it. It made Sun more adamant about UNIX and its future. Most people at Sun did more than join a company; they signed up for a crusade. They were willing to sacrifice for its sake because they adhered to the value system that was concomitant with UNIX—open, pow-erful, distributed systems on the desktops of everyone in an organization, possibly the world. This was the true destiny of computer technology, and their mission was to help bring it about. They wanted to liberate computers from the "high priests" and the men in white coats. If they had to eschew immediate satisfaction for the long-term cause, so be it. As Bill Joy remarked, "We want to make UNIX more successful. It's kind of an altruistic goal."

Much as the Christians of pagan Rome had huddled in the catacombs of the Empire's capital, UNIX devotees began as an underground movement inside the computer industry. They created their own network and shared information freely, in complete contrast with existing approaches fostered by computer leaders such as DEC and IBM. The idea of the proprietary operating system meant more than being restricted to one company. It meant restricted in capabilities and advantages to users. Sun's employees rebelled against this notion.

In a review of this strategy, the youthfulness of Sun cannot be ignored. Nearly every commentator on Sun's early years remarked about how young its founders had been. The majority of the company's first employees were, like the founders, in their twenties, emerging straight from universities, unaccustomed to the perks of business life, content with overcrowding and bare-bones support staff.

Youth is, of course, the best time for idealism. The energy is available to push hard for goals that more-seasoned individuals might shirk. It is not surprising, then, that few doubted Sun's chances of making UNIX an industry standard. Skepticism about unifying such a dispersed operating system was held in check. Establishing a Fortune 500 company built on an operating system that was essentially available to the world did not daunt the workers. In fact, it spurred them to strive for something at the very farthest extent of their grasp. It has become part of the heritage at Sun never to do the expected, easy thing, if a more ambitious and unconventional possibility has a chance of success.

Sun's sense of mission forces it to work closely with its customers. As with any converts, the slightest dissatisfaction with a newly adopted creed can send them reeling back into their old habits, ones that meant buying DEC and IBM products. Sun's technical staff conspires with its customer peer group to refine existing products and define new ones. This approach is not unique to Sun, of course. Every computer company confers with its customers. Few are as good at it as IBM and DEC, in fact. The difference is that Sun infiltrated the IBM and DEC establishments, changing the hearts and minds of users, getting them to accept the Sun credo of open systems. Once that happened, customers felt part of a great awakening in the computer industry and contributed freely to Sun's technical team. Sun's customers, in effect, became part of the conspiracy to undermine proprietary technology. They helped Sun because they knew if Sun were successful, they'd have choices that went far beyond Sun Microsystems itself. That kind of opportunity appealed to more than their sense of altruism; it appealed to their self-interest.

The Sense of Urgency

Few billion-dollar companies were, from their inception, intended to operate in hypergrowth mode, or what some have called the "acceleration syndrome." Sun armed its entire staff of white-collar workers and most of its blue-collar ones with computers or computer terminals. Executives were expected to be well-versed in electronic mail. At Sun, the latest communication technology is almost immediately installed and put to use. Facsimile documents, already a quick way to exchange paperwork, are flashed to recipients at Sun over the network to their workstations, so they don't even have to wait for the hard copy to be delivered to their in baskets. Courier services between buildings, cities, states, and countries are constantly employed.

This technology of timeliness fuels Sun's sense of urgency. People are impatient for responses. They get an idea, send it via e-mail to someone, and expect to receive an almost-immediate reply. One simple UNIX program developed at Sun is called answermail. With it, people who leave on business trips or (rarely) vacations can have their computer respond to the sender with a detailed message. It is a form of politeness for the age of the acceleration syndrome, a phone-machine message for workstations. Some people are so engrossed in the immediacy their systems give them that they actually use answermail when they take off for an afternoon, a long meeting, even lunch.

Time waits for no one and nothing at Sun. This axiom is rooted in the Sun culture. Before the bulky and rather unattractive Sun-1 workstation hit the market in 1982, Sun engineers were well under way on the Sun-2 computer. In fact, just after shipments of the Sun-1 began, there was a pressing need to unleash its successor. Although the Sun-1's lackluster appearance validates the notion that engineers are concerned with function over form, looks alone did not make the Sun-1 immediately replaceable.

The Sun-1 used the Motorola 68000 microprocessor. In 1982 Motorola was releasing its next-generation 32-bit chip, the MC68010. Companies that had incorporated the MC68000 rushed to get their hands on the limited production of the follow-on microprocessor. As is still the case today, established customers were served first, especially those with large orders. Sun, at the time, was new, small, and virtually unknown outside the UNIX community. It got in line with other companies waiting for the delivery of chips, while its larger, more-established competitors—such as Apollo, which used the same Motorola processor—built fast workstations and got them to market quicker.

The Sun-1 was a limited-production-run machine; just over a hundred of the company's first systems left the loading dock. Scott McNealy was director of manufacturing at the time of the launch of the Sun-2, which was to be the first large-scale production effort by Sun. Synchronizing the development of a new computer in engineering with the creation of mass production at Sun instilled a sense of urgency in the company's culture that has never changed.

Sun's young managers and engineers knew that they had only one chance to get it right. If they fumbled the design of the Sun-2, failed to improve its looks, or blew the assembly process, the market was not going to be forgiving. The best UNIX operating system in the world would not compensate for an inadequate workstation. Besides, the competition was clearly out in front. Apollo was proving itself to be a technological leader, attracting key OEM deals and delivering impressive, if somewhat pricey, machines. Sun managers knew their products could compete on price, but being cheaper did not make a company successful. Content was essential, and they had only one chance to deliver it.

By the standards of today, the Sun-2 announcement was modest, almost a whisper amid the normal ballyhoo of new-product introductions. Sun's few customers were invited to see it, and some trade-press reporters got a look at the computer. Shipments followed thirty days after the introduction. Although not without hitches, the coordination between manufacturing and engineering went smoothly. Production of Sun-2s began only a few days behind schedule. Engineering changes were kept to a minimum. And as described in chapter 3, this workstation made Sun a credible force in the industry. With it, Apollo felt its first real challenge.

The successful launch, however, did not dispel the sense of urgency it had created. High technology never hesitates, never stands still. Motorola was already discussing its plans for a faster microprocessor, the MC68020, that eventually powered the Sun-3 series as well as Apollo's machines of the mid-1980s. But Apollo had the jump on Sun once again, getting its MC68020-based products to market first. McNealy, who was then president and CEO, pressed hard on Bernie Lacroute to get the new Sun computer into customers' hands. By falling behind Apollo in new-product availability, Sun was losing the time-to-market race, one that McNealy wanted desperately to win.

Time-to-market philosophy dictates that a company release its products to the world before the competition does. It pressures an entire organization to unleash all its resources toward a single, common goal. The time-to-market mentality assumes that if you're first off the mark, you'll have the advantage to be the first to finish the race. Sun's long-term success against Apollo and other competitors that reached workstation customers prior to Sun belies that attitude. Because it had been so successful in leaping into the fray second or third with its offerings, Sun could have logically rejected time-to-market tactics. But that is not the case.

Sun's management contends that a time-to-market philosophy keeps the company at the top of its industry. Of course, management admits that Sun is not always first with a given technology, but it has to strive to be first out of the gate every time. Time-to-market success reinforces the perception of technology leadership and effective research-and-development activities. It sets the trends for others to mimic. It also brings in revenue quickly. To accept anything less undermines the company's future.

The Sun-3 development and introduction solidified the constant sense of urgency in the company. What had been a tendency became a corporate cultural trait, one that persistently propelled the organization beyond expectations and pushed some people out the door because they were unable to withstand the unrelenting urgency in daily work life. Everything became vital, whether it was designing a critical component for a workstation or developing a nomenclature for it.

For people with low tolerance for stress, Sun was an especially demanding environment. Others, however, thrived in it. The tension and the importance surrounding each task, no matter how apparently trivial, imbued everyone with not only a constant sense of urgency but also a sense of the importance of each element in the development of the whole. Employees knew that if their work was unsatisfactory, they jeopardized the success of the product. Peer pressure to succeed was as strong as, or stronger than, the push from above. The positive aspect of this mentality was that both success and failure were distributed. Every individual felt involved in the corporate *Angst und Sturm*. When the company won, the individual wore the laurels. The downside was the unrelenting anxiety.

The Sun-3 workstation was unveiled to customers in September 1985 at a small hotel in Palo Alto, California, not far from Sun's headquarters. It was late. That is, it had originally been planned for release a couple months earlier, but there had been typical bottlenecks in moving the operating system from the previous-generation Sun-2 machines to the faster Sun-3s.

As September approached, both engineering and marketing requested another delay. Engineering wanted to fix a few more software problems, and marketing people needed more time to devise the promotional literature because Lacroute had vetoed their first efforts. Lacroute, who was one of the drivers of the time-to-market attitude, held firm. The introduction, he told his staff, would take place in September. He insisted that engineering was capable of fixing the software bugs, and he took a direct role in the development of the promotional material prepared for the product launch. His hard line on engineering caused some grumbling, but it also served as a gauntlet for the development team.

Lacroute, bringing to bear the engineering expertise he'd previously gained at DEC, understood the nature of the Sun-3 problem and felt it could be resolved before the announcement. He also knew that numerous customers had already previewed the system and were slowing or stopping their purchases of Sun-2 computers in anticipation of the new workstations. Even though Sun was at the time a private company with plenty of cash in reserve, the company's managers took particular pride in their ability to increase growth and profit in quarter after quarter. Lacroute did not want to break the string by missing the highly anticipated introduction schedule. So he pressured engineering to produce.

Marketing was slightly trickier. Here Lacroute had authority but not the same degree of experience. Carol Bartz was the vice president of marketing during the Sun-3 introduction. Like Lacroute, Bartz was a degreed engineer and had also put in long years at DEC. But she also had a marketing track record. Her team had devised an elaborate set of promotional materials for the Sun-3 announcement and were in full production when, almost as a courtesy, they asked Lacroute to preview the visuals and text of the materials. He politely but firmly rejected their whole plan. He thought they missed the essence of the Sun-3 and the engineering mind of the intended audience. Bartz, who gave her marketers significant independence in working up ideas, argued at length on their behalf. But Lacroute would not budge.

Carl Swirsding, the creative services manager, and his boss, Jackie Rae, the marketing-communications manager, implied to Lacroute that it was too late to have new material conceived, developed, written, produced, and printed in time for the September deadline. Lacroute said that he had complete faith in their talents and suggested they begin immediately. (The fact that marketing's ideas and efforts did not pass muster the first time around did not shock Bartz. In an interview at that time, she told *High-Tech Marketing* magazine, "Sun is not about to become a 'marketing company' in the style of Apple or Lotus.") The revised materials were approved by Lacroute, but he played a more direct role in their development, conferring directly with both the writers and the designers of the collateral materials.

The Sun-3 introduction is indicative of the pressure, frenzy, and last-minute demands pervasive inside the company. Things happen and they happen fast. Involved individuals have to be ready to change course quickly, sustain their energies, and produce quality work. Sometimes the frantic pace derails people unable to keep up or it results in quality-control problems that haunt the company later. Sun is not alone with these problems, and the management has consciously decided that the importance of its time-to-market strategy gains the company much more than the problems it creates. Problems, after all, can be fixed, but an opportunity missed is gone forever.

THE SENSE OF AMBITION

Amid the hectic swirl of day-to-day life at Sun, careers are being built by a generally young work force. People do not accept jobs at Sun with the idea that they will work there until retirement. Although Sun has an excellent history of hiring and retaining intelligent, hardworking women and

men, it also looks for people with ambition—those who may
not remain satisfied with their situation in the company;
those who may view their job as only a stepping stone to a
better position, either inside or outside Sun; those ready to
take risks.

In Silicon Valley, any brilliant engineer, financial wizard,
clever marketer, aggressive salesperson, or manufacturing
expert can land a well-paid job with a large, secure company.
A review of the top employers in the entire San Francisco
Bay Area reveals that the firms that hire the most are based
in the Silicon Valley area. Sun Microsystems is ranked only
twenty-eighth in a *San Francisco Chronicle* survey published
in the spring of 1989. Despite the abundance of résumés that
flood Sun's personnel department, it's clear that not everyone
wants to work at Sun. Similarly, Sun does not accept anyone
simply on the basis of an impressive résumé. It takes something else.

The vice president of corporate resources is Crawford
Beveridge. A Scotsman with a wry sense of humor, Beveridge
encourages his group to search for people with ambition—the
kind of people who may have their eye on their boss's job.
"Hire people who are smarter than you are" is his advice.
Although there are exceptions, most managers adhere to this
dictum.

Ambition is necessary to accept the stress of aggressive
product-introduction schedules, radical new-product functions, and the astounding sales projections. Ambitious employees are challenged by the seeming impossibility of the
task. If they succeed, they will scoop the competition and
surprise the analysts. Often the targets are not met. Products
don't function as planned. Announcement events get behind
schedule. Documentation can't keep up with product
changes. The possible miscues are legion. When this
happens, Sun's management, at the last possible minute,
backs off the goals and sets new ones. Though disappointing,
this retreat from the plan is not viewed as failure. There are
no recriminations or lectures—just new goals that are slightly
less ambitious. The blood pressures are kept high, but there
is no desire to kill the patients.

One way to avoid killing them is to let them vent some steam now and then. The beer bust is a common phenomenon in Silicon Valley. Companies that feature these events buy beer, wine, and food for employees to help them unwind after a long, hard week. Sun started having beer busts as soon as it opened for business. Initially, the company was so small that employees chipped in to buy a few six-packs and snacks. By early 1985, the company was picking up the tab for a keg and some food.

A sense of camaraderie pervaded these weekly events, but a major draw was the monthly cash raffle, for which one had to be present to win. It was simple: An executive (usually McNealy) drew employees' names out of a bin. If employees whose names were drawn were present, they would win an amount of money that was pegged to the number of workstations shipped for the month. This cash prize was split initially among three winners. As the company grew, so did the number of dollars in the raffle.

When McNealy showed up for the May 5, 1989, bust, he had just come from jogging, and his T-shirt and face were drenched with sweat. Someone else had already drawn names for the raffle. The day was warm, and spring was under way, but the nice weather did not account for the overflow crowds spilling out of the cafeteria onto the landscaped grounds. Earlier in the week, Vice President of Corporate Resources Crawford Beveridge had announced via e-mail that this would be the last company-wide beer bust. From now on, busts would be decentralized, leaving the decision of whether or not to have a party up to individual departments and groups.

Most of the questions addressed to McNealy concerned the termination of this company tradition. The primary reason, as Beveridge had stated in his electronic memo, was growth of the company and the concomitant problems of staging the monthly event. As McNealy started to speak, an employee handed him a copy of a petition, which had been circulating since the beginning of the festivities, to retain the beer busts. The president smiled and said, "I've already signed it."

Over the course of the next few days, a debate raged on e-mail about the canceled busts. McNealy even got into the act, explaining over e-mail why the busts had been cancelled. Two reasons: *(1)* "They were getting too big." *(2)* "It was too hard to get to the beer." An e-mail respondent had a couple of answers. To *(1)*: "Solution: so what?" To *(2)*: "Solution: more keggers, dude."

Perhaps no other phenomenon is as representative and symbolic of Sun culture as is e-mail, especially its "junkmail" component. Junkmail is democracy—often anarchy—at its electronic best. Its users can discuss anything from the meaning of life to gripes about speed traps on the highway. Junkmail was instituted as Sun grew larger to avoid clogging the more corporate e-mail with uncontrolled messages.

No one, however, can control a type of junkmail joke pulled occasionally: a prankster's sending a message to junkmail from a workstation whose owner is away from it and has left it operational—rather than logging out or locking the system. One electronic jester did that shtick one better. He sent a message—not just to junkmail but to the *entire company*—from the terminal of an employee who had just turned twenty-one. The message read: "I've just turned 21 and am wondering if anyone out there can recommend a good source of X-rated videos." What was a little disconcerting, said the joke's victim, was the number of serious responses he received, including one from a vice president, informing him where to find smut.

THE SENSE OF CONTROL

When these wild ambitions are achieved—as with the introduction of the SPARCstation 1, which became the fastest, least-expensive RISC-based workstation in 1989—the jubilation in the company is hardly contained. T-shirts are handed out, parties are thrown, celebratory off-site meetings are held, and promotions are doled out. Success is richly rewarded, but failure is not severely punished. This combination gives Sun employees a sense of control over their lives. It is a realistic way of looking at the world. In many companies, failure is not tolerated. Success is the only human trait allowed. At Sun, failure is an acknowledged human capacity—granted, a less desirable one, but one that cannot be wished away.

Andy Bechtolsheim, one of Sun's founders and originator of the high-performance UNIX workstation, was getting bored at his company in 1987. Sun was successful. It had passed Apollo. It was a Fortune 500–class organization. It was public. All of his Sun stock made him a multimillionaire. But he still had some ideas. He got together with Vinod Khosla, the company's former president and the only Sun founder to retire, and considered leaving Sun to form a spin-off firm.

Bechtolsheim wanted to build a computer for the education market, one that would compete with the eagerly anticipated but unseen computer from NeXT, Inc., the company founded by Apple cofounder Steve Jobs. Universities had been pestering computer companies for years to build a computer that met their "3m" needs: megabytes, megaflops, and megapixels—that is, enough memory, performance, and display capabilities for creative teaching inside and outside the computer-science laboratory. And educators did not want the computer to cost megabucks. Bechtolsheim, like Jobs, thought he could design and build a machine to please the university marketplace. The challenge so engrossed him that he considered leaving the firm he had coestablished.

At first, Sun tried to dissuade Bechtolsheim from his project, afraid of losing his talents. They were also less enthusiastic about the education market. Although important to any computer company, especially for research-and-development purposes and beta tests for new products, universities tended to get steep discounts, providing only minimal profits for suppliers. As a public company, Sun now had a responsibility to its stockholders to pursue more-profitable markets, and there was no shortage of places to sell workstations in the late 1980s.

Bechtolsheim held his ground. He argued that a successful

launch of a machine in the university arena would lead to
success in other markets. He pointed to company histories—
including Sun's—that bore out his point.

Noting his adamance and respecting the wisdom of his
plan, Sun offered to be an investor. The new company, to be
called UniSun, reflected the importance of the link between
Sun Microsystems and universities. Khosla was to be president, and Bechtolsheim chief of engineering. They initiated
a trademark search on the new company's name. Public
Relations Director Carol Broadbent prepared a press release
and an announcement plan. Marleen Martin McDaniel,
Sun's director of marketing for education, planned to unveil
the new company's existence at a special meeting for university computer leaders. Slides were prepared. Logos were
designed. The spring 1988 launch of UniSun seemed assured.

During the negotiations, Sun's management warmed even
more to the idea of a specialized machine for universities—so
much so that they wanted Bechtolsheim to stay. It was independence, he argued, that he needed in order to create his
product. He wanted to be out of the burgeoning bureaucratic
loop of a big company. One of the most casual people in one
of the most casual Silicon Valley companies, Bechtolsheim
abhorred the idea of developing his workstation in the traditional R-and-D fashion at Sun.

Sun management countered with a new proposal: What if
we give you your own division? You run it the way you want.
Your schedules. Your staff. Your budget. Your own organization. We fund it. You run it.

With this kind of autonomy, Bechtolsheim realized it was
possible to accomplish his goal. He would not have to worry
about skimping and scraping along, as most startup firms do,
because he'd have the deep pockets of Sun behind him. He
would not have to concern himself with finding new offices
for his employees because Sun would handle that. He could
concentrate on technology, not constructing a company. It
appealed to him, and UniSun faded away with the creation of
Sun's education products division.

At its most extreme, this scenario is an example of how Sun imbues its employees with a sense of control. As often as possible, the company rewards good ideas by giving individuals the responsibility for seeing them through. But more than responsibility is doled out. So is control. Decision making is highly decentralized.

During his tenure, every other Monday, Lacroute and his vice presidents held a morning-long staff meeting known as the "OC," for operating committee. The critical term here is "committee." Individuals run their own groups in the manner they see fit. Few dictates are passed down from on high. Certain general guidelines are established: revenue goals, profit expectations, head-count levels, and introduction dates. But even these can be negotiable. Virtually nothing is cast in stone at Sun. OC meetings are more like a large-scale debating society, in which information is presented and haggled over. Each speaker is treated with the same amount of civility or rudeness as the next. OC meetings have been likened to the Nevada Test Site. Throw out an idea and watch it explode.

The egalitarian decorum in OC meetings feeds the independence of the vice presidents. They propagate their own sense of control inside their own groups—to the point where the decision process reaches deep into the organization. Relatively low-level people inside Sun are able to make significant choices on how to spend money, where to spend it, and what to spend it on. They can decide what to write and publish. They choose how to manufacture something differently. They can redesign a product. Such decisions, of course, do not occur in a complete vacuum without any oversight. Midlevel managers must take responsibility for their charges. But Sun is structured in such a way that some important decisions are made way down on the organization chart.

The most basic structural element in decentralized decision making at Sun is recommendations: low-level workers gather data and pass along their conclusions with the information. Sun thrives on this approach. As a manufacturer of systems that are used in virtually every computing environment, Sun's management expects expertise from the ranks. It cannot have a vice president with experience in every field. Therefore, product managers and market-segment managers develop and guide the introduction of products and influence the selling techniques to their specialized areas. Engineers are encouraged to dream up products that they think will do well in the marketplace. Product development at Sun, then, is not a one-way street with orders coming down from above. It's more like a multilevel, multilane expressway with ideas and decisions coming from all directions.

Examples of this independence are numerous. SunLink products connect Sun workstations to other manufacturers' computers, especially IBM and DEC systems. Comprising a small band of engineers, the SunLink group has been able to develop numerous products that cover virtually every aspect of DEC and IBM computers. Hardly an application exists on an IBM or DEC system with which Sun workstations cannot share data. The ways in which the SunLink team has accomplished this comprehensive communication technology vary. Sometimes the team members start from scratch, writing all the software themselves. Sometimes they incorporate an existing third-party product into the SunLink line. It's up to them.

In December 1985, Sun had outgrown the manufacturing capacity of its plant in Mountain View. Management decided to expand its operations by moving manufacturing to Milpitas, fifteen miles away. This multimillion-dollar project was then handed off to an industrial engineering team. Although oversight by Sun executives existed, management did not interfere with the decisions being made by the task force in charge of implementing the project. "Sun's initial 88,000-square-foot plant [was] operational on time." Noninterference meant that although executives would have preferred to see their own workstations used in the assembly process, the project team concluded that IBM PC ATs were more practical and, therefore, used them. It also meant that although some top-level managers were enthusiastic about investing in the very latest manufacturing technology, the task force opted for "existing technology" with a proven history of reliability.

Every year, Sun attends an increasing number of trade shows. The list of shows from which to choose is virtually endless. Vice presidents, market-segment managers, salespeople, and even engineers all submit their suggestions as to which shows are "critical" to Sun and worthy of support from the corporate trade-show group. Those not deemed "corporate" are passed on to the sales force to attend as regional shows, with nominal financial aid and without a corporate booth. In the fiscal-planning process for 1990, more than eighty trade shows were on the list. The budget, however, provided for less than one-fourth that number. Instead of publicly debating which to drop and which to attend, the trade-show group submitted its own list of the shows it would prepare for. Sun executives accepted the choices, with one exception, from the trade-show group.

In lesser ways, the distribution of decision making is evident at Sun. The people in the facsimile room, for example, had tired of walking around the campus delivering the piles of faxes received daily, so they independently worked with a Sun programmer to develop software that sent the faxes immediately over the network to people with workstations. Decentralization means that although the company is keen on broadcasting a unified company message to the world, nearly every country has its own newsletter. The U.K. office went so far as to produce *Open Computing*, an elaborate four-color magazine that is written, edited, and produced without any guidance or input from corporate headquarters. Decentralization also means a flexible discount schedule on Sun's price list, which gives the sales force significant latitude in putting together highly competitive proposals for customers.

By being decision makers in their everyday tasks, workers at Sun are more productive because they have a sense of control over their lives. This sense of control fuels Sun's sense of mission and the company's sense of urgency, as well as an individual's sense of ambition. With many people having authority for many projects, each person with a somewhat myopic view of a particular project's importance, people tend to become deeply involved with a project's success. They are doing work not merely for the corporation or the boss but for themselves. They clearly see themselves as part of the Sun success story, perhaps in a grander role than they actually deserve. But that self-aggrandizement does little harm, especially in view of the dedication and hard work the company derives from the process of decentralized decision making.

THE SENSE OF HUMOR

It's been another great quarter:
- We swore in a record 15 new vice presidents
- I played golf with Lee Trevino at the Bob Hope Classic in Palm Springs (or was it with Bob Hope at the Lee Trevino Classic)
- Near-average attendance at the AT&T phone training classes
- Summer's almost here

It's achievements like these that make Sun a great place to work. Plus you get to wear sneakers and a T-shirt unlike at IBM, DEC, HP, and all the other dinosaurs chasing us.

So begins the editorial from "Scoot McBreezy, President and CEO" in the April 1, 1989, issue of *Hallucinations*, the parody of Sun's company newsletter, *Illuminations*. No sense at Sun is more pervasive than the sense of fun. It flows from top to bottom and back again. It inspires camaraderie and diffuses the enormous pressure inside the organization. Without its legendary sense of humor, Sun would never have succeeded as well as it has.

McNealy is both the originator and the target of much of Sun's in-house humor. At the company's now-discontinued monthly beer busts, he entertained the throng with lively stories of the past thirty days of business, turning otherwise dull encounters with corporate executives into lighthearted anecdotes. He inspired beer busters with the notion that they were unique in the business world simply because "we're all having a gas of a time." He poked fun at the staid, button-down approach of American business executives, which suited the attitude of the scruffy horde of engineers who produced the workstations.

McNealy once persuaded Phillipe Kahn, the chairman of Borland Corporation, to join him in addressing a beer-bust crowd. Kahn, noted for his own outrageous antics, enthusiastically addressed the assembly. He told them they were destined to succeed because "you're having so much fun. That's why there are cars in the parking lot late at night, early in the morning, all weekend long." He added, "Let's face it, you guys make great toys. The greatest toys in the world." The group cheered. McNealy playfully tried to wrest the microphone back from Kahn. The crowd loved it. And, of course, in the minds of many in the audience, it was true. Sun's computers were like wonderful toys to them, and the company encouraged them to have fun playing with them. Forget the stress, the overcrowding, the unreasonable due dates, the lack of help on projects—Sun was a fun place to work.

With McNealy leading the cast, Sun's executives step into the roles of entertainers regularly. Sales meetings are filled with inspirational, upbeat speeches, as happens in any company. But Sun invariably screens a video or two depicting McNealy and other executives and managers in humorous roles. Most scripts are written by Rich Wyckoff, editorial services manager at Sun. The videos, which cost a few thousand dollars apiece to produce, are worth it, according to Wyckoff. "People appreciate it when the company spends money to improve morale. It proves that the company cares enough about them to make them laugh."

In one video, Wyckoff portrays McNealy as "The Lovable Sundoggy," a parody of the *Gidget* film character Moon-doggy. In it McNealy croons to a young woman, lip-syncing the song "No Sun Is the Next Best Thing to Sun." In the same video, Vice President of Sales Joe Roebuck is seen riding a surfboard as "the Big Kahuna." Wyckoff has por-

trayed his bosses as rock stars hamming it up onstage before
a simulated live, screaming audience. In a lampoon of advertising for "never-before-offered" record albums, Sun vice
presidents Larry Hambly and Larry Baker join other sales
managers in satirical songs about technology such as "Baby,
You Can Use My Mouse" and "Under My Sun." In an
ambitious video to celebrate the company's reaching the
billion-dollar-revenue mark, Sun hired actors to play Sun
executives in a "Star Trek" satire, in which the actors tell
arcane jokes about the technology and the competition. At
the end, when the Sun ship has defeated its opponents,
"Colonel Zander" of the Apollo vessel pleads to come aboard
the Sun spacecraft, saying, "There's no reason to stay aboard
this rotting hulk. Permission to beam aboard and do some
marketing." At the end of the video, Sun executives "beamed
down" live onto the stage, complete with "Star Trek" uni-
forms. The thousands of employees in the audience at the
cavernous Santa Clara Convention Center loved the show.

Sun's management does not need a script, however, to kid
around. In a story published in the *San Jose Mercury News*,
they got a chuckle out of posing for a front-page business
section photo with everyone wearing sunglasses. The headline read: "The Future's So Bright, They've Gotta Wear
Shades," a reference to a popular song at the time. Although
not a public relations coup in the eyes of PR Director Carol
Broadbent, who was trying to portray her bosses as sophisticated and mature members of the Fortune 500 establishment,
the article was widely posted throughout the company.

Sun is most famous for its April Fool's gags. The first was
played on Eric Schmidt, engineering vice president, by a
group of engineers. In 1985 they removed the entire contents
of his office and set them up next to the pond between
Buildings 1 and 5. The next year, Schmidt was again the
target. This time, they disassembled a Volkswagen Beetle and
reassembled it in his office. By 1987 Schmidt was getting
paranoid as March came to a close, but the engineering team
in charge of the pranks, led by Jon Feiber, switched their
attack. They "stole" Bill Joy's Ferrari with the help of Andy

Bechtolsheim and parked it on a platform set just below the water's surface in the pond between Buildings 6 and 7. They provided Joy with a rubber dinghy and a paddle to reach his pricey car. Once in the car, Joy, enjoying the joke, called the AAA auto service from his car phone for help. As with the two jokes on Schmidt, the event made the local media.

In answer to a question about what might happen in 1988 to an unwary Sun executive, Feiber replied, "Well, we've done office in pond, car in office, car in pond: I guess the only thing left is pond in office." Sure enough, the next year, the engineering team took out the wall between McNealy and Lacroute's offices and turned them into a one-hole golf course, complete with pond and sand traps. Other pranks have included turning Bernard Peuto's office into an aviary and covering an entire building with an exterminator's tent and hanging a sign proclaiming the software inside to be "bug free."

Individuals foster humor throughout the company over the local area network. Sun's network carries jokes, limericks, parodies, and biting comments on contemporary issues. On the network nothing is sacred. Anything can be laughed at.

But sometimes the fun gets carried beyond even Sun's liberal boundaries. A few employees have been removed because of their inability to accept the limits of what's toler- ated. Peer pressure generally keeps people in line, but some overzealous and talented engineers have been let go for prob- ing the files of another employee "just for a joke." (One employee was fired for breaking into McNealy's files.) But these are the rare exceptions and do not discredit manage- ment's encouragement, even sponsorship, of a corporate sense of humor.

Without the levity that plays so well to Sun's employees, it is unlikely that Sun would have reached its level of success. Sun keeps its workers so long largely because of the fun atmosphere that prevails. As Lacroute once pointed out to a newspaperman, "We have attracted an engineering team that is second to none in the computer industry. If you attract good people, you can do anything." Part of the attraction of

Sun is more than the technology; it's clear that IBM, DEC, and HP are all developing top-notch products using advanced technology, and Sun's engineers have opportunities to move to those companies and find greater security, less stress, and probably better offices. But they choose Sun for a variety of reasons, not the least of which is the company's deep-seated belief that none of the success would be worth it if they didn't have a good time along the way.

QUO VADIS?

In spite of the petition and the junkmail campaign, beer busts were over at Sun. Was the cancellation symbolic? Did it mean, as one junkmail correspondent suggested, that Sun was on its way to becoming a big, soulless bureaucracy?: "It's starting to get real stuffy around here. Next say goodbye to doughnuts on Wednesdays and then the final straw—no more jeans on Fridays!"

To Sun old-timers, the open feeling of the company is likely to diminish over the years. Bureaucracy is inevitable. Still, by standards of any other Fortune 500 company, Sun is chaotic—even wild. People still contend that their work is fun, but keeping that spirit alive in the years ahead will be difficult.

Sun is unquestionably in the process of a major transition. Sheer numbers indicate that it is no longer the freewheeling startup that some longtime employees fondly remember. The total number of employees is edging toward ten thousand. Sun is a $2 billion, Fortune 500 company. In 1989, for the first time in its short existence, it experienced one of the harsh realities of the corporate world: the prospect of quarterly losses. Even though losses are normal, for a company accustomed to a yearly doubling of revenues, it was a shock.

9

Open Season

Austin Wing Mayer encountered some healthy skepticism when he first discussed the possible financial woes Sun was facing in the spring of 1989, the company's final fiscal quarter for that year. For years, Sun's executives had been cautious about their company's revenue and profit performance. And for years Sun had consistently exceeded everyone's expectations. Mayer's warnings in 1989 were not the equivocations of a conservative director of investor relations, which he was. They were harbingers of hard times ahead for investors and management alike.

Mayer had cultivated good relationships with Wall Street's top computer analysts. His success can be seen in the dozens of reports cited in this book. The financial community was well tutored in the intricacies of Sun, its market, and products, and Mayer believed his most important asset to Sun was his "credibility with the financial community." By alerting his Wall Street contacts early about the trouble Sun faced that spring, he hoped the damage to the company's image and, most important, its stock would be minimized. Mayer thoroughly briefed analysts at Bear Stearns, Sanford Bernstein, and other such institutions as soon as Sun's troubles began to unfold.

The close connection between Sun and America's capital markets preceded Mayer. Even before Sun's emergence as a public company, the company released quarterly financial statements. Cofounder Vinod Khosla established close relations with major investors during his stint as Sun's president and chairman from 1982 to 1984. McNealy enlarged upon relations with investors after he took the company's helm, formalizing the process with the hiring of Mayer and creating the position of investor relations in 1987.

In his office at corporate headquarters, Mayer spends much of his day hooked up to his phone through his headset. Other than Sun's receptionists and telephone operators, few Sun employees need phone headsets, but Mayer is on the phone from early in the morning, when he talks to analysts in London and New York, to late in the day, when he updates markets on the West Coast and in Tokyo. His headset is so much a part of him that he has a hand-lettered sign he displays when he's on an open line.

WHAT WENT WRONG

Even starting in late 1987, when a shortage of dynamic random-access memory (DRAM) chips diminished the entire high-technology industry's profits, Mayer had had the good fortune of reporting better than predicted revenues and profits for Sun. The first three quarters in fiscal 1989 indicated only more of the same: record revenues, record profits. This constant string of pleasant surprises for investors created some doubt in analysts' minds, then, when Mayer first relayed the news that fiscal 1989's closing period would be a disappointment.

News that Sun's fortunes were dipping was not wholly unanticipated by Sun management, largely because the new mainframe-based management information system (MIS) being installed, known internally as the SunBeam project, had foundered. The switchover from the former minicomputer technology to the Cullinet-software–Amdahl-mainframe MIS approach bogged down, then collapsed. Information on parts availability, types of systems ordered, sales forecasts, and other vital figures disappeared. Data from the month of April was irretrievable. May was a mess. As June dawned, management realized that in addition to the confusion within the organization, some very bad news loomed.

On June 1, 1989, McNealy authorized Mayer to release a fourth-quarter advisory. The one-page press release tersely predicted that "the fourth quarter . . . will be significantly below the results for the same quarter a year ago and the company could experience a slight loss depending upon revenue levels." The cause of the trouble was due in part to the change of computer systems. "The conversion to a new management information system in April was not without difficulties," the press release drily stated.

The MIS situation was compounded by the overhaul of Sun's product line. In the workstation market, customers consistently choose a company's top-of-the-line system—that is, the computer with the best performance at a reasonable price. Technology advances so quickly that one company or another is bound to offer a machine that is a little faster, a little cheaper. It's an engineering tradition that keeps workstation R-and-D talent working at a feverish pace. Each company must "out-MIPS" and undercut the competition to keep customers' interest.

Generally, computer companies introduce their new products in piecemeal fashion, avoiding wholesale changes to product families. This policy minimizes the disruption in the sales of established models of computers. Sun bucked that trend with its "Spring Fling," as some insiders sarcastically dubbed the introduction event. In April 1989, Sun unveiled new products that cut into the sales of existing systems, particularly the popular Sun-3/60, the world's bestselling workstation before the introduction of the SPARCstation 1. Customers who ordinarily bought 3/60s would overwhelmingly switch to the SPARCstation 1 because of its clear technological advantage and lower price. How many and how fast were the big questions.

It was here that the SunBeam troubles edged toward disas-

ter. Keeping pace with the supersonic switchover from manufacturing hundreds of millions of dollars' worth of one
product to another depended on swift and accurate information—sales forecasts, part inventories, and the like. And it
frequently wasn't there—or wasn't there fast enough.

Compounding the problem of managing this product transition in a void was, by Sun's standards, a hefty inventory. As
the third quarter rolled to another record close, just under a
half-billion dollars, the backlog of orders was surprisingly
low. The reason was plain: nearly everyone interested in Sun
computers was waiting expectantly for the April announcement before filling out purchase orders. Long before the
introduction event, Carol Broadbent, Sun's PR chief, regularly declined to comment on increasingly detailed stories
about Sun's latest workstations. She complained that when it
came to prematurely divulging information about the products, Sun executives were the most difficult employees to
control. The enthusiasm spawned by Sun's latest computer
made it impossible to button the "loose lips" about which
McNealy was continually warning employees on e-mail.
Long before the official announcement of Sun's new products, everyone in the industry knew about Sun's hot new
boxes.

Aware that something better was imminent, customers
stalled their buying plans. Stalled orders meant a diminishing backlog, which made the company uncomfortable. A
healthy backlog, though tough on customers because it
generally means delays in delivery, is always a good sign in
the workstation industry. Quarter-to-quarter through the
years, Sun had carried a massive, sometimes burdensome
backlog. Entering the fourth fiscal quarter in 1989, Sun saw
scant dollars in the pipeline.

Worried about the product transition and the rising inventories of now-old products, management decided to offer
attractive discounts on systems that the new computers
would replace. These deals were so good that the stall in
buying existing products suddenly reversed itself. Concurrently, sales of the new products, especially the SPARCstation
1, took off dramatically.

All this good news might have been more uplifting had the SunBeam MIS project been wholly successful. But it wasn't. The SunBeam system was a maze of electronic data, and because it was so bogged down, information was difficult or impossible to locate. Employees who tracked orders for products could not keep a handle on who was ordering what. Those who worked in manufacturing could not adequately track material requirements. Because the SunBeam system was supposed to link all relevant groups—sales, order entry, manufacturing, etc.—Sun's manufacturing group was dispirited because its members had to guess as to what and how many of the different products they were supposed to build. Given Sun's huge lists of possible product options, manufacturing became less a science of estimation and more an art of guesstimation.

Two months later, the extent of the damage to the company's balance sheet was clear. Mayer's cautionary warning to Wall Street had turned into a financial horror story. Not only was there a loss, it was "in the $20–26 million range," according to Sun's July 27 press release. Besides the substantial loss in the final quarter, the press release announced, "Sun advised that a return to profitability in the current first quarter cannot be assured."

In the history of Sun, such a situation was unheard of. In a *Business Week* cover story that appeared the week before Sun projected its fourth-quarter downturn, McNealy claimed to have "seen worse times." He told the writer, Jonathan B. Levine, that during his first month in 1984 as Sun's CEO, the company suffered a half-million-dollar loss on two million in sales, while "70% of the computers it made didn't work, and one of the three co-founders [had] quit." McNealy argued that in 1984 the problems could have destroyed the company, while the hard times in 1989, although not insignificant, were not a threat to Sun's survival.

The difference, of course, was one of magnitude. A small company, just getting started, in a niche market, with only a handful of employees and customers and losing less than a million dollars, was not to be compared with a Fortune 500 concern that had supplanted Apple Computer as the model for business achievement. Its success had perpetuated the Silicon Valley rags-to-riches, hacker-to-hero mythology. In revealing its financial problems, Sun once again proved the frailty of the high-technology marketplace. Those companies that are on top one moment can plummet to earth in the next instant—not that Sun had plummeted, but the loss, after so many years of uninterrupted and nearly unprecedented growth, was shocking.

New employees at Sun—and since 1986 that meant more than half the company—had known nothing but unrelenting growth, unparalleled success. With rumors of an upcoming loss afoot, McNealy sent a message over the electronic-mail network on June 1 to assuage everyone's fears and pump up the troops. The message read in part: "I wanted to make you aware of an announcement that will be made this afternoon concerning our fourth quarter net income. . . . Clearly this is serious, but we have some time left in the fourth quarter, which ends July 30. By really cutting your spending to only the necessities and by supporting the sales and manufacturing organizations in every way possible, we may be able to turn this around and not have to announce the first loss in Sun's history. . . . A slight loss or even break-even quarter may be inevitable, but I am not ready to buy it yet. It's June 1. Your actions have always made a difference! The products are great, the customers are excited, and OUR TEAM IS THE BEST!! Let's give it our all and launch Sun into year 8 with style!" McNealy's electronic pep talk wasn't enough, however.

His recollection to Levine about Sun's early difficulties was also intended to assure *Business Week*'s millions of readers that he was capable of handling the crisis—because more than just questions about the firm's financial performance were pouring into the offices of Mayer and Broadbent from Wall Street. Doubts were being expressed about Sun's management team, including McNealy.

TURMOIL AT THE TOP

Immediately after Sun's unquestioned success in introducing the SPARCstation and other new products in April, the first in a series of unpleasant surprises struck: Bernie Lacroute resigned. In the eyes of outsiders, his departure was inexplicable and unexpected. His longtime role as executive vice president had nicely balanced McNealy's tenure as CEO. Lacroute's seasoned presence played well with his boss's youth. While Lacroute's experience at DEC bolstered McNealy's understanding of the market and corporate structuring, the older man gained an exuberance from McNealy, to the point where the mildly overweight vice president took up running in 1986, shedding considerable pounds in the process.

Lacroute's flight from Sun unnerved many, as did his reason for resigning—that he "needed a break from 'the hectic pace' at the company." The follow-on statement from McNealy was no less disturbing. His announcement that he had no intention of replacing the French-born executive did not sit well inside or outside the company. Lacroute had been viewed as a counterweight to McNealy. Although he had not been universally liked inside the company, Lacroute's experience at DEC and at Sun was widely admired.

Although officially Lacroute was to stay at Sun until June, he was written out of the management team almost immediately. It had been considered axiomatic that Sun would jump at the chance to bring in a replacement for Lacroute. For a long time, the company had been thinking about creating a separate office of the president, and this seemed like an ideal time to recruit such a person. The search for a president did not proceed, however, as McNealy was reported to be "relishing his added duties."

In June, McNealy reorganized the top level of the company, handing most of Lacroute's responsibilities over to four people. Marketing responsibilities fell completely into Ed Zander's lap. Research and development decisions were split between Wayne Rosing and Eric Schmidt. Manufacturing operations stayed with Bob Garrow, while Carol Bartz broadened her charter as the head of customer service. In a June 7 memo that McNealy sent to the entire company, this new management structure was obvious: whereas they had once looked to Lacroute for leadership, all these executives now reported to McNealy. With the financial and sales areas already under his wing, McNealy now had overall responsibility for every aspect of Sun's performance—a massive challenge for any CEO, let alone such a youthful one.

Then, one week after the public announcement of the new management team, another key member jumped ship. Joe Graziano, Sun's chief financial officer, dropped the depth charge that he was returning to Apple Computer, the company he had left to join Sun. Earlier in the year, Bob Lux had left the customer service division's top post to become an independent consultant. Barry James Folsom, who had led Sun's East Coast division and was principal champion for the Intel-based workstations, had disappeared more quietly, but in the same period. Some insiders and former Sun managers began chatting freely with the press, casting McNealy as the villain who was overworking his people with his "hard-charging style," a man "so obsessed with working that even while chatting at a party he changes the topic of conversation back to Sun and the market." Sun and its leader, so long the darlings of the trade and business media, were suddenly ripe for criticism; it had become open season on Sun Microsystems. Zander, who had experienced a similar downturn while he was marketing chief at Apollo, had long warned that Sun would "show its true stuff" when it "hit the wall" and got up again. The wall was large and very hard.

Sun's miscue with its new MIS mainframe and software was "ironic" and "embarrassing . . . for a manufacturer of computers." Sun was "suffering from its own success." The loss of some of its management team, especially Lacroute, was cited as a possible reason for the company's troubles. Lawrence Fisher wrote in the *New York Times* that "Sun has grown so large, so quickly that some analysts have worried that it has grown to a size beyond its young founders' ability to manage. Until now Sun's executives have prided themselves on the company's decentralized management style, but some analysts have suggested that Sun might fall victim to problems related to uncontrolled growth." Perhaps recalling the Osborne collapse, analysts and the press quickly leapt on the string of bad news.

With the July 27 announcement indicating the magnitude
of the loss, Sun had reached its bottom. At corporate headquarters, depression among executives was palpable; black
humor predominated, and downturned faces reflected the
downward trend of Sun's stock. Analysts sniped at Sun as if
it were a target. Broadbent counseled McNealy to refrain
from press-appealing antics and keep a low profile. When the
final fourth-quarter results appeared, six weeks after the
quarter's close, the news was bad, but not as bad as it might
have been—a $20.3 million loss on $431 million in revenue.
But by then, halfway through the first fiscal quarter of 1990,
eyes were looking ahead. Past performance, both good and
bad, was forgotten. The hope and the concern were focused
on the future.

WELCOME TO THE NEW WORLD

At its April introduction Sun revealed its technological direction and unveiled its new product lines with the upbeat intro
slogan "Welcome to the New World." Like Columbus coming upon the riches of the Western Hemisphere, customers
and high-tech observers were invited to discover the breadth
and scope of Sun's latest systems. Bright as this impression
may have been, Sun had entered a newer and darker world.
Just as the colonists of the Americas faced, in McNealy's
phrase, "insurmountable opportunity," so too did they en-
counter privation, suffering, and ignominy in their New
World. For the first time in its brief corporate history, Sun
faced sustained and company-threatening problems. How it
responded to the new and more difficult conditions would
determine the fundamental strengths of the organization.

Adding to Sun's financial difficulties, the fiscal 1990 year
began with hot new products from competitors. DEC's 3100
workstation and a new, inexpensive machine from the HP/
Apollo group attracted significant and deserved attention.
Also on the horizon were the new SPARC clones from Taiwan
and Japan. Finally, IBM, a nearly dormant player in the
workstation market, was rumored to be readying a new workstation line that was fast and cheap and ran a version of the

UNIX operating system. Certainly, all of this would spur interest in the workstation market, considered by all analysts to be the fastest-growing segment in the computer industry. Still, the competition was heating up.

In September 1989, as the first quarter of the new fiscal year came to a close, Susan Hathaway, a writer and analyst in Broadbent's PR group, circulated an internal review of the competition. Noting IBM's "huge customer base," she wrote, "If the new [products] are as good as promised, IBM could become a smart buy as well as a safe buy." Accepting the notion prevalent in the computer industry that "no one ever got fired for buying IBM," the report concluded that IBM was "serious competition" and might steal up to 20 percent of the UNIX-related market by 1993.

As if tougher competition, a negative P-and-L sheet, and the defection of senior management were not problems enough, Sun had to face another new reality: the company would no longer be able to use its phenomenal revenue growth to cover its poor management of expenses.

Sun was never an exceptional company at delivering profits. Its margins were consistently in the 7 to 10 percent range, mostly on the lower end of the scale. Building market share at any cost was always the prime objective. The tremendous growth of the industry and Sun's dominance in it allowed the company to funnel its resources into engineering and, to a lesser degree, marketing, at the expense of financial controls. Most Sun managers had long complained about the lack of computer software or trained financial analysts to help them manage their budgets more effectively. As many Sun vendors realized, getting paid by Sun was difficult, because the accounting procedures were weak for a Fortune 500 organization. In fact, a major reason for switching to the new main-frame-based MIS system was to solve these problems. When it faltered during the changeover, the situation in the finance department only got worse.

In the summer of 1989, McNealy refined his growth-at-all-costs strategy. Although not abandoning his market-share philosophy, he recognized that revenue expansion alone would not satisfy the company's insatiable hunger for cash. The doubling of revenues from quarter to quarter had ceased, requiring a different, more cost-conscious management approach.

THE BUCK STOPS EVERYWHERE

Adopting his predecessor's reputation for pinching pennies, McNealy immediately instituted restrictive policies to bring costs down. Almost at once, expense authorizations throughout the company were reviewed. Most were scaled back. Directors who once signed for $10,000 purchases were now begging vice presidents to initial $2,500 requisitions. Controllers for each division had to approve every expenditure. Some managers fumed at the delays this picayune approval process imposed on their projects. Vendors increasingly complained about late payments.

By stalling projects in the queue, whether launching new products or constructing new facilities such as the corporate headquarters in Palo Alto, the company immediately improved its cash-flow situation. Pushing out the date for a product introduction did two things: it clamped down on near-term cash consumption and shortened the time between the product's unveiling and its generation of revenues. Like many high-tech outfits, Sun was constantly under pressure to outengineer its competitors. When DEC or HP trotted out its latest machine with more performance or lower costs, Sun was compelled to equal or surpass the feat. Sometimes that meant accelerating a product launch in order to distract customers from interest in something offered by a competitor but not yet available from Sun. The marketing logic was to assure customers that Sun was ready to match or surpass anything on a competitor's price list.

In the urgent climate of the summer of 1989, new-product announcements were inextricably tied to the date when the products would be available in quantity. This policy meant that Sun suffered an image problem at the high end of its computer line. The more expensive, higher-margin, and faster systems—known as servers because more than one person could use them—were not available from Sun. But DEC, in particular, was ready with its servers.

Despite increasing the engineering resources for these products and a strong reason to announce them, Sun decided to postpone the introduction. The sales Sun lost because these faster computers were not on the market were sizable, but by not selling what could not be delivered, Sun eased the pressure on manufacturing and focused the sales force on selling existing products with immediate revenue potential. The company also saved considerable dollars by rescheduling the announcement date and its attendant promotional expenses.

The most effective cost-containment program was management's communication of the need for controls at all levels in the company. After years of nearly nonstop hypergrowth, the slowdown now gave department managers time to assess each project with new, more cost-sensitive criteria. One of the most visible cuts was the curtailment of glossy brochures, data sheets, books, and reports.

The college atmosphere at Sun had fostered more than a casual, energetic work life. It had brought with it the "publish or perish" mentality so common at U.S. universities. Every product, no matter how obscure, had a product manager who felt obligated to generate printed material to promote or explain the product. As a result, Sun spent millions of dollars on product information—sometimes as absurd as the five-thousand-copy printing of a glossy six-page document that described how Sun put its computers into boxes.

Since most of these costs were borne by Ed Zander's organization but were initiated in sales and divisional marketing groups, Zander instituted a stringent interdepartmental review committee for every piece that Sun sent to a printer. Carl Swirsding, Sun's most knowledgeable person on printing issues, advised representatives from other divisions who were demanding brochures and the like as to what each piece would cost. He discovered that what had once been a pro forma approval of printing projects stopped in the new review committee. Before the review committee was started, each project was scrutinized on a one-by-one basis, so the costs seemed relatively small. But when the review committee finally examined all these projects in aggregate, it became clear how huge the overall bill was. An additional benefit of examining all projects was that redundancy and duplication became apparent. This new examination of projects tended to make even the most profligate of managers ready to cut or scale back programs.

The facilities department, once one of the most overworked groups in the company, dramatically applied the brakes to its programs. Work on the new corporate headquarters in Palo Alto slowed significantly. Moves from building to building were curtailed. Even a move to a new office in the same building required the approval of Crawford Beveridge, the department's senior vice president.

The fastest way to lower expenses, of course, is to cut the payroll, but McNealy was adamantly opposed to layoffs. Sun's success, he argued, was due as much to the enthusiasm and commitment of its employees as to the value of its workstations. To take the simple route to financial stability by lopping off heads seemed wrongheaded. Sun's work force was cut back, but through employee departures and a freeze on hiring.

In the months of July and August, all new—even replacement—personnel had to be personally approved by McNealy. By September Sun had approximately two hundred fewer employees than it had at the beginning of July. Attrition took its toll. Management levels diminished, and the number of managers thinned. Numerous departments and divisions reorganized to meet the more constrained growth pattern. People picked up extra responsibilities. Reassignment to different groups caused some resentment among various individuals. Most, however, took to the arrangement with enthusiasm. Employees who had been around for years noticed that the situation was similar to what it had been in the early days of the company: lots of responsibility and precious few resources to accomplish tasks. Ingenuity as much as an understanding of the tighter controls became the most important traits in a worker.

Cuts came in nearly every area. Travel expenses dropped by 50 percent from the fourth quarter of fiscal 1989 to the first of 1990. Office supplies were cut back. Although full-time employees were spared, temporary workers were released en masse. The purchasing and contracts departments were strengthened. Lawyers helped keep spending at bay by tying up programs in legal limbo. There was even a successful voluntary system to cut electricity use in buildings.

All of these spending bottlenecks were accomplished, in part, because the company continued to resist the option of laying off workers. Overall, the loyalty of Sun employees remained intact. This loyalty was reinforced when the company gave an average 8 percent company-wide salary hike. This commitment to workers on the part of Sun management differed from that of Sun's competitors. When HP had run into difficulties a few years earlier, it had cut salaries across the board by 10 percent. DEC redeployed its work force into sales. Apple and Apollo had both experienced layoffs. By sidestepping those approaches, management had to become rabid about cost cutting. The philosophy of "Whatever it takes to get the job done" had changed. Now it was "If it doesn't generate revenue, don't spend anything for it."

McNealy was tireless in promulgating the new stinginess at Sun. He often used electronic mail to exhort his troops to consider every single purchase. Was it necessary? Can the price be cut? Is there another, equally effective but less expensive way to get the job done?

And it worked. The $20.3 million hemorrhage in the fourth quarter of 1989 diminished by the end of 1990's first fiscal quarter. Revenue for the quarter was a record $538.5 million, 39 percent greater than the same period of the previous year. In one quarter, the company had put itself in the profits column, registering a modest $5.2 million.

Although Sun continued to expand, the pressures of hypergrowth were brought under greater control. The company only broke even during its first fiscal quarter, but that was a tremendous improvement over the preceding quarter. Sun had weathered the storm with no layoffs and even a decent wage hike. Equally important, Wall Street began to put Sun back on the "buy" list.

Sun's officers were confident of the future. They had steered the company through some heavy waters—a big quarterly loss, key management defections, increased competition, and perhaps most important, the psychological blow of losing its reputation for economic invulnerability. Although severely tested, the company survived and would be stronger for it.

The first fiscal quarter of 1990 brought other good news. IBM admitted that it would not be able to introduce its new workstations until early calendar 1990, at the earliest. The delay gave Sun a critical advantage as it expanded into a less technical marketplace. The competitive UNIX operating system from the Open Software Foundation, whose strings were pulled by IBM, DEC, and HP, was late in materializing, giving an edge to Sun and its allies in UNIX International. DEC, Sun's most consistent opponent in sales situations, was not pummeling Sun with its hot DECstation 3100 because "users [were] not yet fully convinced of the sincerity of its intentions." UNIX buyers, the fastest-growing segment in the system-software arena, still looked to Sun, more than to any other company, for products and innovation.

The sales of Sun's SPARCstation 1 exceeded even the most optimistic forecasts. Sun's SPARC product line, in fact, was rapidly replacing its systems built on Motorola chips. That trend meant higher margins for Sun because it owned the SPARC technology and did not have to buy it from other sources. The success of its SPARC technology continued to spread—so much so that SPARC became the main contender in the RISC arena. Sun's top twenty customers, who comprised more than 30 percent of the company's business, were moving to SPARC at a rate of three SPARC computers for every one Motorola-based machine. Clone makers in Taiwan and Korea were revising their commitments to the Intel chip and were adopting SPARC, expanding the market in Sun's favor.

When the profits for the second fiscal quarter were an-

nounced in January 1990, the turnaround was complete. Sun
had earned $20 million on record revenues of $595 million.
Although the tight cost-contract reigns of the previous six
months loosened, lessons had been learned.

The fourth quarter had humbled Sun's executives. The
company that could do no wrong for so long suddenly had
become the whipping boy for industry analysts and pundits.
Reporters who had once camped on Sun's doorstep to write
about the company's latest triumph now gathered to describe
the disintegration of the organization.

The ill will toward Sun came, more than anywhere else,
from Wall Street, where Sun's stock fell by 40 percent—from
22 to as low as 13—on the NASDAQ exchange. The stock
rebounded from time to time but has not, as of this writing,
regained and held the momentum that caused it to split when
it had reached a high of 45 in early 1988. In effect, in a little
over a year, Sun had gone from tripling investors' value since
going public, to halving their worth.

NEW DAWN?
SUDDEN ECLIPSE?

The high-tech business is not meant for those with faint
hearts or weak nerves. The uncertainty and volatility of the
industry make predictions a hazardous game. Success or
failure can be hard to measure. Is Atari a success because
Jack Tramiel pulled it out of oblivion? Maybe yes, maybe no.
The company name is the same. Everything else is different.
Was Apollo a success? Because it was gobbled up by HP in
the midst of economic chaos, no one will ever know.

Sun has confronted its troubles by sticking to its strategy.
It has adhered to standards. It has continued to promote open
systems by licensing its own in-house technology. It has
invested heavily in new, highest-performance technology. It
has fought aggressively for more market share. Hard times,
however, have instilled something new in Sun's management—intimations of fallibility. Like latter-day Icaruses,
they fell back to earth.

Sun's comeback from its worst-ever quarter impressed
investors, analysts, and the press alike. Whether Sun will

regain its status as the *wunderkind* of the industry is un-
answerable. It may continue to leap up the rungs of the
Fortune 500 ladder. It may be absorbed in some as-yet-
unhatched scheme of megaacquisition. Whatever the out-
come, the importance of Sun Microsystems will transcend its
place as a corporation. As the computer industry's major
proponent of open technology, it has changed the way computer makers develop, build, market, and sell their wares.
Sun forced the computer industry to wake up to the information-processing needs of users. Sun dragged its competitors
into the real world, in which users live with the frustration of
having millions of dollars' worth of incompatible equipment.
It forced vendors to offer, at least as an option, standard
technologies. Sun made open systems profitable, for both
vendors and users. That is the company's vital legacy—Sun
tapped into the future of technology and made it turn a buck.

In the 1990s and into the next century, computer users will
increasingly profit by the marketing and development philosophy perpetuated at Sun. They will use systems from numerous manufacturers. They will buy them for various price,
function, and performance reasons. But they will use those
machines effortlessly, not even certain which computer is
processing which task. Users will buy and use software and
hardware as if they were putting a compact disc into their
CD player or plugging in a new stereo component. Companies will become information-efficient because the problematic aspects of networks, user interfaces, even the computers
themselves will gradually disappear. Technology will become
invisible, allowing easy and instant access to information.

This computing environment will emerge because of Sun
and those that followed in its profitable footsteps. If Sun
skates through its current difficulties and holds its leadership
position, it may see a new dawn of possibility, with the
intriguing new products and technologies under development. But even if the company should somehow be eclipsed,
its part in technology history will be noted. Open systems,
once an obtuse expression of an obscure company, is now the
buzzword for computing in the 1990s, the *glasnost* of high
technology—controversial, but worth waiting for.

Authors' Coda

No book lacks bias. This volume does not break that tradition. We conceived and wrote *Sunburst* while we were employees of Sun Microsystems. During the writing of the book, no executive or manager attempted to influence its contents. The company did not authorize or discourage the work.

It's impossible to be part of something and claim to see the whole of it objectively. And it's not easy to separate emotions, negative or positive, from experiences when writing a book; even the selection of material indicates bias. The best we can do is reflect on events and present them in as impartial manner as possible. *Sunburst* is our interpretation of our high-gear experiences inside one of America's most astonishing business success stories.

We came to Sun in the spring of 1985 when the company was a $100 million rising star in the computer industry and left in the spring of 1990. It had grown quickly in its first three and a half years of existence, but not nearly as fast as it would in the next four and a half years. Despite being part of the process, we, like most sentient and sane observers, were amazed and impressed by this unprecedented growth. Amid the long hours and hard work, there was an unbridled ambition and an intensity of intellect inside Sun that begged to be reported to the world. Magazines, journals, newspapers, newsletters, and even television told bits and pieces of the story. But the limits of space and time in those media produced incomplete versions of the Sun story.

It was the incompleteness of all these articles and essays that led us to spend our early mornings, nights, weekends, and even vacations at home, working on the book for the better part of a year. A more complete tale needed to be told if people were to profit from the lessons learned inside Sun.

Glossary

Certain terms appear frequently in the speech and writing of people at Sun. Although some of the following terms are common throughout the computer industry, they crop up so frequently in Sun communications that they are an integral part of Sun *culture*, and some have even taken on meanings specific to Sun.

acronyms and abbreviations: The computer industry is one of the biggest generators of acronyms (other major competitors being the federal government and the military). Sun does not stint on its contribution, and a complete list of the acronyms and abbreviations in everyday use at Sun could comprise an entire chapter of this book. This list below includes some of the most common and most interesting. Those followed by an asterisk were coined at Sun; the others are in widespread use throughout the industry. (A few other acronyms, with comments, are interspersed throughout this glossary.)

ASIC (application-specific integrated circuit)
CAD/CAM (computer-aided design/computer-aided manufacturing)

CASE (computer-aided software engineering)
CIM (computer-integrated manufacturing)
CISC (complex-instruction-set computer)
ECAD (electrical [or electronic] computer-aided design)
GKS (graphical kernel system)
ISV (independent software vendor)
LAN (local area network)
MIS (management information system)
NeWS★ (Network/extensible Window System)
NSE★ (Network Software Environment)
OEM (original equipment manufacturer)
PHIGS (programmers' hierarchical interactive graphical standard [or system])
RISC (reduced-instruction-set computer)
SOC★ (systems for open computing)
SPARC★ (Scalable Processor Architecture)
SunView★ (Sun Visual Environment for Windows)
TLA★ (three-letter acronym)
VAR (value-added reseller)

alias: An electronic-mail (e-mail) list of people with a common interest. Some aliases are "bldg6@sun" (all inhabitants of building 6), "allsales@sun" (everyone in the sales organization), "mktng@sun" (everyone in the marketing organization), "music@sun" (music lovers), "film@sun" (film buffs), "conscience@sun" (political interest group). Aliases are of two types. The first consists of those, like the above, that are set up and maintained by system administrators. To have their e-mail address added to or deleted from any of these aliases, employees must contact "aliases@sun." The second type of aliases are those set up by individuals (for example, a group of several people who meet regularly to discuss a product introduction).

application: One of several words that are frequently not used in their true lexicographic sense. Most often when people at Sun employ the word, they mean a product or package, not a use to which something is put. Actual examples of applications are word processing, computer-aided design, and illustration. A word-processing program is an application program, but at Sun the program becomes an "application"—as in, "Those engineers [who are developing a database program] are developing a new application."

architecture: A fundamental design. SPARC, for example, is an architecture upon which to build RISC microprocessors. Architectures can be of the hardware or of the software variety.

bang: The exclamation point (!). Also, an important event. Prior to the SPARC introduction in the summer of 1987, workstation division Product Marketing Director John Hime had helped draw up a list of planned product announcements and other events, known as "bangs;" the list was called the "bang list." The major events were referred to as the "big bangs."

barrier to entry: This phrase was heard a great deal, starting in early 1986, when Sun was in the throes of trying to effectively position itself against the competition. Having Bill Joy at Sun, for example, is a barrier to other companies' attempting to get into the workstation market.

box: The hardware component of a workstation, including the boards, disk, and enclosure. One company's box is essentially indistinguishable from another's. What differentiates them is the software they can run.

bundled: Included as part of another product at no charge. Sun bundles its programming languages with its operating system—in essence, giving away something customers might normally pay for from a competitor.

client: At Sun a client can be three things: *(1)* A workstation that is requesting data over an NFS network from a server, such as a program to run on another workstation. *(2)* A window on a computer's display that sends information about the contents of the window to a window server. *(3)* In the marketing-communications department, all internal work done for clients.

clone: A workstation from another company whose avowed purpose is to produce workstations that have the same functionality as Sun's but at lower prices; to produce such workstations. A clone maker is able to bypass the R-and-D costs and go straight to a product, an approach that allows the clone-maker to charge less money. In keeping with the philosophy of open and giveaway technology, Sun encourages clone makers, one of which is Solbourne.

code names: Code names at Sun, like elsewhere, have no particular rhyme or reason. Some are: Campus, Carrera, Hydra, Lego, Office, Pegasus, Roadrunner, Sirius, STAGE, Sunray, Suntan.

collateral: At Sun, *collateral* does not mean assets pledged in return for payment; it comes instead from the phrase *collateral materials* and substitutes for the entire phrase. Synonyms: brochures, data sheets. Many of Sun's collateral pieces are hybrids—part specification sheet, part marketing brochure. Someone in marketing once suggested, in jest, calling these pieces "datachures" or "brosheets." The former term caught on and is now actually being used in earnest by some marketing people.

culture: The Sun way of life, of thinking, of doing business. Entrepreneurialism and junkmail are key components of Sun culture.

desktop: When people from Sun talk about a desktop, most likely they mean *desktop computer* (one small enough to fit on top of a desk), not the top of the desk itself. In a marketing sense the desktop is what one "wins" after a sale is made.

disconnect: Lack of communication. For example, if two people walk out of a meeting with a different interpretation of a task to be done, they are said to have had—when the different interpretations are discovered—a disconnect. (Think of prison warden Strother Martin in *Cool Hand Luke* saying to recalcitrant con Paul Newman: "What we got here is a disconnect.")

distributed computing: As defined by Sun's one-time executive VP, Bernie Lacroute, distributed computing—or network-based one-on-one computing—is the "fourth generation of computing." The preceding generations were:

- First generation, or "back-room, one-on-one computing," which stemmed from the invention of the transistor and the later introduction of batch operating systems in the 1960s

- Second generation, or "shared interactive computing," which was created in the 1970s by minicomputer companies such as DEC and HP

- Third generation, or "isolated, one-on-one computing," which came about in the mid-1970s as a result of the invention of the microprocessor

Distributed computing, according to Lacroute, emerged in the early 1980s as the result of five major technological advances:

- High-performance 32-bit microprocessors

- High-speed networking

- High-resolution bitmapped displays and mice

- Windows software

- Networkwide, multitasking operating systems, such as UNIX

e-mail: Short for "electronic mail." Like many companies, Sun has a system by which its employees can send each other messages, files, etc., electronically. Recipients of these electronic missives can call them up and read them on a computer screen. To send such a message is "to e-mail." E-mail is both a blessing and a curse. It guarantees delivery of (though not necessarily response to) messages, it is a useful productivity tool, and it helps maintain a sense of cohesiveness in a company with thousands of employees. Conversely, it can be a time and productivity waster, and it can prompt clashes among the impetuous. See *flame*, *junkmail*, and *snail-mail*.

end-user: The final user of a computer in a trail that stretches from manufacturer through VARs and OEMs. Essentially synonymous with *user*.

environment: This word is often tacked onto names of products or "applications" to make them appear organic or more impressive than the term alone would appear. A database, for example, is a database; but its gestalt is a "database environment."

flame: An angry or impassioned response to a provocative e-mail message. To send such a response is "to flame."

functionality: Frequently serves as a substitute for *function*. Functionality actually denotes "ability to function."

graphical user interface: The screen display with which people interact when using a computer.

heterogeneous network computing: Use of a local area network that connects computer systems from different manufacturers.

high-five day: A personal day off from work. A high-five day is a McNealy-endorsed method for employees to reward themselves for particularly hard work or a particularly noteworthy accomplishment. Derives from the propensity of the CEO to deliver high fives to executives when an auspicious event has occurred. (Ideally limited to one a year.)

implement: Rarely will you hear at Sun the more prosaic *do*, *accomplish*, *build*, or *perform* in reference to something realized.

insurmountable opportunity: This McNealyism refers to the limitless potential out there for those who work hard, long, smart, and fast.

integrate: To assemble diverse entities to work together. For example, the Sun386i (integrated) allows its users to work with both DOS and UNIX.

interface: A surface, literal or figurative, where two entities meet. The user interface is the area of interaction between person and computer. To interface means to link or connect; it can also mean to talk to or interact with—as in "I'll interface with you about that."

Interleaf: Interleaf is a page-composition package that runs on Sun workstations. To use the package to compose pages is "to interleaf"—as in "I'm going to interleaf that report."

interoperability: The ability of disparate systems to work reciprocally—an extremely important capability to have in heterogeneous networked environments.

JAWS: As an example of how little each box differed from the others, jaded denizens of the workstation industry tended to greet the arrival of the latest ballyhooed product with "Just Another Work Station." Sun's product-marketing manager from 1985 through 1987, John Hime, had as his e-mail address, jhime@jaws.

junkmail: A form of e-mail by which people can share ideas, tell jokes, proselytize, flame, or otherwise express their opinions. Junkmail is open to any Sun employee with a workstation or terminal.

OEM: An original-equipment manufacturer buys Sun workstations and incorporates them into the OEM's product. Interleaf, Inc., uses Sun workstations as the basis for its publishing system, which also includes Interleaf software, a laser printer, and a scanner.

off line: This is one of many terms originally used to describe computer phenomena and then transported to the realm of human interaction. Say you're in a meeting, and someone who's not involved in the meeting indicates he wants to discuss another issue with you. You respond by saying, "I'll talk to you about that off line."

open: Nonproprietary. Some of Sun's open products and philosophies: Open Network Computing, Open Systems Computing, Open Windows. Some others: OPEN LOOK, Open Software Foundation. Open terminology has become the lingua franca for computer companies in the 1990s.

open system[s]: Nonproprietary systems. See chapter 9 for more on open systems.

platform: Generally, product line. "This product runs on the Sun platform" translates roughly to "This product works on Sun workstations." Occasionally used in the traditional sense of plan, design.

port: Move. If your software product runs on, say, DEC minicomputers, and you port it to the Sun platform, you move it over from DEC to Sun—although it may still run on the DEC machines. Upon success, you have completed the port. Porting may involve major recompilation, reconfiguration, etc.

proprietary: Specific to a given company; developed by that company to function only with its own products. Closed.

server: A computer with large amounts of memory and data storage space. This computer can serve the needs of users of diskless systems, such as the Sun-3/50, by storing files (file server), or it can boost the computing power of a modestly outfitted workstation (compute server). These are two of several services a server can render.

snailmail: The USPS. It can also refer to interoffice mail. Contrast with the immediacy of electronic mail.

standard: A device, software protocol, or set of rules that determines how computer hardware and software work. Standards make it possible for hardware and software to work together. They can be *de jure* (by the sanction of some standards body) or *de facto* (by widespread adoption). Products based on standards cost less because more companies produce them. They often perform at a lower degree of efficiency because they address common computer problems, not specific ones.

Sun: In large part because Sun cofounder Andy Bechtolsheim was a grad student at Stanford when he designed what would become the Sun workstation—and because the design called for networking capabilities, and Bechtolsheim tapped his creation into the university's network—the company he helped start was named after the Stanford University Network, or SUN. The company soon downplayed the acronymic origin, however.

support: As a verb, *support* generally means "work with" or "use"—as in "Sun workstations support databases." The verb is often rendered in noun form: "Sun workstations provide support for databases."

technical professional: The original customer base targeted by Sun's marketing department (now eschewed as Sun moves into markets other than engineering, science, and universities).

The Network *Is* the Computer: Essentially means that in a heavily networked environment of computers—all sharing files transparently—the resources available to a user over the network make the network a single, powerful, resourceful computer. Said user has access to computing power much beyond that which sits on his desk.

timesharing: The ability of more than one user to simultaneously tap into a computer (usually a minicomputer).

transparent: Invisible—as in "The process is transparent to the user." Though *transparent* implies that you can see right through the process and ascertain how it works, what users of this term really mean is that the process is hidden from the user's view and the user is not even aware of it.

window: An area of a workstation screen in which a task or application runs. If three windows are open on a screen, the user can perform three different tasks, switching among them at will. This word has given rise to the ersatz gerund/ gerundive "windowing."

workstation: More powerful than a personal computer, and more expensive, too, a workstation is essentially a desktop computer with at least as much CPU speed as a VAX 780 minicomputer. The distinctions between workstations and more powerful PCs is blurring. The amorphousness of this word is a cause of concern for Sun because companies such as Apple—known as a maker of personal computers—are calling their high-end products workstations.

Notes

Chapter 1: Insurmountable Opportunity

Page 8. **Joy "is also a . . ."**: Cheryll Aimee Barron, "The Gospel According to Joy," *The New York Times Magazine: The Business World, Part 2*, March 27, 1988, 30. Virtually everyone who meets Joy is impressed by the scope of his knowledge. Although freely giving his knowledge and opinions on any subject, his style precludes judgments of him as a "know-it-all."

Page 8. **With Joy, the Sun team . . .** : An abbreviated version of this story can be found in Mary Eisenhart and Steve Guttman, "The World According to Sun: President/CEO Scott McNealy Sets the Record Straight," *Micro Times*, mid-December 1988, 41–42. Also important is an unpublished transcription of an interview with Vinod Khosla, "Vinod Khosla and Sun Microsystems (A)," *Harvard Business Review*, no date.

Page 9. **ten-thousand-dollar workstations**: The company's first price list carried an $8,900 amount for the basic system. But that wouldn't get a user up and running.

With computer memory, a local area network attach-
ment, and mass storage subsystem, the more realistic
price was around $30,000, still considerably cheaper than
comparable workstations from the competition.

Page 12. **The board of directors insisted . . .** : Cynics inside
Sun thought Brown could become the company's major
headhunter, scouring the hallways of DEC in search of
top-flight employees. In fact, Brown was instrumental in
identifying Carol Bartz and Bernie Lacroute, who both
joined Sun in 1983 in senior positions, Bartz as director
of marketing (later, vice president) and Lacroute as vice
president of engineering (later, Sun's only executive vice
president).

Page 14. **"put us on the map"**: Steve Kaufman, "A Shining
Success," *San Jose Mercury News*, July 16, 1984, 13E.

Page 15. **Apollo had lost its first . . .**: In recounting the story
to audiences today, McNealy uses it to underscore the
importance of never taking no for an answer. It is, however, inconceivable to most people to imagine either
McNealy or Khosla, now both older and successful executives and millionaires, cooling their heels in anyone's
lobby, even IBM's.

Page 15. **"insurmountable opportunity"**: McNealy, known
for his aphorisms, uses this phrase often.

Page 16. **After a close look at Suns's books . . .** : Peter Nulty,
"Computerdom's Heavenly Brawl," *Fortune*, January 4,
1985, 38.

Page 16. **tight-fisted Khosla**: Even as Sun reached the $40
million-plus plateau, Khosla insisted on approving any
purchase over $500, which seemed to undermine mana-
gers' authority and impaired the company's ability to
react swiftly.

Page 16. **They chose him . . . over Paul Ely, Jr.** : Jonathan B.
Levine, "High Noon for Sun," *Business Week*, July 24,
1989, 72.

CHAPTER 2: HIGH-FIVE DEAL MAKING

Page 21. **Analysts estimated . . . $300 million**: Patricia Lau-pheimer, *Equity Research, Basic Report: Sun Microsystems, Inc.,* Shearson Lehman Brothers, January 12, 1988, 27; Timothy R. McCollum, "Investment Focus: Sun Microsystems," *Design Automation and Instrumentation Review: April 1988 Portfolio Managers' Monthly Summary,* Dean Witter, April 22, 1988, 44. See also *1988 Annual Report,* Sun Microsystems, Inc., September 1988, 3, 11.

Page 21. **UNIX**: Sun's operating system was based on UNIX, developed at AT&T in the late 1960s. In large part because of Sun's tireless efforts, UNIX became de rigueur in the computer industry. See chapter 4 for more details on UNIX.

Page 21. **The deal solidified a business relationship . . .** : Sun seemed to be taking the advice of business-success guru Tom Peters to heart. "Down with barriers, up with alliances" was how *CIO* magazine in part characterized the August 1989–issue interview with Peters. "Partnerships [or] alliances . . . will be the norm. The idea of organizations as islands to themselves is a notion only associated with losers," said Peters in the interview. Alan E. Alter, "Peters' Principles," 13.

Page 21. **Since its founding . . .** : Most Sun systems were purchased in relatively large quantities by volume buyers. These systems were often incorporated into larger systems—generally for specialized purposes—so users of the Sun machines frequently were not aware that they were using a Sun workstation. Single sales to individual users were more rare, although by 1989 the company was beginning to make efforts to enter retail channels.

Page 22. ***Distributed computing . . .*** : John P. Rohal, "Sun Microsystems, Inc.," *Communications & Information Systems Group.* Alex Brown & Sons, December 8, 1988, 3.

Page 25. **It also set Sun apart . . .** : Sean Silverthorne, "Growth Expected to Continue in Workstation Market," *Investor's Daily*, September 8, 1988, 38.

Page 25. **Sun kept its margins . . .** : Mark Stahlman, "Sun Microsystems, Inc.," *Research Notes*, Bernstein Research, August 11, 1988, 11.

Page 25. **In Europe . . . Sun's sales . . .** : "More Young Millionaires, Please," *The Economist*, February 4, 1989, 13.

Page 25. **The importance of attaining . . .** : "Sun has pursued a correct strategy of focusing on the long term and growing market share at the expense of margins." David Wu, "Engineering Workstations," *Quarterly Computer and Design Automation Review*, Warburg Securities, November 1987, 16.

Page 26. **Sun's managers had set their sights . . .** : Philip J. Gill, "Sun Rises Above Its Stations, May Shine As All-Purpose Vendor," *Information Week*, January 26, 1987, passim. Gill quotes both executives at Sun and industry analysts who confirm Sun's chances of becoming "more than a workstation company." See also Scott McNealy's letter to stockholders in the *1988 Annual Report*, 4.

Page 27. **From 1979 to 1985, LAN companies . . .** : "This Market is Hot," *Micro Communications*, April 1984, 17; "The Year of the LAN," *Micro Communications*, May 1985, 11.

Page 27. **"Minis thrived . . . "**: Geoff Lewis, "These Minis Could Be Out of Fashion for Good," *Business Week*, November 21, 1988, 106.

Page 28. **But Sun . . . held its advantage . . .** : McCollum, "Investment Focus . . . ," 11.

Page 28. **Even after Sun later increased . . .** : Cowen Institutional Services, *Perspectives*, Cowen & Company, February 18, 1988, 4.

Page 29. **"one of Sun Microsystems' strengths"**: John Rutledge, "Research Wrap-up," *Weekly Review*, Dillon Reed, October 19, 1987, 2. See also Stahlman, "Sun Microsystems . . . ," 9 and Cowen Institutional Services, Perspectives . . . , 2.

Page 29. **Don't worry about the hardware**: Conventional commercial wisdom in the computer industry is that a computer without good software makes a very effective boat anchor. In fact, many people at Sun actually considered the company to be, primarily, not a workstation vendor, but a software firm.

Page 29. **"The Open Systems environment . . ."**: John C. Levinson, "Sun Microsystems, Inc.," *Investment Research*, Goldman Sachs, September 12, 1988, 1, 3.

Page 32. **TOPS softwave was one of . . .** : "*MacWorld* Best Sellers," *MacWorld*, February 1989, 392.

Page 32. **Adobe's Postscript**: Though technically referred to as a "page-description language," Postscript is overwhelmingly used to define the fonts used to print pages of text.

Page 32. **Although such a combination . . .** : "We are firmly convinced that Sun is unique and is going to be the computer growth company of the 1990s. . . . The company is gaining market share and is growing more rapidly than any other computer company in the industry." John L. Rutledge, "Sun Micro Again Leads the Way for the Computer Industry," *Weekly Review*, Dillon Reed Equity Research, April 11, 1988, 2.

Page 34. **When the Sun386i debuted . . .** : *Ibid.*, 1.

Page 35. **By November of that year . . .** : "Fifty New Independent Vendors Port to Sun386i Platform," Sun Microsystems press release, Las Vegas, November 14, 1988.

Page 35. **Concurrent with . . .** : Ultimately, the Sun386i was only a modest success, and debate raged inside the company for over a year as to whether to continue with the product line. At this writing, the system remains one of Sun's workstation offerings.

Page 36. **To enforce this compliance . . .** : Mark Hall, "Factory Networks," *Micro Communications*, February 1985, 14–20. Byron Belitsos and Jay Misra, *Business Telematics*, Dow Jones–Irwin, 1986, 141.

Page 36. **The Sun engineer, who referred . . .** : John Barry, "Bringing Products to Market," *Sun Technology*, Spring 1988, 35–36.

Page 37. **"Sun workstations on Wall Street . . . "**: Rich Edwards, *Weekly Research*, Robertson Colman & Stephens, March 19, 1987, 1.

Page 40. **People's Republic of China**: The China sales occurred before the crackdown on student demonstrators in June 1989.

Page 40. **number-one workstation company in that country**: Rich Edwards, *Research Notes*, Robertson Colman & Stephens, August 17, 1988, 15.

Page 40. **Industry analysts have consistently . . .** : Patricia Laupheimer, "Company Comment," *Equity Research*, Shearson Lehman Brothers, January 25, 1988, 3; Rich Edwards, "The Impact of Downsizing and Industry Standards," *Computer Systems Industry Research Highlights*, Robertson Colman & Stephens, February 1988, 9; McCollum, "Investment Focus . . . ," 44.

Page 40. **No single institution . . .** : Edwards, *Computer Systems . . .* , 9. McCollum, "Investment Focus . . . ," 44.

Page 44. **Sun had taken the market lead . . .** : *Electronic Publishing: Background Information*, Sun Microsystems, Inc., September 1988, 3.

Page 44. **$40 million in fiscal 1988**: *Oil Exploration and Production Market: Background Information*, Sun Microsystems, Inc. October 1988, 3–4.

Page 45. **SunOS was so prized . . .** : In 1988 Data General bought more than a hundred Sun workstations for operating system development for its next-generation workstation, which would compete with Sun's products.

Page 46. **"Cooperating with technology leaders . . ."**: Stuart Gannes, "Sun's Sizzling Race to the Top," *Fortune*, April 17, 1987, 27.

Page 47. **In the more esoteric realms . . .** : In the deal with Schlumberger, Sun adopted Schlumberger's object-oriented programming and AI software. Giving computer commands by typing in long strings of cryptic characters is giving way to commanding the machines by manipulating stylized, easily identified pictograms (objects) on a screen. In the parallel-processing deals, Sun allied itself with companies that were pioneering work in which more than one microprocessor works on the same problem— usually problems that would require incalculable amounts of a single processor's time—simultaneously.

Chapter 3: The Performance Game

Page 50. **What differentiated Sun . . .** : Those in attendance were in a good position to judge the competition. Bartz and Lacroute had come to Sun from DEC. Lux had been wooed from Apollo. Roebuck and Rosing were Apple alumni. Hime hailed from Data General.

Page 54. **Even in IBM's mainframe world . . .** : Andrew Pollack, "A New 'Fast Lane' in Computers," Business Day, *New York Times*, February 23, 1988.

Page 55. **RISC technology**: Robert Garner, "Scalable Processor Architecture," *SunTechnology*, Summer 1988, 43. Garner provides an extensive bibliography on RISC technology. See also Bernard Lacroute, "The ABI Story," *SunTechnology*, Winter 1988, 9.

Page 55. **MIPS Computer**: John Hime, one of the participants in the meeting outlined at the beginning of this chapter, went on to become a vice president at MIPS. Silicon Valley is much like professional sports, with employees continually changing employers—much like free agents.

Page 55. **RISC . . . executed one instruction . . .** : Herb Brody, "RISC-y Business," *High Technology Business*, August 1988, 20.

Page 55. **"RISC chips can be made . . ."**: Stuart Gannes, "Sun's Sizzling Race to the Top," *Fortune*, August 17, 1987.

Page 55. **Memory a . . . commodity**: An inaccurate prediction that proved troublesome to Sun three years later when the market ran short of 1-megabyte DRAM chips. Dynamic random-access memory, or DRAM, chips hold the program or the data being used by the CPU. In 1988 the 1-megabyte DRAM chips were the most popular, used by Sun, Apple, IBM, and the rest of the industry. Through either collusion or poor planning, the 1-megabyte DRAMs nearly vanished from the market. Controlled by Japanese manufacturers, the DRAM shortage caused most of the computer industry to raise its prices. At Sun, where products were already priced aggressively at the expense of margins, the lack of DRAMs caused a backlog headache for both Sun and its customers. See also George Gilder, "How the Computer Companies Lost Their Memories," *Forbes*, June 13, 1988, 79–84.

Page 55. **billion-byte memory systems**: At Princeton University a researcher connected a billion-byte board set to a Sun workstation.

Page 56. **In Joy's mind, RISC and UNIX . . .** : Laura Conigliaro and Richard Whittington, "RISC Has Come of Age . . ." *CAD/CAM & Technical Workstations*, Prudential-Bache Securities, October 7, 1988.

Page 57. **General Motors and Ford**: Wu, "Engineering Workstations," . . . 16.

Page 57. **In 1985 the best and biggest . . .** : *Ibid.* Weighing AT&T, the originator and owner of UNIX, and Sun, Wu concludes: "Sun will be the company to exploit it commercially." And what Wu understood in 1987, Sun's engineers firmly believed long before. McCollum, *Design Automation and Instrumentation Review*, Dean Witter, April/May 1988, 24.

Page 57. **"You can never have too many MIPS . . ."**: In 1964 Intel founder Gordon Moore answered a question about the number of transistors that could be put on a chip. He gave a formula of 2 raised to the power of the current year minus 1964. So for 1980 the number of transistors on a chip would be 2^{16} ($2^{1980 - 1964}$), or approximately 65,000, which has remained an accurate, if off-the-cuff, formula for twenty years. Bill Joy's corollary to this is his "Law of MIPS," which posits that a microprocessor's speed will be 2 to the current year minus 1984.

Page 57. **"Reducing all the features . . ."**: Mark Stahlman, "Significant Research Conclusions, "*The Myth of Price/Performance*, Bernstein Research, March 1987, 3–4.

Page 59. **"took the latest microprocessor technology . . ."**: Michael Leibowitz, "Workstation Wars: The Battle of the Big 7," *High Technology Business*, November 1987, 23.

Page 59. **"a computer that would combine . . ."**: Peter Nulty, "Computerdom's Heavenly . . . ."

Page 62. *Business Week* **kicked off 1985 . . .** : Marilyn Harris, et al., "Can Apollo and Sun Hang On to Stardom?" *Business Week*, January 14, 1985, 126J.

Page 62. **Industry prognosticators were confident . . .** : Charmaine Harris, "Engineering Workstations," *Information Week*, September 9, 1985, 27.

Page 63. **HP had more sales than . . .** : David Card, "What's Hot and What's Not in Workstations," *Electronic Business*, March 15, 1987, 64–65.

Page 63. **HP's products carved up . . . :** Edwards, "The Impact of Downsizing . . . ," 7.

Page 64. **HP's presence in the market . . . :** Card, "What's Hot and What's Not . . . ," 64.

Page 64. **HP joined in . . . :** Peter D. Schleider, "Engineering Computer Update," *Institutional Research*, Wessels, Arnold & Henderson, May 9, 1988, 5.

Page 65. **DEC was a favorite . . . :** John Verity, "A Bold Move in Mainframes," *International Business Week*, May 29, 1989, 44–50.

Page 66. **DEC had "the most to lose . . .":** Leibowitz, "Workstation Wars . . . ," 27.

Page 67. **DEC would get upward . . .":** Denise Caruso, "Workstation Makers Brace for IBM and DEC," *Electronics*, October 21, 1985, 35.

Page 67. **Ironically, Gallup's withering . . . :** M. Harris, "Can Apollo and Sun . . . ," 126J.

Page 67. **In addition to making Sun . . . :** Karen Freeze, "Sun Microsystems," Harvard Business School, 9-686-134, 1986, 5.

Page 68. **VMS was not available:** In a briefing to Sun marketing people in July 1989, Vicki Brown, an analyst at International Data Corporation, noted that VMS did work on DEC's 3100 and 2100 in the company's laboratories. It was only a matter of time, she thought, before DEC gave their users a choice of operating systems.

Page 70. **In their first three . . . $57 million in revenue:** Frederic H. Cohen and Walter J. Winnitzki, "Sun Microsystems, Inc.: A Rising Performer," *Company Research*, L. F. Rothschild, Unterberg, Towbin, Inc., July 10, 1986, 6–7.

Page 71. **The Sun computer cost 15 percent less:** *Ibid.*, 4.

Page 72. **When Sun's vice president of finance . . . :** Every quarter until Sun became a publicly held company,

Smith compared Sun's financial progress with that of Apollo. Each quarter showed improvement, and in Sun's second fiscal quarter in 1987, he was able to crow that Sun had raced by Apollo. Smith did not provide a similar comparison to other competitors. Sun, although privately held during these years, freely announced its quarterly results to the press and financial community.

Page 73. **Unlike Apollo, which was . . .** : Philip J. Gill, "Sun Rises Above Its Stations, May Shine as All-Purpose Vendor," *Information Week*, January 26, 1987.

Page 73. **"on only three third-party . . ."**: Gordon Bock, et al., "The Workstation Sweepstakes: It's IBM, Coming Up on the Outside," *Business Week*, February 3, 1986, 66.

Page 74. **Sun had to accept . . .** : International Data Corporation was the only major market researcher that still gave Sun the top spot after the HP-Apollo deal. Its figures show Sun with 37.2 percent of the calendar-year 1988 workstation shipments, while the combined strength of HP and Apollo accounts for only 28.7 percent. In January 1990, DataQuest revised its estimates, returning sun to the top spot.

Page 74. **HP losing market share to Sun and DEC**: "Pairing: How HP/Apollo Shapes a New Competitive Lineup," *The Monosson Report on DEC and IBM*, April 1989, 3.

Page 74. **HP deemed the purchase . . .** : Larry Hicks, "Maturing Industry Leaves Less Room for Start-up Firms," *San Francisco Examiner*, May 7, 1989, E1.

Page 76. **As the "giant footsteps" of . . .** : Bock, "The Workstation Sweepstakes . . . ," 66–67. M. Harris, "Can Apollo and Sun . . . ," 126J. Caruso, "Workstation Makers Brace . . . ," 34–35.

Page 77. **"snake oil"**: Glen Rifkin and George Harrar, *The Ultimate Entrepreneur: The Story of Ken Olsen and Digital Equipment Corporation* (Chicago,: Contemporary Books, 1988), 305.

Page 77. **This latter point is ironic . . .** : *Ibid.*, 71.

Page 77. **Olsen**: "Olsen on DEC," *Information Week*, September 12, 1988, 41.

Page 77. **His scorn for desktop machines . . .** : "Behind the financial downturn, DEC's three-legged personal computer strategy was toppling . . . . DEC intended to ship 55,000 Pros in 1983 and 215,000 in 1984. The revised estimates specified 13,000 in 1983 and 60,000 in 1984. Profits were forecast at $13 million in 1983, $302 million in 1984. The new plan: $78 million loss in 1983, $46 million in 1984." Rifkin and Harrar, *The Ultimate Entrepreneur* . . . , 237.

Page 77. **Finally, the continued success . . .** : DEC's initial computer line, the PDP series, continues to sell well. In early 1989, DEC estimated that the sales of PDP minicomputers alone "produce[d] enough revenue to be considered a Fortune 500 company on its own." "Fueled by Development, PDP-11 Product Line Accelerates into the Future," *Product Insight*, January 1989, 13.

Page 78. **Edwards**: Rich Edwards, "Standards and Open Systems—What Customers Are Demanding (and Why They Choose Sun)," *Sun Microsystems, Inc.,* Robertson Colman & Stephens, July 23, 1986, 7.

Page 79. **"We will never compete on price"**: Rifkin and Harrar, *The Ultimate Entrepreneur* . . . , 233.

Page 80. **DEC introduced . . . Sun-killer machines . . .** : Ron Wolf, "Digital Throws Down Workstation Gauntlet," *San Jose Mercury News*, January 8, 1989, E-1.

Page 80. **14 MIPS**: Some analysts questioned the veracity of the 14 MIPS claims, noting that the RISC chip maker MIPS Computer maintained that its CPU reached only a 12 MIPS clock speed.

Page 80. **Since, as Olsen has admitted . . .** : Wolf, "Digital Throws Down Gauntlet . . . ," E-3; "Olsen On DEC," 41.

Page 81. **. . . the vice presidency once held by Bartz**: The odyssey of Carol Bartz typified the opportunities for movement within the Sun organization. She went from vice president of marketing to take over the vice presidency of Sun's federal systems division—a wholly owned subsidiary that sold Sun systems to the government and the military. After her stint at "Sun Fed," she left the company to have a baby. Just when some people thought her days as a career woman were over, Bartz resurfaced as the vice president of the customer service division, replacing Bob Lux, who had vacated the position.

Page 82. **"was now open season . . ."**: It was in this meeting that Zander glibly remarked that he'd like to see Sun immediately run an advertisement inviting VAX/VMS customers to look at SPARC, Sun's RISC workstation product family. Later in the day he got McNealy to agree to the idea. That night Sun's marketing communications director was up late relaying copy points over the phone to typesetters at the *Wall Street Journal*. The ad ran on the back of section B the next morning and provoked considerable attention in the business press. See Don Clark, "Technology," *San Francisco Chronicle*, January 12, 1989, E-3; "Sun Micro Opens Counterattack," *San Jose Mercury News*, January 13, 1989, 15E. The day after the DEC "Sun-killer" introduction, McNealy and Sun's chief financial officer, Joseph Graziano, were boasting to New York financial analysts about yet another quarter of record revenues and earnings. McNealy was quoted as saying, "People ask me if I'm afraid of a price war. I say let it begin."

Page 82. **Strecker**: Stuart Gannes, "IBM and DEC Take on the Little Guys," *Fortune*, October 10, 1988, 108.

CHAPTER 4: THE RELIGION OF UNIX

Page 85. **a pitched battle**: "It could have been a declaration of war," begins one article. Charles Pelton and Charles von Simson, "OSF, AT&T Square Off," *Information Week*, October 24, 1988, 12.

Page 86. **UNIX was the industry's standard . . .** : "The competitive environment for standards-based computers (i.e., those with UNIX) is heating up considerably." John C. Levinson, "Notes from Our Morning Research Conference Call," *Research Notes*, Goldman Sachs, October 7, 1988, 3.

Page 86. **With Sun and AT&T allied . . .** : Barry F. Bosak, "Sun Microsystems," *Company Report*, Eberstadt Fleming Inc., March 11, 1988, 3, 6.

Page 87. **Wiegner**: Kathleen K. Wiegner, "They Are Not There Waiting for the Plane to Land," *Forbes*, June 27, 1988, 49.

Page 87. **International Data Corporation . . .** : Gannes, "IBM and DEC . . . ," 109.

Page 87. **Lowe**: *Ibid.*, 112.

Page 90. **Stahlman**: Marc G. Schulman, *IBM and DEC: The Battle for Supremacy in the Computer Industry*, Salomon Brothers, Inc., April 1988, 1–3.

Page 91. **DiNucci**: Gannes, "IBM and DEC . . . ," 114.

Page 91. **"the gospel of UNIX"**: "Role for UNIX Expands in High-End Integration," *Computer Systems News*, November 12, 1987, 10.

Page 93. **Moving the operating system . . .** : Dean Witter, *Equity Report #917*, May 18, 1988.

Page 94. **What does this word *UNIX* mean?**: Because it is a computer-related term and because the computer world loves acronyms, *UNIX* at first glance appears as though it might be an acronym. It's not. The order of the four letters that comprise the word has, however, been reversed to form one: a Berkeley company—apparently wanting to differentiate itself from the operating system—called itself Mt. Xinu; Xinu stood for "Xinu is not UNIX."

Page 94. **"name applies to a family . . .** : Paul S. Wang, *An*

Introduction to Berkeley UNIX, (Belmont, CA: Wadsworth Publishing Company, 1988), 1.

Page 95. **"guru"**: The investment community doesn't necessarily share this exalted view: concerning Joy, Paine Webber's June 23, 1988, technology group investment newsletter, entitled *UNIX: The Tower of Babble*, said, "Guru is too mystical."

Page 96. **Patterson**: Interview with Dave Patterson for the Summer 1988 issue of *Sun Technology*. Patterson was an apostle of reduced-instruction-set computing (RISC). He was later to bring his expertise to Sun as a consultant on Sun's RISC-based SPARC (Scalable Processor Architecture) chip.

Page 96. **"hacker ethic"** . . . **"Access to computers . . . "**: Stephen, Levy, Hackers: *Heroes of the Computer Revolution* (Garden Grove, NJ: Anchor Press, 1984), 26–36.

Page 97. **"There are currently more versions . . . "**: Paine Webber, *UNIX: The Tower of Babble*.

Page 100. **he reported to no one**: In the real world after the departure of Bernie Lacroute, Joy existed on McNealy's organization chart reporting to Sun's CEO.

Page 101. **Sun press release**: "Sun Offers First Phase of Converged UNIX Operating System," August 5, 1986.

Page 102. **Sun wished to increase its penetration . . . **: "Amdahl and Sun Microsystems to Integrate Workstations and Mainframes under the UNIX System," Sun press release, February 9, 1988.

Page 102. **Blumenthal**: Sun/Unisys/AT&T press release issued by Sun on March 9, 1988.

Page 103. **Blumenthal/McNealy/Cassoni**: *Ibid.*

Page 103. **Berkeley, where DARPA . . . **: As Peter Nulty points out in "Computerdom's Heavenly Brawl," Bill Joy received a DoD grant for his work on UNIX at Berkeley.

Page 104. **the mission of an army procurement officer . . .** :
One of the authors, who was employed by *Info World* at
the time, discussed the officer's computer needs with
him.

Page 105. **any computer company that bid . . .** : Mark Hall,
"The Monthly Report," *UNIX Review*, April 1985, 8.

Page 105. **Ultrix could not make the grade . . .** : Bear Stearns,
"AT&T's UNIX Metamorphosis," October 5, 1988.

Page 105. **wreaked havoc on the DoD's Arpanet**: The *San
Jose Mercury News*, which reported on the incident in a
page-1 story entitled " 'Virus' Hits Nation's Research
Computers," noted that the virus was launched on In-
ternet, a "network of networks" connecting six hundred
sites, including research universities, think tanks, and
government agencies (among the latter, the DoD and
NASA).

Page 105. **"A virus is . . ."**: John Markoff, " 'Virus in Military Computers Disrupts Systems Nationwide," *New
York Times*, November 4, 1988. The *San Jose Mercury
News* reiterated the vulnerability of Sun systems in this
incident: Dan Stober, "VAX and Sun computers were
hardest hit by the virus," November 4, 1988, 1. The *San
Francisco Chronicle* also noted that Sun systems were
hit.

Page 106. **Reports indicated that . . .** : Brenton R. Schlender,
"Computer 'Virus,' Infiltrating Network, Shuts Down
Computers Around World," *Wall Street Journal*, No-
vember 4, 1988.

Page 106. **Cole**: Markoff, "Virus in Military Computers. . . ."

Page 108. **Henry McGilton, a writer . . .** : McGilton's motive,
he says, for getting into the UNIX-book market was the
poor quality of UNIX books existing at that time.

Page 109. **"solely on word of mouth"**: Nulty, "Computerdom's Heavenly Brawl. . . ."

Page 109. **Actually, pioneering work . . .** : Douglas K. Smith and Robert C. Alexander, *Fumbling the Future* (New York: William Morrow and Co., 1988).

Page 110. **"Pizza Computer"**: At a Roadrunner meeting held in Building 7 in 1986, Sun's vice president of the East Coast division, Barry James Folsom, showed the assembled group a short film featuring Muppets characters. One nerdlike fellow attempted to write a complex program to make his computer dial a pizza place and order a pizza. He kept getting a "syntax error" message on the screen. Finally, his exasperated friend picked up the phone and called the pizza place. Within seconds, a chef popped through the screen, bearing the pizza. The moral of the story was that computers—even UNIX-based ones—should be easy to use. Roadrunner became informally and irreverently known among some of the film's viewers as the "Pizza Computer."

Page 111. **Your plane lands . . .** : Jon Kannegaard, "OPEN LOOK: Industry Outlook and Overview," *Sun Technology*, Autumn 1988, 58–62.

Page 111. **"this chaos is . . ."**: *Ibid.*

Page 111. **"moved out of the lab . . ."**: *Ibid.*

Page 111. **With the OPEN LOOK . . ."**: *Ibid.*

Page 111. **With an acknowledgment to Xerox . . .** : Apple, on the other hand, had incorporated much of Xerox's development work, and a few years after the product debuted in 1984, Apple was brazenly claiming that it had virtually invented object-oriented interfaces. It looks as though the U.S. judicial system will settle the controversy.

Page 113. **Joy's message said . . .** : Reported in Paine Webber, *UNIX: The Tower of Babble.*

CHAPTER 5: SUITS AND SANDALS

Page 115. **Sun T-shirts**: T-shirts at Sun are legendary. Nearly every department has its own. Most of them have multiple versions. Events are marked with T-shirts. Project completions are celebrated with T-shirts. The publication of a book is noted with a T-shirt. Even parties get T-shirts. There have been T-shirt contests at Sun. There is even a black market for old, rare T-shirts. They are used as status symbols, with veteran employees flaunting their early-year T-shirts in front of jealous rookies. The pervasiveness of T-shirts gave rise to jokes that during the tough fourth fiscal quarter of 1989, the company would have been able to make record profits if it had just stopped making T-shirts. In fact, when the first fiscal quarter of 1990 began, one of the cost-saving programs for the company was a moratorium on the making of T-shirts. One waggish employee suggested that the company sponsor a "T-shirt retrospective."

Page 117. **"contriving or planning . . ."**: *Webster's Ninth New Collegiate Dictionary* (Springfield, MA: Merriam-Webster, Inc., 1983).

Page 118. **Stanford was a hotbed . . .**: In 1981 *Psychology Today* ran an article entitled "The Hacker Papers" in which the author researched and reported on the hacker mentality at Stanford University.

Page 119. **Ethernet, invented at Xerox's PARC**: The leader of the Ethernet development team, Robert Metcalf, went on to found 3Com Corporation, just down the street from Sun. Metcalf, like so many other Silicon Valley success stories, is an engineer who understood technology and its place in the market. 3Com is now a half-billion-dollar outfit that specializes in local area networks for computers, a multibillion-dollar industry that virtually did not exist before the 1980s.

Page 120. **"He reports to . . ."**: John Markoff, "The Joy of Computer Design," *San Francisco Examiner*, November 1, 1987. As Cheryll Aimee Barron put it in "The Gospel According to Joy" (*The New York Times Magazine*, March 27, 1988): "Officially, he answers to the title of vice president of research and development. In fact, he is a sort of freewheeling corporate guru and the driving force behind a strategy to turn the industry upside down."

Page 120. **Joy grew up . . . UC Berkeley**: Barron, "The Gospel According. . . ."

Page 120. **True to his roots . . . devoted followers**: Markoff, "The Joy of Computer. . . ."

Page 121. **"Sun would not be anything . . ."**: Frank Rose, *West of Eden* (New York: Viking Press, 1989).

Page 124. **Some later formed . . .** : Legato Corporation of Palo Alto, California, and Go Corporation are two promising offshoots of Sun that are peopled with early-year engineers from Sun.

Page 125. **Network Software Environment**: The NSE addressed two realities of large software-development projects: *(1)* Many programmers worked on discrete parts of the overall program, which had to be successfully merged to make the entire program work successfully. *(2)* These phalanxes of programmers work over networks, exchanging much data in the process. Among other things, the NSE would keep track of the most up-to-date version of the program, avoid duplication of effort, and help locate and eradicate bugs.

Page 126. **"programming in the large"**: John Barry, "The Secrets of Success," *Sun Technology*, Spring 1988, 29–30.

Page 131. **"docubox"**: The docubox is the so-called manual set from Sun. Its alleged purpose is to help users understand their Sun workstations. But in the spirit of Bernie Lacroute's new-employee video, it was a huge daunting work that was useful primarily to established technologists. Neophytes who did not kill themselves while lugging the docubox into their offices would certainly succumb to the overpowering "techno-speak" of the thousands of pages of excruciating detail with precious little context.

Page 132. **an alphabet soup**: Lou Delzompo, a Sun product manager, refers to these letter strings that cannot be pronounced as "TLAs," or three-letter abbreviations.

Page 138. **McNealy**: *The Computer Industry in 1987* (Mahassett, NJ: CMP Publishing, 1986), a collection of editorials written by computer industry executives.

Page 138. **When Lacroute left . . .** : Herb Greenberg, "An Executive Eclipse at Sun Microsystems," *San Francisco Chronicle*, June 7, 1989, C1.

CHAPTER 6: GIVEAWAY TECHNOLOGY

Page 144. **"major market shifts . . ."**: Jonathan Fram and Louis Giglio, *Bear Stearns Report on Sun Microsystems*, September 28, 1987, 2.

Page 144. **"strategy makes it . . ."**: Bob Herwick, *Spot Report*, Hambrecht & Quist, Inc., April 7, 1988, 1.

Page 144. **"Sun Microsystems was founded . . ."**: William P. O'Connor, *Portfolio Opportunity 14*, December 1, 1987, 1.

Page 146. **In an essay . . .** : Bernard Lacroute, "Computing: The Fourth Generation," *SunTechnology*, Spring 1988, 9–10.

Page 147. **Big, diversified companies . . .** : Mitch Irsfeld, "Role for UNIX Expands in High-End Integration," *Computer Systems News*, November 2, 1987, 10.

Page 147. **Morgan Stanley**: Rick Ruthven, "Sun Microsystems: Pointing the Way to the Promised Land of Open Systems," *Investment Research*, Morgan Stanley, September 6, 1988, 6.

Page 147. **Marc Schulman**: Marc G. Schulman and Sanjiv G. Hingorani, "The Computer Industry—Dawn of a New Era," *Stock Research: Computers*, Salomon Brothers, Inc., May 18, 1988, 1–3. These analysts go on to explain that it is the formation of the Open Software Foundation (OSF) that will deliver these multivendor systems. The OSF, Salomon Brothers believes, has the computer clout to establish effective standards. They seem miffed that Sun, along with AT&T, "spurned" the OSF, and Salomon concluded that the best interests of DEC, IBM, and HP were not uppermost in Sun's plans when developing a new unified UNIX or introducing other industry standards.

Page 148. **NFS . . . was licensed by . . .**: One can see the difference in Sun's confidence by reviewing old press releases the company sent to editors as each new licensee jumped onto the NFS bandwagon. One announcement in September 1985 is modestly headlined "Sun Network File System Gains Ground as Standard." In it, three relatively minor companies proclaim their adherence to NFS. But no total number of licensees is referred to in the copy. A year later, in October 1986, an NFS-related announcement brags about 80 licensees. In early 1987 the company's press release positively crows with the headline about Apollo's conversion to NFS—"Sun Continues Leadership in Open Systems; Apollo Joins NFS Ranks." A year after that, when IBM and Control Data Corporation buy into NFS, the press releases show a restrained self-confidence but do not neglect to point out the 175 organizations that support NFS.

Page 149. **Today, this technique . . .** : John Hime, "NFS Brings Common Specs to Computing," *Systems and Software*, July 1985, 44–48; Fram and Giglio, *Bear Stearns . . .* , 3.

Page 149. **From that point the popularity . . .** : Brian Robinson, "Sun's Network File System Draws More Supporters," *Electronic Engineering Times*, February 10, 1986, 1, 18.

Page 150. **At least one company . . .** : Mike Saul, Larry Lace, David Robinson, and Jerry Toporek, "Development of a

NFS VAX/VMS Server," *SunTechnology*, Winter 1989, 85–88.

Page 150. **With NFS, Sun returned . . .** : "Inside Report," *The Anderson Report*, Anderson Publishing Company, July 1986, 5. In this unsigned analyst's review of the market, Scott McNealy is reported to have said that NFS was thrown "over the wall" to the market. The analyst remarks that NFS "could have been held close to the chest for proprietary advantage (but) has instead virtually become a de facto standard."

Page 151. **It adopted the international . . .** : Leslie Goff, "Sun Brings Out IBM Links, Outlines NFS-TOPS Meld," *MIS Week*, June 8, 1987, 5; "Sun Unveils NFS for AT&T's UNIX System V," *Computer Systems News*, December 8, 1986, 2; Abigail Christopher, "Mac-to-DEC PC Connections in Sun Network," *MacWeek*, June 8, 1987, 12.

Page 151. **McNealy**: "Sun Outlines Computing Strategy," Sun press release, June 1, 1987.

Page 151. **In fact, in a later . . .** : Sun's promotional pitch changed to "Systems for Open Computing" in 1988–89.

Page 151. **Despite the success . . .** : Helen Pike, "Sun, Apollo Spar over Whose Network Software Is Best," *Electronic Engineering Times*, June 22, 1987, 7; Lynn Haber, "Sun's NFS, AT&T'S RFS to Compete for Recognition," *Mini-Micro Systems*, May 1986, 22–23.

Page 152. **NCF**: It appeared that the companies were trying to "out-TLA" as well as outengineer and outmarket each other.

Page 153. **The small company figured . . .** : Denise Caruso, "Inside Silicon Valley: Upside Goes Inside the Valley," *San Francisco Examiner*, June 11, 1989, D-3.

Page 156. **If for no other reason . . .** : David S. Rosenthal, "Toward a More Focused View," *UNIX Review*, June 1986, 59.

Page 157. **NeWS combines the . . .** : For the most complete description of NeWS, see James Gosling, David Rosenthal, and Michelle Arden, *The NeWS Book* (New York: Springer-Verlag, 1989).

Page 158. **"the window system of choice . . ."**: "Sun Microsystems and Intel to Demonstrate Window Technology," *Computer Daily*, November 24, 1986, 4.

Page 158. **"a replacement for ASCII . . ."**: "Windows of Opportunity," *UNIX Review*, January 1987, 74.

Page 159. ***Computer Graphics World***: Barbara Robertson, "What's NeWS at Sun?" *Computer Graphics World*, November 1986, 14.

Page 160. **Bernie Toth**: Jeff Moad, "Three Hats in the Ring," *Datamation*, October 15, 1986, 32.

Page 160. **At the announcement . . .** : Priscilla M. Chabal, "Sun Unveils Windowing for Networks," *Infoworld*, October 20, 1986, 1.

Page 160. **lead time**: Sun's tradition is to announce a product only when it is ready to be in the customer's hands within thirty days.

Page 160. **In April 1987, Sun unveiled . . .** : Markoff, "The Joy of Computer Design," . . . D-3.

Page 161. **"The Revolutionary . . ."**: Brenton R. Schlender, *Wall Street Journal*, March 18, 1988, 1.

Page 162. **Achilles' heel**: Marc G. Shulman, *Open Systems: Facts and Fallacies*, Salomon Brothers, July 25, 1988, passim. Schulman denigrates the entire notion of open systems in this scathing analysis of Sun. His predictions a year after the report's publication, however, failed to materialize in many areas—the introduction of OSF products, a new IBM version of its UNIX (AIX), and the failure of Sun in the RISC market.

Page 163. **The long-term goal was . . .** : However, the SPARC license/royalty scheme has generated significant income.

The multitiered license structure allows some companies to invest at the chip-development level. Semiconductor companies, such as Cypress and Bipolar, are in this category. These organizations can bring SPARC up on new, faster media that they can then sell to the market. Another tier offers a license to computer makers. This agreement lets them build SPARC computers, but not engage in any CPU enhancements. Solbourne Computers falls into this category. Solbourne pays less for its license, but it pays a royalty to Sun for each system it sells. That royalty is close to the margin of profit Sun would make if it sold its own computer. This plan means that even though Solbourne and other clone makers may cut into Sun's revenue stream, they will actually add directly to Sun's profits, altering in a positive way Sun's reputation as a company with low margins.

Page 164. **In effect, the SPARC strategy . . .** : Rich Edwards, *Sun Microsystems, Inc.,* Robertson Colman & Stephens, October 21, 1987, 3.

Page 164. **If they had a true . . .** : Patricia Laupheimer, "Advanced Computing: Understanding BIs, ABIs, Open Look, and What's Happening With UNIX," *Equity Research: Industry Comment*, Shearson Lehman Hutton, April 15, 1988, 3. She writes: "Sun hopes to replicate the success of the Intel/MS-DOS dominated PC market, where the power of a binary standard accelerated market growth and penetration."

Page 165. **"exactly what Sun should . . ."**: John C. Levinson, "Sun-4: Good or Bad News?" *Investment Research*, Goldman Sachs, July 20, 1987, 3–4.

Page 165. **More important, with an increase . . .** : Alfred Rosenblatt, "King of the Third World?" *Electronic Products*, November 15, 1987, 9. The article's title refers to an expression Vittorio Cassoni used at the announcement of AT&T's adopting SPARC. At the New York press conference that day, he told attendees that IBM and DEC represented the First and Second Worlds of proprietary computing. SPARC, he claimed, was the liberating force of the Third World. Although it was a tidy and provocative metaphor, public relations staffers at Sun and elsewhere quickly discouraged its use, feeling it was potentially loaded with Western cultural myopia and might be misconstrued.

Page 167. **Even IBM . . .** : Rich Edwards, *The RISC Wars: An Investment Perspective*, Robertson, Colman & Stephens, July 20, 1988, 1–4.

Page 167. **"one architecture . . ."**: A Sun brochure, *Sun and Open Systems*, lays out the theory that UNIX is the architecture and that the underlying hardware, the "instruction set" of a CPU's registers, is meaningless. No one cares about the low-level microprocessor, the document purports, so long as it's fast. Everything else is software magic.

Page 167. **Sun executives wanted . . .** : Norm Alster, "How Intel and Motorola Missed the Sun Rise," *Electronic Business*, November 1, 1987, 32–34. Motorola went on to introduce its 88000 RISC processor. Intel competed with its lackluster i860 RISC chip.

Page 167. **gate-array technology**: This technology involves arranging the circuits on a microchip in such a way that the chip can be easily customized for specific applications. This approach worked well for SPARC, which was scalable, or customizable.

Page 167. **Bill Joy**: Alster, "How Intel . . . ," 34.

Page 168. **"Scott McGreedy"**: Denise Caruso, "Inside Silicon Valley: Trading Patriotism for Profit," *San Francisco Examiner*, June 4, 1989, D-3.

Page 168. **Innovative SPARC products . . .** : "Computer Technology: Land of the Licensing Sun," *The Economist*, June 3, 1989, 68.

Page 168. **"the U.S. is not that tough . . ."**: Tom Inglesby, editor, "An Interview with Scott McNealy," *Manufacturing Systems*, April 1989, 14.

Page 169. **"SPARCintosh"**: Henry Bortman, "Sun Makes SPARCs Fly," *MacUser*, July 1989, 220. Others also used the term in reference to the SPARCstation 1. The term was bandied about inside Sun for months—not in reference to the SPARCstation but to yet another, less expensive, faster machine on the drawing boards of Andy Bechtolsheim's group. The word filtered to a *USA Today* business writer, who used it in a leaked story on the SPARCstation 1.

CHAPTER 7: MANAGING HYPERGROWTH

Page 172. **It was one of the key . . .** : According to one respected business journal, the hiring of Lux, Rosing, and Bob Garrow was Sun's "preparation for major-league competition." John W. Wilson, "Sun Microsystems: The New Hotshot," *Business Week*, February 3, 1986, 67.

Page 172. **Bill Joy, Eric Schmidt . . .** : Rosing and Bechtolsheim have been seen only once at Sun wearing suits. The momentous event was the 1988 shareholders meeting.

Page 173. **hypergrowth**: The term *hypergrowth*, which means excessive or exaggerated growth, derives from a self-published book of that name by Adam Osborne and John C. Dvorak. (See "Preventing the 'Osborne Syndrome'" later in this chapter.)

Page 174. **Osborne's business plan . . .** : Paul Freiberger and Michael Swaine, *Fire in the Valley* (Berkeley, CA, Osborne/McGraw-Hill, 1984), 54–66.

Page 175. **Ethernet was one . . .** : In Kenneth Thurber's *Local Area Network Handbook of 1983*, he lists more than a hundred different companies offering a variety of LANs. Virtually all of them linked minicomputers together.

Page 175. **Since IBM did not . . .** : IBM eventually introduced a PC LAN from 3Com's neighbor, Sytek, which was located directly across the street. But IBM's marketing and technical people were not thrilled with the product, and it eventually died a quiet, unheralded death. See "IBM Jostles PC LAN Market with Broadband LAN Entry," *Micro Communications*, October 1984, 7–8.

Page 177. **"places substantial stress . . ."** : Frederic H. Cohen and Walter J. Winnitzki, "Sun Microsystems, Inc.: A Rising Performer," *Company Research*, L. F. Rothschild, Unterberg, Towbin, Inc., July 10, 1986, 3.

Page 177. **So Sun introduced . . .** : Cowen Institution Services, *Perspectives*, Cowen & Company, February 18, 1988, 3. Patricia Laupheimer, "Company Comment," *Equity Research*, March 17, 1988, 1–3.

Page 177. **Sun doubled its sales . . .** : "A Sun Rising in the West: An Interview with Carol Bartz," *High-Tech Marketing*, December 1985, 56.

Page 178. **In fiscal 1988 . . .** : Sanjiv G. Hingorani, "Sun Microsystems, Inc.—Rapid Expense Growth and Slowdown in Workstation Market Could Lead to Severe Earnings Disappointment," *Computers*, Salomon Brothers, October 17, 1988, 1.

Page 178. **Warburg**: Wu, "Engineering Workstations," . . . 16.

Page 178. **Dillon Reed**: Rutledge, "Sun Micro Again Leads . . .," 2.

Page 178. **Prudential-Bache**: Laura Conigliaro, "Sun's Thinking: Long-Term, Strategic, and Impressive," *Sun Microsystems: Company Update*, Prudential-Bache, August 31, 1988, 1.

Page 180. **They quickly found . . .** : Steve Kaufman, "The Future's So Bright, They Gotta Wear Shades," *San Jose Mercury News*, January 26, 1987, 4E.

Page 180. **experienced men**: There has never been a woman on Sun's board of directors.

Page 181. **"the level-headed . . ."** : Jonathan B. Levine, "Sun Microsystems Turns On the Afterburners," *Business Week*, July 18, 1988, 62.

Page 181. **Bean also avoided . . .** : David Card, "The Maturing of the Workstation *Wunderkind*," *Electronic Business*, March 15, 1987, 43. See also Fram and Giglio, *Bear Stearns Report . . .*, 37.

Page 181. **It was embarrassing . . .** : At Lacroute's farewell party in June 1989, Eric Schmidt regaled the audience with "horror stories" of "Bernie knowing more than anyone" about the technical problems with a new system or new software. It behooved people to be prepared when offering an excuse to Lacroute, he said.

Page 182. **Analysts referred to . . .** : David Wu, "Computers," *Research Notes*, S. G. Warburg & Co., Inc., August 11, 1987, 2. Peter Schleider, "A Supporting Note," *Report*, October 11, 1988, 10. John Rutledge, "Research Wrap-Up," *Weekly Review*, Dillon Reed Equity Research, October 19, 1987, 2.

Page 182. **So fast was . . .** : The building site, it turned out, was considered to occupy wetlands, even though the entire area had been dredged and filled years ago.

Page 183. **"Silicon Glen"** : Facing the possibility of financial losses in the last quarter of 1989, Sun, according to the *San Jose Mercury News*, slowed down renovations of the Ford building, plans to develop the Newark site, and preparations for starting up the Scottish manufacturing operations in Linlithgow. Plans for East Palo Alto were not affected, according to the article's authors, Jim Bartimo and Michelle Levander, who cited PR spokesperson Kim Miller in their article, "Sun Puts Clamps on Costs." July 13, 1989, 1F, 12F.

Page 184. **Hiring freezes were not . . .** : John Levinson, "Notes from Our Morning Research Conference Call," *Research Brief*, Goldman Sachs, August 2, 1988, 7. The reputation for control of expenses permeated Sun. In the 1985, 1986, and 1989 hiring freezes, everyone, from receptionists to CFOs, was encouraged to devise ways of saving cash.

Page 186. **At the same time, Sun's own managers . . .** : The best-known leak happened at the January 1989 Sun user group meeting. At the gathering, held in Miami, nearly eight hundred attendees learned the specifics of Sun's new product offerings in a speech by Lacroute. Although it excited his listeners, it infuriated Sun's public-relations and product-marketing people, who had been laboriously lecturing others to keep their mouths shut about the upcoming product introduction in April. McNealy occasionally sent out electronic mail to everyone in the company warning people about the necessity of keeping proprietary information under wraps. His messages were more like pleadings for help than lectures to loose-lipped employees.

Page 187. **In just one day, Microsoft's . . .** : John Schwartz, "Hard Times for Software," *Newsweek*, April 3, 1989, 42–43.

Page 187. **Even as revenues . . .** : Levine, "Sun Microsystems Turns On . . .," 62.

Page 189. **"Software is crucial . . ."** : Paul Freiberger, "Software Companies Can Make or Break Newest Computers," *San Francisco Examiner*, June 18, 1989, D1.

Page 189. **Sun instituted . . . employee-training hours**: William Bluestein, "How Sun Microsystems Buys for Quality," *Electronics Purchasing*, March 1988, 38.

Page 189. **It also made Sun's products . . .** : "Engineering/Technology: Sun Microsystems," *Research Notes*, Wessels, Arnold & Henderson, September 15, 1988, 8–9.

Page 190. **He also hoped . . .** : Almost everything did work, except for a panel that was supposed to lower on a cue from Bechtolsheim to reveal the SPARCstation 1. He gestured, waiting until finally the recalcitrant panel descended. A demonstration of the machine's audio system flopped, as did Bernie Lacroute's joking reference to another troublesome panel in the previous day's rehearsal. Lacroute appeared to be referring to one of Sun's new 68030 systems when he said, "It didn't work yesterday: it kept going up and down."

Page 192. **This scenario scared . . .** : Don Clark, "Sun Gets Taiwan Clones," *San Francisco Chronicle*, June 22, 1989, C3.

Page 192. **Despite this franchise's . . .** : John Schneidawind, "Sun Microsystems Inches Toward Retail Marketing," *San Francisco Chronicle*, June 20, 1989.

CHAPTER 8: WORKING IN A REVVED ENGINE

Page 196. **"80-hour workweeks . . ."** : Michael S. Malone, "Coins of the Realm," *West*, November 6, 1988, 30–31.

Page 196. **"you lose weight just . . ."** : Leigh Weimers, "Ever Wonder Where World of High-Tech Keeps Its Dictionary?" *San Jose Mercury News*, April 5, 1989, D-3.

Page 199. **Sun also proposed . . .** : Chris Kenrick, "Here Comes the Sun (Microsystems)," *Peninsula Times Tribune*, November 26, 1988, C-2; Klaus Kramer, memo to Sun employees, December 20, 1988. In 1989 Sun hammered out a deal with the town council of East Palo Alto to provide funds to study the possible move of Sun's headquarters to East Palo Alto. The city, which has high unemployment, poverty, and drug problems, was initially less than eager to embrace Sun. But after much haggling, an agreement to proceed with development plans was worked out.

Page 199. **In June the East Palo Alto . . .** : Michael Shapiro, "East P.A. City Council Backs Sun's Development Plan," *Peninsula Times Tribune*, June 6, 1989, B1.

Page 199. **The company was still adding . . .** : Steve Kaufman, "The Future's So Bright . . .," 4E.

Page 200. **In blind hallways . . .** : In spite of the space constrictions, "the environment" was listed as one of the three best things about working at Sun in a summer 1989 "quality of life" survey conducted by the corporate marketing department.

Page 200. **In Malone's satire . . .** : Malone, "Coins . . .," 31.

Page 201. **"Sun is considered . . ."** : Carla Lazzareschi, "Sun Microsystems Blazing a Red-Hot Trail in Computers," *Los Angeles Times*, January 31, 1988, IV 2.

Page 201. **The company did, of course . . .** : Kaufman, "The Future's So Bright . . .," 4E.

Page 202. **Even with its modest share . . .** : "System Failure," *The Economist*, March 11, 1989, 70.

Page 203. **Bill Joy**: Lazzareschi, "Sun Microsystems Blazing . . .," IV 1.

Page 204. **"acceleration syndrome"** : Tony Schwartz, "Acceleration Syndrome: Does Everyone Live in the Fast Lane Nowadays?" *Utne Reader*, Jan/Feb 1989, 36–43. Originally appeared in *Vanity Fair*, October 1988.

Page 209. **Bartz**: "A Sun Rising in the West . . .," 56.

Page 210. **Sun Microsystems is ranked . . .** : Sabin Russell, "Area's Largest Firms Slimming Ranks," *Chronicle 100*, March 27, 1989, 16–17. Silicon Valley companies that employ more people than Sun include Lockheed, IBM, Hewlett-Packard, Stanford, Varian, Apple, Amdahl, Ford Aerospace, and National Semiconductor.

Page 213. **NeXT . . . Steve Jobs**: Jobs had been ousted from the company he started by John Sculley, the man Jobs brought in from Pepsico to rescue Apple Computer from the doldrums.

Page 216. **"Sun's initial 88,000 . . ."** : Kathleen M. Holmgren, "Workstation Producer's New Plant Provides Manufacturing Flexibility to Introduce or Switch Products," *Industrial Engineering*, March 1988, 32.

Page 219. **Kahn, noted for . . . antics** : In one instance, Kahn personally slipped copies of *New England Monthly* under the hotel doors of attendees to the PC Forum. The magazine carried an unflattering article on his rival company's boss, Jim Manzi of Lotus Development Corporation. This prank caused no end of embarrassment to Kahn's exasperated public relations people and was one for which he eventually apologized. Denise Caruso, "Inside Silicon Valley," *San Francisco Examiner*, Sunday April 2, 1989, D-3.

Page 219. **Sun's computers were like . . . toys . . .** : Cofounder Bill Joy might be considered an archetype of the technologist who works for fun. In a magazine interview, he described research and development as a place where "we can just try things. That's fun." His decision to switch from his early work in mathematics to engineering was based on his idea that the latter "was fun." David Smith, "Bill Joy: Fun at Work and Play," *VLSI Systems Design*, October 1987, 16.

Page 219. **Wyckoff**: Interview, April 5, 1989.

Page 220. **"The Future's So Bright . . ."** : Steve Kaufman, "The Future's So Bright . . .," E-1.

Page 221. **"We have attracted . . ."** : *Ibid*

Page 222. **"doughnuts on Wednesdays"** : A Sun tradition is the appearance each Wednesday in every building of free doughnuts and bagels for employees. It has proved to be a good incentive: people tend to show up a little earlier on this day of the week.

CHAPTER 9: OPEN SEASON

Page 223. **"credibility with the financial community"**: "Austin Mayer at Sun Microsystems Talks About Credibility and Coverage," *Investor Relations Report*, Vol. 1 No. 2, July 1988, 4.

Page 223. **Mayer thoroughly briefed . . .** : Christian Hill and

William Cellis III, "Sun Microsystems Sees Quarterly Plunge in Net or a Loss, Cites Management Snags," *Wall Street Journal*, A3.

Page 224. **a shortage of . . . chips diminished . . . profits** : George Gilder, "How the Computer Companies Lost Their Memories," *Forbes*, June 13, 1988, 79–84.

Page 224. **The switchover from . . .** : Kathleen Burton, "Sun Microsystems, Inc. Reports Net Income Loss in 4th Quarter," *Investor's Daily*, June 2, 1989, 30.

Page 226. **Long before the official announcement . . .** : Virtually all of the trade magazines carried articles, each with various descriptions of the new products. Even *USA Today* ran an article about the so-called SPARCintosh.

Page 227. **Sun's huge lists** : Sun's Byzantine price lists, running to hundreds of pages and thousands of configurations and options, bewildered some customers and struck terror into the hearts of those who had to update them— an all-too-frequent occurrence.

Page 227. **Sun's July 27 press release** : The release, headlined "Sun Updates Fourth Fiscal Quarterly Advisory," listed both Mayer and Carol Broadbent as the key contacts. Most of Sun's press releases did not bear Broadbent's name, as she prefers that her staff field the calls and gain the experience. This particular release demanded direct personal action.

Page 227. **"70% of the computers . . ."** : Jonathan B. Levine, "High Noon for Sun," *Business Week*, July 24, 1989, 70.

Page 228. **McNealy sent a message . . .** : McNealy used the e-mail system regularly to communicate to Sun employees. Generally, his missives concerned mundane topics such as wearing badges, attending picnics, and officer announcements. But he never avoided more incisive issues on e-mail. Electronic mail was a critical element of Sun's culture and served as a excellent forum for Sun's CEO.

Page 229. **"needed a break . . ."** : Sonja Steptoe, "Sun Microsystems Stock Price Cools As Company Foresees Loss
for Quarter," *Wall Street Journal*, June 5, 1989, C6.

Page 229. **a separate office of the president** : Scott McNealy
holds the offices of president, CEO, and chairman of the
board.

Page 229. **"relishing his added duties"** : Herb Greenberg, "An
Executive Eclipse at Sun Microsystems," *San Francisco
Chronicle*, June 7, 1989, C1.

Page 230. **"hard-charging style"** . . . **"so obsessed . . ."** : Juli
Cortino, "Sun Struggling with Own Success," *PC Week*,
June 19, 1989, 6. Michelle Levander and Steve Kauf-
man, "Another Top Official Turns His Back on Sun,"
San Jose Mercury News, June 16, 1989, 14D.

Page 230. **"ironic"** . . . **"embarrassing . . ."** **"suffering . . ."** :
Mark Lewyn, "Sun Microsystems May Post Loss," *USA
Today*, June 2, 1989, B3. Ron Wolf, "Sun Microsystems
May Report Loss," *San Jose Mercury News*, June 2,
1989, 10D. Louise Kehoe, "Sun Microsystems Warns of
Possible 'Slight Loss,'" *Financial Times*, June 2, 1989
section 2, 25.

Page 230. **"Sun has grown so large . . ."** : Lawrence M.
Fisher, "Hiccup for a Computer Superstar," *New York
Times*, June 2, 1989, 9.

Page 230. **Perhaps recalling the Osborne collapse . . ."** : *Ibid..*
Kehoe, "Sun Microsystems Warns . . ." 25. Wolf, "Sun
Microsystems may report . . .," 10Ð.

Page 231. **black humor predominated** : During the aftermath
of the fourth-quarter cash crunch, McNealy happened to
wander into an office where a group of employees was
playing with an obnoxious electronic toy called Mr.
Game Show. The "contestants" were asked questions and
answered by pushing the appropriate button on the base
of the one-foot-high electronic doll. When the players
noticed the CEO, they asked him whether he wanted to

join in the fun. McNealy replied, "No, thanks. I've already lost enough money this quarter."

Page 231. **Broadbent counseled McNealy . . .** : Sun's CEO had often exasperated his public relations crew with "stunts" such as wearing his sunglasses for a business photo or mocking a Steve Jobs pose in another press shot. "He's just so nervous and tight before these interviews and things that he lets go," said one PR staffer about McNealy's playfulness.

Page 232. **accounting procedures** : Graziano's arrival in May 1987 was supposed to help solve the problem with Sun's controls. He failed, obviously. Soon after Graziano was on the job, he bragged to Austin Mayer that he would turn around quarterly information to stockholders in two weeks after the books closed. He said Sun's current six-week time frame for revealing its quarterly numbers was "laughable." Two years after his arrival, Sun still took six weeks to publish its period results.

Page 233. **Adopting his predecessor's reputation . . .** : Sun's first chief executive, Vinod Khosla, was adamant about keeping track of every dime. As one person put it, "He watched pennies, pencils, and people very carefully." The *San Jose Mercury News* reported that McNealy was reputed to keep "a strict eye on the bottom line. . . . He nickels and dimes and expects miracles." Levander and Kaufman, "Another Top Official . . .," 14D.

Page 236. **DEC redeployed its work force . . .** : Those marketing managers who didn't suddenly want to move from Maynard, Massachusetts, to become sales assistants in Fargo, North Dakota, were quietly eased out of the company.

Page 236. **In one quarter, the company . . .** : "Sun Microsystems Rebounds," *San Francisco Chronicle*, October 26, 1989, D3.

Page 236. **Sun had weathered . . .** : Don Clark, "Record Sales

Spark Turnaround at Sun," *San Francisco Chronicle*, October 4, 1989, C3.

Page 237. **Equally important, Wall Street . . .** : Herb Greenberg, "Sun Micro—Analysts Embrace It Again," *San Francisco Chronicle*, October 2, 1989, C1.

Page 237. **"users [were] not yet . . ."** : Peter D. Schleifer and Thomas R. Woods, "Engineering/Technical Workstation User Survey," *Institutional Research*, Wessels, Arnold & Henderson, June 21, 1989, 1.

Page 237. **Clone makers in Taiwan . . .** : Richard March, "Daewoo to Offer SPARC Clones," *PC Week*, August 28, 1989, 13. Dori Jones Yang, "Taiwan Isn't Just for Cloning Anymore," *Business Week*, September 25, 1989, 208.

Page 239. **It may be absorbed . . .** : Like most companies, Sun had adopted a poison pill of sorts to prevent such unfriendly takeovers. It also has its complex stock-ownership deal with AT&T that would make a greenmailer or honest capitalist hesitant to muscle into the company.

Index